Motherhood and Infertility in Ireland

Understanding the Presence of Absence

Motherhood and Infertility in Ireland

UNDERSTANDING THE PRESENCE OF ABSENCE

JILL ALLISON

First published in 2013 by
Cork University Press
Youngline Industrial Estate
Pouladuff Road, Togher
Cork, Ireland

British Library Cataloguing in Publication Data
A CIP catalogue record for this book is available from the British Library.

ISBN 978-1-78205-003-2

Typeset by Tower Books, Ballincollig, County Cork
Printed and bound by CPI Group (UK) Ltd, Croydon, CR0 4YY

www.corkuniversitypress.com

To my beloveds – David, Alex, Duncan, Charlotte and Brendan –
for giving me the strength in my journey and believing in me;
and to the people who shared their stories with me
about journeys toward presence and absence

Contents

Acknowledgements

It is a daunting task to try to adequately acknowledge all the people who provided support and inspiration for the work that has resulted in this book. I apologise if I have failed to mention people who were instrumental in the project or its vision in some way.

First, I must acknowledge that without the people in Ireland who have faced infertility and its challenges and were willing to share their stories this book would not have been written. I thank all my research participants for their generosity and courage. Your stories of overcoming those challenges and of finding new meanings in the role of motherhood inspired me to take my research and the book in different directions. I hope I have represented your lives and experiences adequately and with the respect you deserve. I thank the clinicians and professionals from various clinics who shared their perspectives. I also acknowledge the support and steadfast dedication of the National Infertility Support and Information Group (NISIG) who provided information, encouragement and context for the research.

This book has come about with the help of many other people in the world of academia. I was always a bit of a reluctant academic and found encouragement from many of my teachers at the University of Regina and Memorial University of Newfoundland. I want to thank Dr Robin Whitaker, Dr Sharon Roseman and Dr Fern Brunger for their generous and invaluable advice, mentorship and support as members of my dissertation committee. I also acknowledge the late Dr Peter Hart for his support on my committee. In our last conversation together, he encouraged me to develop a book from the dissertation. Dr Robin Whitaker took me on as a graduate student even as my interests were somewhat less political than her own. I thank you for taking up the challenge Robin. We made it work. I also thank all the faculty, staff and fellow graduate students of the Anthropology Department of Memorial University for academic and collegial support.

I also thank the funding agencies who supported my work. My PhD studies were supported by an F.A. Aldrich Scholarship from Memorial

University and a Social Sciences and Humanities Research Council Doctoral Award. I also received a Wenner Gren Foundation Dissertation Fieldwork Grant to support the research in Ireland.

My thanks to the anonymous reviewers for their comments on an early draft of the book. A very abridged version of chapter 5 was published as an article titled 'Grieving Conceptions: Making Motherhood in the Wake of Infertility in Ireland' in the *Journal of the Motherhood Initiative.* 1(2): 201–214 (2010). I thank everyone involved in the publication of material from my research. I appreciate the patience of Mike Collins and Maria O'Donovon at Cork University Press.

Most of all I thank my family for being patient, supportive and loving. My parents, Murray and Doreen MacKay, taught me that life is a journey worthy of constant exploration and never to fear change. My husband, David Allison, shares my thirst for new roads and adventures. He has encouraged me to pursue my dreams and always believed in me. My children, Alex, Duncan, Charlotte and Brendan, have been a source of joy and strength and the reason motherhood and family were such important subjects to explore. They endured my PhD studies and the writing of this book. They have been my inspiration.

Acronyms

ART   Assisted Reproduction Technology
CAHR   Commission on Assisted Human Reproduction
CSO   Central Statistics Office
ECHR   European Commission on Human Rights
ECtHR   European Court of Human Rights
GIFT   gamete intrafallopian transfer
HARI   Human Assisted Reproduction Ireland
hCG   human chorionic gonadatropin
hES   human embryonic stem cells
HFEA   Human Fertilisation and Embryology Authority
IAA   International Adoption Association
ICSI   intra-cytoplasmic sperm injection
IHRC   Irish Human Rights Commission
IUI   intra-uterine insemination
IVF   *in vitro* fertilisation
MNI   ManNotIncluded.com
NaPro   Natural Procreative Technology
NISIG   National Infertility Support and Information Group
RTÉ   Raidió Teilifís Éireann
TESA   Testicular Sperm Aspiration
UCD   University College Dublin

Introduction:
Conceiving the Presence of Absence

The presence of absence explains the paradox, the sensation and the life experiences of infertility in Ireland. There are few experiences in life more culturally contingent than conceiving and giving birth. Deeply embedded in the meanings of family, gender, community and nation, the politics associated with conception, birth and motherhood are rich subjects for anthropological study. Fertility matters. Fertility is not simply a biological fact, but rather a process of becoming that is shaped by relations of power, ideas of personhood and subjectivity.

As a human condition with a biological basis, infertility also matters. It is also an experience of contrast and contradiction deeply marked by the social conditions that shape the way people define parenthood and family.[1] An inability to conceive poses challenges to the way biology and nature have come to underscore the social and moral meanings of reproduction. Moreover, infertility produces very real human dilemmas, challenges to notions of self and identity, and crises of faith in the foundations that underwrite the social meanings of procreation – religion, science and nature. In this book I explore how these difficulties are deeply connected with the social and political context in Ireland. This book is also an exploration, from an anthropological point of view, of infertility as a *presence of absence* – a lingering and complex sensation of both being and not being – experienced by women and men who endure and overcome the challenges infertility poses in their lives. I explore the way presence of absence shapes and is shaped by the significance of motherhood in Irish society, past and present, and the way assisted reproduction technologies (ART) are employed, defined and redefined, and debated (or not) as part of the cultural repertoire in which the presence of absence is constituted.

Defining the Presence of Absence

The presence of absence, as an experiential motif, was given to me in the story told by Elsa. As an artist, Elsa's creative expression of her own

1

infertility experience exposes the places where power is naturalised and 'nature' is empowered in the politics of reproduction. Seeing the aesthetic representations of infertility in her work challenged me to push my exploration beyond the impact of reproductive technologies toward the meaning of infertility in the places where contrast and contradiction were sometimes less obvious. Elsa translated her experiences with infertility, her critical perspectives on ART, and her perceptions of social pressures and moral values through the medium of her artwork. She also shared with me the simple, elegant, yet powerful trope for conveying the feelings associated with an inability to conceive. This theme became the title of a handmade book she called *The Presence of Absence*.[2] Just as Elsa's artwork reveals much about her experience of infertility, so would the stories of infertility I gathered in my research reveal a great deal about the meanings of fertility, conception, motherhood, family and reproductive politics in Irish society. More importantly perhaps, these stories expose the way existing values and social conventions are both challenged and endure in the face of what many perceive to be vast changes in gender relations and the social institutions of education, medicine, religion and politics in twenty-first-century Ireland.

The idea for the presence of absence came to Elsa as she began to play with the potential impact of the Madonna image, seeing it as the foundation for a more critical conceptual work on the contradictions experienced by infertile couples in Ireland. This connection proved to be the pivotal point for development of a project that involved hand-painting over reproductions of old masters' works to remove the baby Jesus, a technique where she was adding the paint to remove something. Her addition was, from an artistic and conceptual point of view, a 'presence of absence' – the addition of something missing.

> ELSA: *So then I kept thinking 'what is the ultimate image of motherhood?' And that's where the Madonna image came in. And how can I work with that? I photocopied it . . . And I just took a brush and painted over the baby sort of very quickly. Then I said, hang on now, if I do that so that you can't see the baby anymore but she still has the clothes and everything, if I keep painting over that . . . Well it was just very powerful. I mean in the exhibition with the paintings on the wall a lot of people didn't even cop on that the child was missing, even though my painting is very obvious, you know? . . . It kind of seemed to work on a level that I could explain it on our terms [those who are infertile].*

The failure to notice what was 'absent' seemed to Elsa a sign of how frequently people misunderstand or fail to take notice of the impact of infertility on those around them. They do not fully appreciate the impact of this absence, as a very real presence and tangible reality in the day-to-day lives for those who do not conceive children.

Elsa had recently left a career in tourism to explore a latent creativity through courses at a local art college. Somewhat reluctantly at first, she decided to portray her experiences with infertility through the medium of her art. Her work received high praise from both teachers and the public in a show at the college and one of her major pieces, the hand-made book entitled *The Presence of Absence*, was purchased for the permanent collection at the school. As we spoke there was a definite reticence to cross what was often described to me as a public and private divide when talking about infertility. Elsa's inspiration and passion revolved around her desire to 'get it out in the open'. At the same time, she sought to critique the social forces that keep infertility mired in secrecy, shame, guilt and misunderstanding and contribute to feelings of marginalisation.

The irony of this marginalisation is that it is at least partly a product of infertile people's own perception of themselves as being outside the norm. It is their sense of discomfort in a social world that revolves around children and reproduction that produces and perpetuates the feeling of exclusion or isolation. The ongoing silence on the part of many infertile people does little to challenge the paradigm of fertility as a given – a paradigm that underscores the hetero-normative basis for a definition of family life in Ireland that includes raising children. Elsa certainly struggled with such issues but felt it was worth the risk of exposing her own struggle to conceive in order to provide an avenue for public dialogue and generating awareness.

> ELSA: *With all the artwork I dealt with it [infertility] and did put it out there. It's a very strange feeling with the paintings. I just kind of put it out and you're standing there and exposing yourself to the world. It's often something, you know, that's hard to deal with.*

Elsa's artwork beckons us to look at what is behind infertility as it relates to subjectivity, the ideology of motherhood, experiences of embodied dysfunction, loss and grief, social exclusion, moral contradiction and political ambiguity. An overarching principle in her work, and perhaps most important to explicate in mine, is that reproductive potential has furnished the naturalised basis for the construction of gender difference and gendered identities, biological bodies, concepts of 'natural' reproduction, and the ideals of hetero-normative relationships that underwrite so many of Ireland's institutional discourses. And yet infertility stories challenge the presence of a universal reproductive potential on which these constructs of difference rest.

Through the presence of absence, this book interrogates both the role and the importance of motherhood, marriage and family in the context of social change in Ireland. I also examine the cultural contingencies that govern the production and reification of certain kinds of knowledge in reproductive medicine. Infertility highlights the contested image of nature as either value laden or value free in its use as a part of the moral fabric of reproductive decision-making. I use infertility as a lens to, first, explore the ongoing importance of motherhood, family, procreation and gender difference in both the politics of day-to-day life and the politics of a purportedly modernising Ireland; and second, to reveal the movement of long-held social values and moral tenets into new, but equally culturally contingent and politically expedient, uses of assisted reproduction technologies.

The Presence of Absence in the Wake of Social Change

Infertility is not a new phenomenon in Ireland or anywhere else but rather one that is experienced in context. In Ireland in the early twenty-first century it is experienced as part of the wave of social change, at once sustaining and exposing the refractory nature of social values embedded deeply in the politics of reproduction even as the social institutions that sustain the politics are in a state of flux. This book is more than a cultural account of infertility: it is a cultural account of the meaning of conception in an era of possibility and change – both social and technological.

My research lies at a critical intersection between the social meanings of fertility, reproduction and motherhood, and the institutional and political discourses that use, shape and depend upon those meanings. Neither the meanings nor the institutions can be seen as static. At this particular time in Irish history, a number of significant changes have precipitated an opportunity to examine the meaning of reproduction and its place as a symbol of Irish political and social identity. In *Naturalizing Power*, Sylvia Yanagisako and Carol Delaney describe how social and political change can disrupt the meta-narratives and origin stories through which people make sense of the world and give order to things. In nineteenth-century Euro-America, challenges to Christian accounts and social structures emerged in response to rapid social and economic change. In addition, colonial expansion in conjunction with a new emphasis on theories such as evolution forced people to reconsider the simplicity of conceptual premises based on religious doctrine. Yanagisako and Delaney point to the shift from a reliance on creationist accounts to a dependence on science and nature. Prior social and economic arrangements, concepts of social class, kinship, reproduction and gender difference were not simply replaced, but rather absorbed into the new accounts that now posited that power was derived from nature rather than from God.[3] As Yanagisako and Delaney charge, it is important to expose how the boundaries of nature and culture have been drawn and to 'challenge the assignment of sex and reproduction to the category of "biology"'.[4] Infertility provides a medium through which we can challenge not only the biological designation of sex and reproduction but the multiple layers of meaning that biology itself entails.

Embodied and Engendered Subjects

The presence of absence, portrayed in Elsa's artwork, is also deeply embedded in the collapsing of the subject positions of woman and mother. The puzzle of the subject lies in what Paul Rabinow calls 'subjectification'[5] or the 'way a human being turns him- or herself into a subject'.[6] Subjectivity is the position from which we make sense not only of ourselves but of what we experience, even as the framework for doing so is itself a product of relations of sociality and power. Biehl, Good and Kleinman note that while 'modes of subjectivation' are produced through institutional relations and discourses that shape the subject, 'subjectivity is not just the outcome of social control or the unconscious; it also provides the ground for subjects to think through their circumstances and feel through their contradictions . . . [as] the means of shaping sensibility'.[7] Feminist debates around the importance of acknowledging subjectivity have arisen in response and in relation to postmodernism – a theoretical position that challenges the validity and constructedness of all categories and structures.

Seyla Benhabib points out that the purported 'death of man' or death of the subject threatens to undo the work of feminism that has challenged longstanding social inequalities based on the recognition of difference and the subject position 'woman'.[8] Judith Butler, on the other hand, argues that Benhabib's concern with an overarching universality or elimination of subject positions seemingly inherent in postmodernism is better understood as 'reliev[ing] the category of its foundationalist weight in order to render it as a site of permanent political contest'.[9] Subjectivity is significant as people narrate, act and experience through the very real conditions of their existence. Louis Althusser describes how we are 'always-already subjects' both formed by and experiencing through the ideologies that shape us.[10] So powerful is the ideal of the motherhood identity in daily life in Ireland that people like Elsa feel the presence of unborn children in their personal relationships even before they begin actively trying to conceive. Ragoné and Twine argue that ideologies of motherhood are part of a wider hegemony that 'posits the unquestioned existence of racial matching, exclusively heterosexual family formations, and unassisted or "natural" reproduction, unequal economic privilege, and the idea of "perfect" babies'.[11] And yet, Elsa's work challenges the multiple institutional and discursive relations of power that shape both an ideology of motherhood and the experiences in which people are constituted as infertile.

Reproduction has been part of this complex of social, religious and family politics that incorporates assumptions about womanhood as synonymous with motherhood and essential gender roles. Two additional issues arise from these assumptions. The first is an unproblematised link between the biology, or 'nature', of sex and the social relations of procreation, and the second is a conflation of biology and reproduction in determining the rules for building family, community and nation. At a moment in time in Ireland, when everyone is talking about social and economic change, stories about infertility reveal, with particular acuity, how deeply naturalised these socially constituted connections have become.[12]

The discursive construction of sex as an immutable category has had enormous consequences on the naturalisation of sexual/ gendered difference, and reproduction has played an important role in sustaining such discourses. Earle and Letherby point out that 'expectations, experiences and representations of reproduction are central to our understanding of gender and identity, or who we are and how we are perceived by others'.[13] In her argument against such irreducible attributes of a material body, Judith Butler asks, 'how is it the materiality of sex is understood as that which only bears cultural constructions and, therefore, cannot be a construction?'[14] Butler argues that we must look beyond the division of biological sex and culturally constituted gender to deconstruct the foundational element. She suggests that if feminism is about exposing and challenging the constitutive basis for gender inequality, it must unmake all the binaries along which gender can be discursively organised, including the 'biological' division of sex. While I agree with Butler's call to deconstruct the biological basis for gender difference at the social and political level, I also see the biological body, with all of its sexual characteristics and reproductive physiology, as key in subjectification as the sensation of self is embodied.

As a source and site of experience, the body is an important analytical component in understanding and making meaning, particularly around issues of health and illness. Thomas Csordas sees embodiment as a 'paradigm' capable of overcoming seemingly disparate method-ological and theoretical positions on 'bodily being' as both culturally and biologically constituted; he argues for an anthropological perspective that '*gives access* to experience as the meaningfulness of meaning'.[15] Even as biological difference is employed as a basis for constructing social dif-ference, it is an important part of how people experience infertility. Bodily experiences and socially constituted meanings become embodied sensibilities. Thus while I agree with Butler's emphasis on the need to deconstruct the social implications of biological categories, I refuse her dismissal of biological sex as a mere discursive construction. I will, however, emphasise the ways that infertility does constitute a challenge or a rupture in the structural and discursive foundations of binary cate-gories such as gender or sexuality. I focus attention on how infertility stories include the reproductive body as a crucial site that participates in the shaping of experiences. While this is obviously socially mediated, the meanings attributed to bodily experiences also contribute to a sense of embodied difference. The reproductive body serves as a map on which the biological and physiological aspects of 'normal' reproduction are drawn, and infertility is medicalised as unnatural and unhealthy.

From a feminist standpoint, is it possible to acknowledge distinctive biologies in reproductive bodies without reifying the sex/gender cate-gories that so-called biological facts constitute as naturally given?[16] It is crucial to account for the importance of biological difference in the *meaning* of any and all experiences of reproduction without resorting to the structures that link woman to nature and man to culture, or gendered divisions of labour in public and private spheres. As many feminist scholars note, these frameworks were used to explain and sometimes justify differential access to power in many cultural accounts of the past.[17] But for many of the women I spoke to, the biological differences they iden-tified as 'natural' were embodied and significant to them as part of their experience of infertility and thus are important aspects of their narratives.

What is important about an embodied sense of biological difference, from the feminist perspective, is the way power becomes embedded in the constitution of the subject, shaping our sense of self through the body as the 'existential grounds for culture and the self'.[18] No experience, bodily or emotional, and no political perspective remains outside or uninhabited by the play of power. Joan Scott argues that 'we need to attend to the historical processes that, through discourse, position sub-jects and produce their experiences. It is not individuals who have experience, but subjects who are constituted through experience.'[19] But experiences emerge from within the body as well as the social milieu and are textured by bodily sensations as material fact. Bodily difference and

reproductive experiences are sites where the discourses of power are particularly potent in fostering that process Foucault describes as the
self-formation of the subject. In other words, men and women are subject
to discourses of difference, comparison and discrimination in the very
process of recognising and experiencing biological functions in the body.

Elsa's depiction of the Madonna without her child and the failure of
people to notice what was missing is, to her, symbolic of a social context
where people take fertility and family largely for granted without challenging the underlying politics of meaning. Fertility and conception have
come to represent political and social coherence as well as physical and
moral well-being in ways that, paradoxically, can be traced most clearly
by exploring the meanings of their absence.

Local Moral Worlds

The presence of absence and the seemingly unified subjectivity of
woman as mother in Ireland are products of a complex moral discourse
in which the Irish state has traded in a sense of shared values, and moral
and ethical tenets drawn from a close association with the Catholic
Church. Tom Inglis has argued that the Catholic Church has lost its
former 'moral monopoly' in the past two decades.[20] However, there is
evidence to suggest that, in the politics of reproduction and family formation at least, the church remains an important part of peoples'
decision-making and 'local moral world'.[21] It also remains a part of the
institutional and discursive backdrop to what Jarrett Zigon describes as
embodied moral sensibilities.[22] Gender difference and sexual politics
based on moral propriety and marriage continue to influence everyday
life, evident in narratives of contestation and resistance. In many stories
about infertility, the importance of the family and people's perception of
its changing dimensions are grounds for debating moral meanings in
social life in Ireland. But here, too, the contested place of nature and
biology, science and technology participate in the formation of local
moral worlds as moral frameworks, counter-discourses and explanatory
models for family formation as a moral enterprise.

I explore morality as complex, fluid and nuanced by individual and
historical circumstances with respect to infertility and family formation,
following a number of scholars who also focus on the importance of
morality in the social context.[23] The centrality of religion as a basis for
making reproductive decisions has not disappeared even as science and
technology seek to make morality seem essentially rational. In fact, rather
than an insignificant factor, religion continues to be of concern all around
the world and continues to exert a dominant influence over issues of

reproductive decision-making, and no less so in the wake of advances in reproductive technologies.[24]

Ethical questions about the use of assisted reproduction highlight the intersection, and occasional collision, between science and technology and religious faith. In light of Ireland's history of legislating and regulating matters of reproduction based on religious moralising and idealism, such collisions have implications for both individuals and institutions. Institutions such as medicine, the state and the church have all employed the concept of 'nature' as a basis for constituting and perpetuating moral authority with respect to the new technologies; nature provides a measure of continuity and moral reassurance as such technologies provoke concerns about changing social values associated with procreative endeavours. This is not new or unique since '"nature" continues to serve, as it did prior to the Enlightenment, as a moral touchstone'.[25] This institutional dialogue has become part of a complex politics or a 'moral economy of science', as it applies to the realm of science and technology.[26] Lorraine Daston argues that social values are absorbed into scientific discourse as part of its claim to truth. At the same time, however, these values are reshaped in ways that make them appear as if they are intrinsic properties of science rather than drawn from the wider social context of their origin.[27] I take Daston's exploration of the way social values are subsumed to enhance an inherent sense of rational goodness in science. From this standpoint I examine where state and medical institutions might fill in the moral authority void around reproduction by positing the values of rationality, nature, objectivity and empiricism in reproductive medicine.

Advances in the science of reproductive medicine have created new meanings in kinship and new kinds of procreative relations and in some cases new biological entities or new meanings for biology itself.[28] Rayna Rapp notes that the scholarship in this area has virtually thrust reproduction from 'invisible centrality' to the visible centre of social theory and public discourse.[29] But equally important is the need to explore how the meanings of fertility, conception, birth, motherhood and family have been similarly thrust from 'invisible centrality' into the centre of relations of power, politics and commerce in Ireland, particularly when the interests of various institutions collide.

The National Infertility Support and Information Group (NISIG) in Ireland reported in 2003 that, statistically, approximately one in six couples (15%) in Ireland, as in other EU nations and North America, will experience some form of 'infertility'.[30] New technologies aimed at assisting people to overcome fertility challenges are both universal and particular as they emerge within a medical context shaped by both reproductive and social politics. Challenges to old assumptions about the 'nature' of family relationships, kinship terms and sexuality are another aspect of a dramatic process in which people are struggling to locate new ideas on an old moral and ethical compass in the wake of the declining moral authority of the Catholic Church.

The Introduction of IVF and Its Controversies

The use of assisted reproduction technologies such as IVF has grown worldwide since the first 'test tube' baby, Louise Brown, was born in 1978. Her conception in a clinic in England was the result of highly experimental techniques by IVF pioneers Robert Edwards and Patrick Steptoe. The treatment is now used to overcome a variety of fertility problems including blocked fallopian tubes, hormonal imbalances and low sperm counts. It involves stimulating a woman's ovaries with hormones to produce a number of eggs at once, removing those eggs with an ultrasound-guided needle, and mixing them with sperm in a Petri dish. The highly technical process is designed to facilitate fertilisation (penetration of the egg by the sperm) and produce as many embryos as possible in the laboratory. The embryos are then incubated for a few days and placed in the woman's uterus in the hope that they will implant and begin an otherwise normal pregnancy. Because the treatment can result in many more embryos than can be safely (or sensibly) placed in a woman's body, technology has been developed to freeze or cryo-preserve embryos for a later cycle of IVF. This process has been ethically and politically challenging for many people, and a number of countries have implemented some form of regulation at the national, medico-legal or local clinical level.[31]

From the standpoint of pronatalist politics and pro-family ethics that remain important in both social and political discourse in Ireland, a technology that enables procreation would seem to be a positive and welcome option for people trying to build a family. However, the Catholic Church has been fundamentally opposed to nearly all aspects of assisted reproduction. Much of the objection arises from the separation of the sexual act from the procreative intent – the basis for the church's prohibition of contraception among Catholics. The Catholic Church is also opposed to IVF, because men generally need to masturbate in order to produce sperm. They also oppose embryo freezing, on the grounds that embryos are lost in the freezing and thawing process or can be used for purposes other than procreation.

Despite the objections of the Catholic Church, assisted reproduction technology, in the form of IVF, has been available in Ireland since 1986 when it was introduced at the Clane Hospital by Dr Peter Brinsden, a clinician who also works in the clinic at Bourne Hall where Louise Brown was conceived.[32] Since this time there have been upwards of 2,000 couples a year seeking treatment and more than 1,000 children born through IVF in Ireland.[33] At the time of writing there are nine clinics across the country providing a variety of services ranging from simple donor inseminations to *in vitro* fertilisation (IVF) with donor eggs. Apart from Poland and Romania, Ireland remains the only EU nation without an independent committee or regulatory body concerned with ethics, regulation and legislation around ART. Other nations have struggled with the political issues around regulation of ART; most recently Canada, where legislation was enacted in 2004, ten years after the process began, had its regulatory body, Assisted Human Reproduction Canada, disbanded because of challenges that regulation interfered with provincial authority for managing healthcare. The move was also undertaken under a very conservative (and Conservative) government that has made a number of changes to social policy.[34] Britain has established the Human Fertilisation and Embryology Authority (HFEA), an independent regulatory body concerned with monitoring, providing information, and promoting public debate as well as informing regulation and legislation.[35]

In Ireland the practice of embryo freezing for example has been regulated only by a set of clinical practice guidelines and a professional consensus on this issue has been difficult to reach.[36] This leaves the practice of reproductive medicine largely unregulated by any independent authority and, moreover, allows little or no opportunity for public debate and awareness.[37] In a nation where morality and religious values in reproductive health have been primary concerns in matters related to the Constitution and national identity, such regulatory gaps leave practitioners and potential beneficiaries of ART oddly exposed to legal, moral or ethical criticism. This creates a level of uncertainty about the future with respect to the introduction of new techniques in reproductive medicine, or the ongoing provision of some current ones.

In an effort to address this gap, the Irish government established the Commission on Assisted Human Reproduction (CAHR) in 2000. The commission was mandated to explore 'approaches to the regulation of assisted human reproduction and the social, ethical, and legal factors to be taken into account in determining public policy'.[38] The most contentious issue facing the CAHR has been attempts at a legal and moral reconciliation of assisted reproduction practices with Article 40.3.3 of the Constitution, which guarantees protection of the 'right to life of the unborn'. While this clause is aimed first and foremost at prohibiting any provision of abortion in the Irish state, it is also the source of much ambivalence and dissent in attempts to regulate the use of ART in Ireland. The commission's work was ongoing but nearing completion as I began my research in Ireland in early summer of 2004. The CAHR's report, signalling the completion of the Commission's work, was also issued while I was conducting fieldwork in 2005. Its report, the public discourse and, more importantly, the lack of public debate around these findings, particularly with respect to defining the meaning of 'unborn' vis-à-vis embryos created *in vitro* and stored in clinical settings, have all been important context for my work. The fact that, at the time of writing, there has still been no legislation produced in light of the CAHR's recommendations points to the ongoing and deeply rooted challenges assisted reproduction poses in the Irish political and social contexts.

Asking Questions in a Field of Absence: Some Notes on Methodology

I began the research with an interest in how medicalisation and the highly technical medical treatment for infertility might be embraced or contested in a post-Catholic Irish state.[39] I quickly realised that the contentious aspects of *in vitro* fertilisation, and related technologies like embryo freezing and donor eggs, were only a tiny piece of the story. This realisation necessitated a shift in focus beyond the medical issues to include the broader impact of an inability to conceive, for women in particular, and the persistence of an ideology of motherhood in everyday contexts in Ireland. From an anthropological perspective, I was seeking to locate a deeply unsettling aspect of some people's lives within the broader cultural context in which that sensation both originated and persisted. This meant that I was following the problem, as George Marcus would suggest, through a multi-sited ethnographic study.[40] I could link individual subjectivity and identity based on procreation to broader social institutions and political ideals built around the meaning of family formation and reproduction in both biological and social dimensions.

As the mother of four children conceived with no difficulty, I did not share any infertility experiences with my participants. While I was always mindful of how significant this could be in my work, there was a particular moment of intensity in the midst of an interview with a woman who had unsuccessfully undergone IVF several times. Lara was very decisive in her explanation of the impact of infertility on her life. She told me bluntly early in the interview that 'there were two kinds of people in the world, fertiles and infertiles'. She felt strongly that those in the 'fertile' camp could never understand the isolation, pain and frustration of those who were infertile. I pondered the implications of her having carved out a particular social niche for herself from within the social imagination that assumes all men and women are capable of becoming parents. Clearly this woman sought to constitute those who had *not* shared her experiences as 'the other'. The binary identity of fertile/infertile took on a heightened measure of discomfort when the woman's husband joined us briefly and asked not only if I had children but how many. The woman looked rather distressed at my response and said to her husband 'oh, she's a fertile'. That feeling of being on the margins of a world I wanted to understand overtook me. A brief period of silence was followed by her concession that, 'well, at least she's an "enlightened" fertile'. I took a deep breath and the interview continued.

The primary focus of my research interviews was women who had experienced difficulty conceiving a child, but in a quarter of my interviews couples participated together. Based on the obvious fact that conception ideally occurs in women's bodies, infertility treatment, while seeking to bypass any number of the biological roadblocks to conception, involves tinkering with women's hormones and often invasive medical procedures on women's bodies. As a result I thought their experiences and decisions would be of prime significance from a feminist medical anthropology perspective.

I chose to allow couples to self-select. I interviewed forty women, ten of whom participated with their partners.[41] Four women agreed to a second full interview and I kept in regular contact with ten others as they kept me abreast of their progress or provided additional thoughts to our discussion on an ongoing basis. Several other women wrote to me giving me accounts of their experiences but were unwilling to commit to an interview, often citing the heavy emotional and social toll they had already paid as a result of their experiences.

The people I spoke to about their experiences were a fairly homogenous group. The women ranged in age from late twenties, the youngest being twenty-eight, to nearly fifty. The majority lived in urban centres, were in their thirties or early forties and all but two of the women were in a stable relationship with a partner. All had careers and all of them had undertaken some kind of post-secondary education at a trade school, college or university, and about half of the male partners had university education, although not all of the men had post-secondary education. My participants were thus all financially secure and decidedly middle class. None of the people in my study represented a minority population in Ireland such as the Traveller community or the immigrant community.[42] In spite of my efforts to recruit people from these groups, I was unable to find willing participants.[43]

All but one couple had been raised in families that were practising Catholics. Although there were different levels of participation and commitment in the past and the present, most described a significant influence by the Catholic Church in their families as they were growing up. Two couples described leaving the Catholic Church for another Christian denomination and another couple had been practising members of a Protestant church all their lives.

In addition, I spoke with six physicians who practised assisted reproduction and fertility medicine, one embryologist, a medical laboratory technician working in a hospital clinic, alternative medical practitioners, a scholar of medical law, a number of priests, support group volunteers, a manager at the Adoption Board, and people working in family planning clinics. I also attended conferences and public meetings, lectures and symposia on various aspects of fertility medicine, family issues and abortion politics.

Of course the best laid plans oft go astray and I was confounded early on in my research by the silence, hidden experiences and lack of accessibility that are hallmarks of infertility in Irish society. As this silence engulfed me and my research in the first months of the project, I found myself immersed in the invisibility and secrecy that defines so much of the infertility experience, unable to find people to tell me their stories and discouraged by a legion of unreturned phone calls to clinics and practitioners. Silence did not only pose a challenge to my research, it represented an odd contradiction, since there were multiple places in which people engaged in discussion in very public forums, such as websites and online bulletin boards. At the same time, this participation was always under the cloak of anonymity and clearly with the assumption that the boards were private space. This illusion of public and private was both sustained and troubled in a number of ways around the telling of infertility stories. For example, the National Infertility Support and Information Group (NISIG), while providing a means for connecting with others, turned out to be less wide-reaching and more 'private' in its approach than I initially realised. While the focus was on reaching out to people and creating support, their public meetings were, in fact, constituted as private gatherings and their emphasis as a 'network' was on individual support, also sustained by the notion of privacy on telephone lines. The founders of the organisation explained that they were initially reticent to speak in public or to even use their own addresses or phone numbers out of a concern that they might be picketed or targeted in some other way. As I have described elsewhere silence is often delib-erate and present; it too is a presence of absence.[44] This issue of silence was important because the project was directed towards the experi-ences of people in community, family and the everyday; it required ever-widening strategies for finding people who would share these experiences with me.

The most significant data in my project was collected in the taped interviews. A narrative emerges in the space between speaker and lis-tener as the story is made and brought to life. It is reshaped between writer and reader as they both colour it in with back stories and emo-tions of their own. The stories I collected thus developed in a process in which I was both participant and observer. My use of narrative as a tool for qualitative research follows many studies of reproductive health and gender issues where the complexity and multi-sitedness of the issues can only be understood as part of a wider context of lived experiences.[45] Another important facet in interview-based research is the negotiation of identities. Katherine Pratt Ewing notes attention must be paid to 'identity negotiation and power dynamics that go beyond the covert content of what people say to specify the conflicts, compromises and multiple intentions' that are part of the 'complex, often ambiguous positioning of speaker and interlocutor'.[46] Unlike many scholars who have studied infertility with a degree of personal experience,[47] any emotional engagement I might draw into an ethno-graphic empathy will necessarily come from other kinds of experiences. But this does not preclude my ability to make what Ruth Behar describes as the 'efforts to map an intermediate space . . . a bor-derland between passion and intellect, analysis and subjectivity, ethnography and autobiography, art and life'.[48] I often felt the emo-tional weight of having participated in the construction of a story that was laden with tears and pain and I took seriously the obligation to portray this aspect as accurately as I could.

Conceiving Issues in Irish Infertility

The book explores two distinct themes that contribute to the presence of absence as an Irish experience. The first section, chapters 2–4, examine the role of motherhood, and the enduring significance of marriage, family and reproduction in political and social life in Ireland. Infertility enables a multi-dimensional or *bas relief* perspective that exposes those values and normative assumptions about the meaning of reproduction that are otherwise invisible to people who have no basis for challenging or feeling excluded. In Chapter 2 infertility provides a medium through which people explore the changing meanings of the powerful ideology of motherhood in relation to family, the role of mothers, and morality in narratives about their own family relationships. Chapter 3 presents case studies as examples of the way women are embracing motherhood and empowering themselves through new ways to overcome fertility challenges associated with not having partners or having a partner of the same sex. The case studies present the stories of single women and lesbian women who embark on motherhood through assisted reproduction and adoption, as well as powerful stories of agency and resistance to constructs of failure among women who claim motherhood in spite of an inability to conceive. Chapter 4 focuses on the importance of contextualising and giving meaning to feelings of grief and loss from different perspectives in the infertility experience. I explore the contradictory sensibility of motherhood in the absence of children. I will describe the performances and narratives in which some women who have not conceived resist the social construction of themselves as failing to become mothers. In this sense they are resisting a social perception that a 'failure' to conceive is failure to be a woman.

The next three chapters examine the social, institutional and political challenges posed by infertility treatment in Ireland. In Chapter 5 the use of *in vitro* fertilisation and its related technologies is placed in the Irish social and political context. Through the stories of women and men who have contemplated or undertaken fertility treatment I explore the way treatment constitutes gender difference and moral identities, and poses particular challenges to the social ideals of procreation and sexuality that have been a residue of the Catholic Church's moral authority. Chapter 6 focuses on sperm and egg donation, the meaning of exchanges of gametes, and the contested role of biological 'substance' as a basis of kinship and family. Chapter 7 looks at the contested position of embryos created in the treatment of infertility as they pose challenges not only to a powerful pro-life ethos but also to attempts by the state to define and regulate ethical and social meanings in their use. I examine how ambivalence creates a space for ethics in which people can accommodate a number of contingencies and choices.

Stories about reproduction are historically situated, politically significant and socially and morally nuanced. And like many other aspects of the politics of reproduction and the battle for choice, infertility often crosses over difficult social terrain marked by gender differences and moral dissonance or ambivalence. As people narrate their stories about infertility they provide important commentary on the changing meaning of fertility and reproduction in Ireland as part of 'imagining the past and remembering the future'.[49] These narratives highlight the unevenness and disproportionate experience of change among women who challenge the model of motherhood that is currently the norm. Through their narratives on infertility, people challenge as often as they reaffirm norms and values, sometimes revealing uneasiness or ambivalence about change and the search for a new moral or ethical compass in the wake of shifting institutional influences. The place of change in narrative signifies the importance of fertility and birth but also the imagined place that family holds in the lives of men and women both in the past and in Ireland today.

I began this project from the premise that reproduction is a powerful site where cultural and political meanings are both produced and experienced; where difference is both real and constructed; where ideals are both affirmed and challenged, and cultural logic is established and disrupted. This project also situates these questions in the changing social, political and historical circumstances in Ireland in which pro-life and pronatalist values and politics are reanimated in new debates sparked by medical technology aimed at assisting conception.

The presence of absence sums up very succinctly the situation of couples in Ireland who find themselves overwhelmed by the tide of social expectation and the pressure to conform to those social ideals of family and parenthood. It is in the stories of infertility that we come to see most clearly the meaning of fertility and conception to ideals of stability and identity in both nation and individual. In such stories we also see the significance of fertility to individual projects of material success and social conformity against a backdrop of growing prosperity, increasing societal heterogeneity and wider global networks of politics and citizenship. And perhaps most importantly, we can discern the resistance and agency of women and their partners as they struggle to participate in a complex of social identities and processes grounded in an ideal they desire, embrace, even embody, without being able to actualise it.

1. Famine's Traces:
Hunger for Motherhood, Family, Fertility

Barren, never to know the load
of his child in you, what is your body
now if not a famine road?
Eavan Boland (from *The War Horse*, 1975)

In her evocative poem called 'The Famine Road', Eavan Boland draws poignant connections between history and the presence of absence, comparing the Famine Road with infertility. Here the woman's sense of self worth and her concept of her own body as valueless space or a project with no purpose are deeply marked with the history of loss, social suffering and oppression that has informed much of Ireland's national imaginary. The history of poverty, social inequality and colonial politics in Ireland also runs parallel to the history of a unique Irish familism, the politics of reproduction, the political trope of 'woman' and the ways these converged in the politics of producing the nation itself. More important for this inquiry, perhaps, is the historical production of motherhood as an important symbol of renewal and identity and the emergence of family as the site of moral certitude in the Irish state. Boland's poem alludes to the way history lives in embodied meanings of reproduction and motherhood – meanings that are drawn from the past, narrated as if remembered or imagined in personal life stories, and represented as natural facts in institutional discourses. Ireland's history is, of course, experienced differently by those who embody it as they walk the old famine roads in various ways.

Family Conceived in History

Katherine Conrad describes the significance of the family in Ireland through her multi-layered description of the 'family cell' in which people are bound to and captive within the seemingly organic hetero-normative framework defined by marriage and reproduction.[1] The family became a symbol of stability, a means of defining what was foreign or outside, and what was to be accepted as normal, acceptable and safe. Conrad also draws on Foucault's analysis of the family as a site for sexual regulation where the 'family cell' was an 'effective means of control and reproduction, both literally and figuratively, of the social order [. . .] and remained as an idealised structure in both nineteenth- and twentieth-century Irish nationalist *and* unionist discourse and eventually enshrined as the cornerstone of the new Irish nation-state'.[2] Influential in this process was the relationship that grew between the Catholic Church and the emergent postcolonial Free State and ultimately the Republic of Ireland. In many ways then, the current story of a changing Ireland begins before the Famine of 1845–50, in a chain of events through which reproduction and family have become touchstones in Irish history and politics.

Margot Backus (1999) links the political attention focused on the family in Ireland to the legacy of both Christian patriarchy and colonial protection of economic interests rather than a product of Catholic social teaching. The family remains an important institution whose political expedience and symbolic value has been exploited by both Church and state. Repeated episodes of famine in Ireland during the colonial period led to developments in agricultural practices and politics that intensified the political, social and economic significance of the family. The movement towards land reform and greater control over the productive capacity of family farms emerged, at least in part, as a response to the history of mass starvation, poverty and emigration during years of famine in the nineteenth century.[3] For women this shift was particularly significant since they were subject to what Ruth-Ann Harris describes as a 'double jeopardy' in a patriarchal tenancy system that meant their economic dependency was tied to male landowners through male partners and largely by virtue of having children.[4] Women were thus not only desperately poor in many cases, but also tied to a marital relationship and motherhood as key to survival.

Changes in land holding led to parallel changes in family dynamics that, some argue, redefined the meaning of marriage as an economic strategy when dowries and property values became grounds for creating new households. Women did not have to marry to be economically self-sufficient, but without a dowry or a place on their parents' farm they often either emigrated or took up a religious vocation. The relationship between family formation, population growth and fertility led to patterns of high rates of marital fertility and sustained birth rates that were offset by this pattern of emigration and a significantly high rate of permanent celibacy.[5] Low rates of marriage may have constituted a reactive contraceptive strategy in light of the repressive sexual attitudes of the Catholic Church.[6]

The importance accorded the idealised family in Irish political and social life in the twentieth century begins with the emergence of an influential monastic hierarchy and institutional traditions of the Catholic Church during much of the nineteenth century. The Catholic Church played a dual role in constituting the ideals of marriage, motherhood and family. At the level of individual and social life, Tom Inglis describes how the Catholic Church came to exert what he describes as a 'moral monopoly'.[7] The church's influence in the past extended beyond the making of moral decisions, to decisions in virtually every facet of day-to-day life, as if there were concrete rules that could be applied in every situation; consultation with a priest over the most trivial matters like where to sit or what to wear in church was not uncommon, often utilising the medium of the church newsletter.[8] By the end of the nineteenth century and into the early twentieth century, the Catholic Church had become involved in the delivery of social welfare, health and educational programmes that helped foster a mutual political relationship between church and state.[9]

Throughout the nineteenth and twentieth centuries, the church promoted its doctrine by valorising motherhood and promoting marital fertility but, at the same time, enforcing a rigid code of sexual morality that meant opportunities for legally and morally sanctioned reproduction were restricted. Fertility and family were encouraged, but at the same time the structural constraints on family formation meant fewer people would have large numbers of children. The church's prohibition on contraception was only one strand of the complex fertility picture as family farm economies, concern over emigration patterns and the delayed movement to an urban industrial economy contributed to the fertility picture.[10] What is clear is that the combination of church, state and economics in Ireland produced a rather unique and complex family picture with sometimes contrary formations and patterns of reproduction.

A drive towards modernisation in Irish family life in the early twentieth century, encouraged by the hierarchy of the Catholic Church, further emphasised the division of gender roles consolidated in the Constitution. Claire Wills argues that a combined 'ideology of motherhood and domesticity' also helped constitute domestic space as a site of resistance to 'secular individualism'.[11] The increasing status of men as providers in the household was reinforced by encouraging women to concentrate their labour in domestic space, emphasising the value of a new middle-class definition of the household with a focus on hygiene and order, making it appealing to a better-educated generation of women.[12] This ideal of domesticity was marshalled into the politics of Catholic-nationalism, bolstering the patriarchal social vision that was later reflected in the Irish Constitution in 1937.

The meaning of motherhood has also travelled the Famine Road as history contributed to the complex and institutionalised constructions and uses of the concept and relationship. 'Mother Ireland' is a gendered construction associated not only with the feminising of Irishness in colonial representations but also the modelling of the state after patriarchal family structures.[13] Much has been written on the kind of gendered identity that emerged, in broad representational strokes, in the relationship between Britain, as colonial patriarch and Ireland. On one hand, Ireland was portrayed as weak, inept and backward by its colonial political oppressors. On the other hand, a feminine Ireland also featured in nationalist portrayals of a nation that must be fought for – sometimes 'Mother Ireland' as a national femme fatale that needed to be rescued and protected[14] and sometimes as a lover whose virtue is at risk but whose moral character is beyond reproach.[15]

Motherhood played a dual role in the continuity of rural Irish life, providing not only heirs to the property but also a point through which church authority and influence could be directed most efficiently. The ongoing and deeply hegemonic insistence that mothers were the moral arbiters and carriers of the faith within families, while not unique to Catholicism or Ireland, constituted them as the 'organisational link between the Catholic Church and the individual'.[16] Catholic teaching was not only the purview of women in family homes but was carried out through 'oral transmission of religious tradition [and] was mostly the responsibility of older women'.[17] In this way women were constituted as allies of the Church. At the same time, their reproductive capacity was the site for much moral denigration, and women describe being forced to hide in their homes after giving birth until they could be ritually cleansed or 'churched' to expunge the sin of childbirth.[18] This conflicted representation of birth as a reminder of the sinfulness of sex in light of the importance placed on fertility and motherhood is one of many contradictions that resonate for infertile women in the present.

The role of the Catholic Church in the politics of motherhood was thus most effective in relation to sexual morality. The infamous Magdalene Laundries that were asylums for prostitutes, women and girls who were pregnant out of wedlock, were enabled by a society convinced that morality could be decided along the lines of sexual activity and family politics. Catholic social teaching not only encouraged but empowered families to commit 'fallen' or at risk girls to asylums and even refuse to return for them once the penance had been served.[19] Motherhood was expected but within the social enclosure of marriage and family.

The Constitution of Family

Origins of the more recent regulatory debates around divorce, reproductive choice, abortion and assisted reproduction technologies can
be traced through historical developments wherein Catholic social
teaching came to dominate much of the early state policy-making and
the writing of the Constitution in 1937. The 1937 Constitution was
framed partly around the need to convey the contrast between Britain
and Ireland and affirm politically an alliance with Catholicism – the
religion to which more than 90% of the population adhered.[20] These
assumptions emerge as recurring themes in the historical construction
of gendered Irish state policies on sexuality and reproductive choice,
particularly those in which contraception, divorce, homosexuality
and abortion were made illegal. The banning of divorce and prohibition of contraceptives in 1935, while reflecting church doctrine and
based on the constitutional validation of the family, were both framed
as nationalist political measures to protect the nation against the
immoral influences of Britain, Protestants and the outside world.[21]
The reproductive heterosexual family unit, as both the symbol and
source of social stability, was of course also further enshrined and
protected.

The Constitution of 1937, written by Éamon de Valera of the newly
formed Fianna Fáil party and taoiseach (prime minister), was based on
the two significant elements that became social ideals with enduring
impact on the reproductive politics of the state – patriarchy and
Catholicism. Recognising 'the Family as the natural primary and fundamental unit of Society, and as a moral institution possessing inalienable
and imprescriptible rights', it 'guarantees to protect the Family in its constitution and authority, as the necessary basis for social order and as
indispensable to the welfare of the Nation and State'.[22] The Constitution
also established that common good and social responsibility take precedence over the individual aspirations of women as citizens. Article 41.2
of the Constitution establishes the position of women in Irish social, economic and political life:

> the State recognises that by her life within the home, woman gives
> to the State a support without which the common good cannot be
> achieved . . . The State shall endeavour to ensure that mothers shall
> not be obligated by economic necessity to engage in labour to the
> neglect of their duties in the home.[23]

Women were excluded from public life in many ways in Ireland at
the dawn of its independence, beginning with the historical construction

of motherhood as producing rebellious sons and nationalist heroes rather than participating in political struggles themselves.[24] The constitutional ascription of a domestic role for women had a concrete application with the implementing of a 'marriage bar' in the 1930s. Married women's participation in the labour market was discouraged by an extensive ban on public-sector employment. This practice was not unique to Ireland and was a response to high unemployment, restricting women's access to jobs in the white collar sector, largely, but also limiting access to industrial employment.[25] What is unique is that the structural constraints on women's employment persisted in Ireland until 1973 when the ban was lifted. Women's workforce participation has remained consistently lower than that of women in Northern Ireland.[26] The residue continues today as studies indicate that women in the Irish workforce gain fewer benefits for their investment in education than men, gain fewer benefits from employment experience than men and tend to enter lower-paying fields of study.[27]

Gerardine Meaney suggests that '[t]he identification of the family (rather than, for example, the individual) as the basic building block of society is more than pious rhetoric in the Irish Constitution. In postcolonial southern Ireland a particular construction of sexual and familial roles became the very substance of what it means to be Irish.'[28] Reproduction and family have remained hallmarks of Irish society. Indeed, virtually any media story in Ireland today describing individuals – whether victims of a tragedy or the centre of human interest pieces – includes the number of children to whom they are a 'mother' or a 'father'.

As a political document of its time, the Irish Constitution was steeped in a discourse and ideology of patriarchy – providing for children, the logic of material wealth as inheritance, and protecting mothers and children – that is often a basis for narrating the values that underpin reproductive choices and family formation in Ireland today. What the document also does in its collapse of women and mothers is affirm an assumption that women are essentially fertile and leaves little room for an autonomous identity of womanhood outside this assumption.

Current Concepts of Family

In recent years, changes in family composition have continued to be linked to changing economic factors. Finola Kennedy suggests that the family, economics and reproduction remain inextricably linked and are thus important indicators of political and economic change. Changing agricultural patterns, shifting political relationships with the European

Union and altered meanings for economic independence combined with an increasing standard of living culminating in the Celtic Tiger in the late twentieth and into the twenty-first century have all had an impact on the shape of families and the role of children within families.[29] Close family ties endure, promoting different kinds of social and economic networks in particular communities, even if such networks of family relations are reconfigured in their meanings.[30]

The Irish government has, it seems, acknowledged the changing social fabric by undertaking a constitutional review to explore whether the terms of reference in the constitutional framework remain valid. This began with two committees struck in 1996 and 1997 aimed at, among other things, re-evaluating the definition of family and the impact of such definitions on public policy.[31] Since all amendments to the Irish Constitution must be ratified by referendum, any changes are carefully considered. The Constitutional Review Group's tenth report, which addresses the issue of the family specifically, suggests that any amendment to 'extend the definition of family' would be divisive and unlikely to be supported by the population in referendum.[32] The report suggests instead, based on submissions from a wide spectrum of the public, that the main concerns in the current definition could be addressed by legislative rather than constitutional changes.[33] The Irish Human Rights Commission (IHRC) has criticised this decision since it leaves couples who are outside the hetero-normative definition on the margins. They argue that any legislation designed to protect the interests of 'de facto families' such as cohabiting couples (same sex or heterosexual) can be overridden by constitutional laws that still rely on the traditional definition, creating a two-tiered definition of family.[34] As a political idiom, 'traditional' marriage still forms the backbone of hetero-normative definitions of family even if the pattern, in reality, differs from the idealised picture.[35]

This influence lingers into the twenty-first century in the policies that are products of the Constitution and that most directly influence family formation and the perpetuation of a hetero-normative ideal. The Catholic Church in Ireland was not omnipotent but certainly influential. At the same time, the significance of familism, gender and notions of tradition as features of the national identity are also important in the making and meaning of ideals and the shape of individual identities within families in Ireland.[36] And yet, the story of change in Ireland is an old and enduring story with institutional discourses shifting in and out of positions of influence and state policies being crafted and re-crafted in order to sustain the iconic Irish family as the source of social and economic stability.

In fact, Ireland continues to have the highest fertility rate among all EU nations. While the numbers indicate that Irish women are having fewer children than they did even a decade ago the statistics also indicate an important demographic shift in the average age of women giving birth, either for the first time or subsequent times. Overall, fewer teenagers and women in their twenties gave birth to children, while a greater proportion of women who gave birth in 2004 were in their later thirties and early forties. This trend continued in 2012 and represents a shift from past years when the greater proportion of women giving birth were less than thirty years of age. Another important change has been in relation to the type of family in which children are born. Since nearly a third of all children born in Ireland in the last decade are born to women who are not married to a partner there is evidence that motherhood is no longer tied to marriage. Single mothers are as likely to be in their thirties and forties as are married mothers. However, Cormac Ó Gráda specu-lates that this rise in age might be associated with 'planned' extramarital births and therefore presumed to be within 'stable and viable family units'.[37] Ó Gráda does not define exactly what he means by a 'stable' family unit but the phrase suggests that he means a relationship that involves a partnership and perhaps the hetero-normative ideal of a man, a woman and their children.

Defining the Unborn

The influence of the Constitution is perhaps felt most distinctly in the historical events of the abortion referendum. In 1983, a national refer-endum was held to decide on a constitutional amendment to secure the 'right to life of the unborn'. This event has had a profound social, polit-ical and symbolic impact on the way conception and motherhood are perceived in relation to many facets of identity from personhood to cit-izenship. It has also resonated into the present as women and men seek to use the services of assisted reproduction. The meaning of the 'right to life' with respect to such practices as *in vitro* fertilisation, embryo freezing and embryo donation remains uncertain. And indeed, legisla-tors and legal experts have all noted the challenge in interpreting the meaning of the unborn in relation to technologies that were not common or did not exist in 1983. The abortion referendum campaign was divisive and hard fought but ultimately the addition of Article 40.3.3 was accepted. Voter participation in the 1983 referendum on the Eighth Amendment to the Constitution was 54% of those eligible and the amendment was accepted when 67% voted in agreement. As Tom Hesketh notes, Ireland represents a somewhat unusual case in that it did not move from 'restrictive to permissive – a feature common to most European countries – but rather moved to entrench constitutional force where there were already laws in place'.[38] The concern among pro-life advocates was that constitutional backing was the only way to ensure that legislation could not be introduced that might pave the way for legal abortion. Criminal laws could be changed more easily than the constitution, which requires a nationwide referendum to ratify changes, and pro-life supporters were cognizant of the power of court challenges to change laws.[39]

The following passage taken from the 1983 Dáil Debates around the issue indicates the desire of legislators to distance themselves from the responsibility of defining the terms of political and moral obligation associated with when life begins. The passage is taken from a statement issued by the Fianna Fáil deputy Dr Woods, whose lengthy statement in favour of strengthening the constitutional protection of the unborn by referendum was questioned at one point for being read from notes. The debate itself centred on the issue of language and the need to leave some room to manoeuvre in the wording of the Bill as noted below:

> Despite what would undoubtedly have been the wish of the pro-moters of this amendment and the majority church in this island, there is no attempt in the wording of the amendment to define the moment at which the life of the unborn begins. The amendment does not attempt to make this definition. Most, of course, would argue that it begins at the time of conception, but this is a matter of theological and scientific argument and in preparing the wording of the amendment we felt it was not appropriate to the Constitution to have such definitions.[40]

What is germane to my project is not only the obvious reticence on the part of legislators, in the past, to make clear the definitions on which they were basing their proposed constitutional protection, but the sug-gestion that the ongoing debate and responsibility for the definition should reside with the science and theology. The underlying assumption is that religious and scientific or medical institutions represent static values and interests and have, themselves, formulated a singular unproblematised definition of such terms as 'unborn'. At stake are the grounds for determining moral authority. While science and theology are not necessarily, or always, in opposition in their positions on when the 'life of the unborn begins', the institutional interests and implications for these groups differ greatly; the work of science in the area of repro-ductive medicine is at risk of complete curtailment should the Constitution be interpreted in favour of the interests of many theologians who argue that life begins at the moment of fertilisation.

The fallout of a refusal to define the terms is at least partly behind a number of cases that have tested the moral mettle of a universal ban on abortion in the Irish social context. In 1991 the debate on abortion and the 'right to life of the unborn' extended into wider political arenas as Ireland prepared for the referendum on ratification of the Maastricht Treaty on European Union. The Irish government added a protocol to the treaty ensuring no interference with Article 40.3.3 by the European Union.[41] However, even as Ireland took measures to ensure EU policies could not override its policies on reproductive choice, publicity about the 'X' case forced a re-examination of national policy on abortion from within.

The case involved a court injunction issued to prevent a suicidal fourteen-year-old sexual assault victim from travelling to Britain to terminate a pregnancy.[42] Following a public outcry sparked by women's groups around the country, the ruling was ultimately overturned by the Supreme Court and the girl's parents were permitted to take her to Britain. However, constitutional debates have continued over the rights of citizenship and gender equality in reproductive choice. Since that time several other cases have come before the courts resulting in a very public re-examination of the legal but, more importantly, the moral and social limits of compassion for women when it comes to reproductive choice and the integrity of body and self. Two referenda, in 1992 and 2002, attempted to reverse the impact of the ruling of the 'X' Case by restricting a woman's right to travel and proposing to exclude risk of suicide as sufficient grounds to allow a legal abortion. More than twenty-five years after Article 40.3.3 was inserted in the Constitution, Morgan Healy argued that the ongoing appearance of a pro-life national politics is part of the 'authenticity' of Irish identity.[43]

Assisted reproduction technology represents one such challenge to the church's attempts to consolidate a moral hegemony through the conservatively written Article 40.3.3 of the Constitution. Definitions of who constitutes 'the unborn' must now be clarified in light of the capacity to separate conception from sex and the body. At the same time, the negative position taken by the Catholic Church hierarchy on ART suggests the church is unwilling or unable to address adequately the problem infertility represents for individuals and families in Ireland.

ART and the Irish Context

From the standpoint of pronatalist politics and pro-family ethics that are present in Ireland, a technology that enables procreation would seem to be a positive and welcome option for people trying to build a family. In 2005 there were nine clinics providing assisted reproduction services in Ireland. In 2012 there were eight clinics but one provides satellite services in three locations in addition to its Dublin clinic. At the turn of the new millennium the Irish government was faced with a growing number of clinics delivering an ever-increasing number of services based on technologies designed to assist in conception and reproduction. While the state has always maintained a paternalistic involvement in reproductive medicine, there was a rather quiet onslaught of increasingly invasive and contentious treatment options available to couples suffering infertility in Ireland. Senator Mary Henry had put forward a private member's bill in the *Oireachtas* in 1999 enti-tled 'Regulation of Assisted Human Reproduction', in which she called for the establishing of a regulatory ethics committee to oversee the serv-ices provided in Ireland.[44] Her concerns stemmed, at least in part, from the possibility of exploitation of couples in a situation where no regula-tions protected their interests. The bill was defeated but the Commission on Assisted Human Reproduction was created in the year 2000 by then Minister for Health and Children Micheál Martin. Following the practices of other states such as Britain and Canada, both of which had similar commissions to establish a basis for regulatory frameworks, the government of Ireland appointed a commission headed by Dr Dervilla Donnelly, an organic chemist from University College Dublin (UCD).[45] The terms of reference for the CAHR were 'to prepare a report on the possible approaches to the regulation of all aspects of assisted human reproduction and the social, ethical and legal factors to be taken into account in determining public policy in this area'.[46] Since the release of the CAHR report and recommendations in 2005, the Oireachtas Committee for Health and Children has discussed its implications on several occasions, always arriving at the same con-clusion that more time is needed or that some other level of institutional redress is required before any attempt at drafting legisla-tion. Some of the specific findings and recommendations of the CAHR report will be explained, where pertinent, in later chapters, but one of its most important points was the immediate need for legislation to govern the use of medical technologies in the field of reproductive medicine. However, legislation has been publicly promised on numerous occasions but, at the time of writing, is not forthcoming.

Issues such as stem cell research, access to medically necessary abor-tion and assisted reproduction appear regularly in the media and in institutional debates and discourse. The Catholic Church hierarchy uses new platforms to ensure its voice is heard in an increasingly secular society where the pulpit and the confessional can no longer be relied on as sites for the exercise of moral authority. Old patterns of institutional response to ethical issues are reanimated in new ways as committees, councils and commissions are struck and reorganised, mandated to develop a consensus before each new challenge can be regulated, but never quite resolving one issue before the next one emerges.

What has emerged from this constitutional construction is a reproductive politics that has not only essentialised gender roles but has marshalled women's reproductive capacity as a rhetorical device to distinguish Ireland from the UK and its EU neighbours as part of the politics of national identity. The distinction is built upon and reinforces a number of facets of Ireland's moral nationhood. These include Catholicism as the religion of the majority, pronatalism and familism as dual prongs of social policy, and the postcolonial imperative toward self-determination.[47] This is evident, as Lisa Smyth suggests, where 'the stimulus for anti-abortion politics in Ireland has emerged from a concern to mark Ireland out, using the liberal apparatus of global human rights, as a morally distinct nation-state'.[48] Against this political backdrop, my research explores how the reproductive politics of the past might shape the quest for motherhood and the use of new reproductive technologies in Ireland's present.

The meaning of infertility is linked to the historical constitution of reproductive idioms in Irish politics, the social meanings of family and the emergence of an idealised 'traditional' model of marriage and family. Behind the statistical story of fertility rates and birth rates in Ireland's history there lies a complex story inscribed in the lives of those who did not reproduce, or left Ireland before they became reproductive individuals – members of religious orders, the unmarried/permanently celibate, the large number of emigrants in the nineteenth and twentieth centuries. The stories behind these patterns in Ireland's past are part of a wider history in which fertility has been socially defined and confined through a 'biopolitics' aimed more often at sustaining social and political ideals than a growing population census.[49] The combined politics of pronatalism, population pressure, lack of access to contraception and efforts to make the family farm a sustainable livelihood in post-Famine Ireland resulted in a complex balance in which fertility was controlled through restricting access to sexual relationships in marriage.[50] At the same time, women who did marry had high fertility rates. What has changed is the accessibility and popularity of nuclear family formation – whether through marriage or cohabitation. However, even those who seek to conform to the idealised nuclear family formation may have difficulty realising their aspirations.

These historical institutional formations and discourses are part of the continuum of reproductive politics, the making of gender difference and the importance of the heterosexual family based in marriage as they pertain to the issues in the chapters that follow. I use the term continuum deliberately since the discourses of church, state and medicine with respect to reproductive politics and the moral and ethical imperatives of reproduction in Ireland are far from static. In fact there is a constant state of flux in which the meanings of reproduction and motherhood, family and morality allude to the past and anticipate and respond to changes in Ireland's social conditions, relationship to the EU, and the global politics of biomedicine in which assisted reproduction plays an important role.

2. Motherhood Contested:
Re-thinking the Woman/Mother Paradigm in Ireland

Whether or not a woman is lesbian, infertile, post-menopausal or child-less, in modern western cultures she will be assigned a subject position linked to a body that has perceived potentialities for birth.[1]

In the post-Celtic Tiger moment of the early twenty-first century, Ireland seemed caught between a lament for tradition and the embrace of social change. In fact, what everyone wanted to talk about was change imagined through the conceptual frame called tradition – a reference that marks the present more distinctly than the past. The seemingly rapid gallop into modernity and prosperity in the past two decades was not easily reconciled with the day-to-day experiences of family life, reproduction and livelihoods in Ireland. For many women, overcoming fertility challenges also meant navigating uncertainty between the multiple overlapping and changing meanings of mother-hood – an experience, an identity, a relationship and a social role. More importantly perhaps is the changing sense of responsibility and social expectation within the meaning of motherhood. In the last chapter I described how maternal identity and the importance of con-ception have come to be imagined in relation to notions of communal morality, social identity and the history of the nation. In this chapter I examine how this production of identities and social values based on women as mothers is experienced in the interplay of subjectivity, agency and the local moral world in modern Ireland.

Perhaps more importantly, I will show how many women envision themselves, through the lens of their own experiences with infertility and reproduction, as part of a wave of social change in the politics of family formation in Ireland. Seeing themselves as both agents and beneficiaries, they mark change, tradition and resistance through relationships to family, institutions such as the Catholic Church and access to reproduc-tive health information and choices. Their stories also mark how fertility and infertility are defined and redefined against the politicised and nat-uralised meanings of birth, family and motherhood in Ireland. Some of my early experiences with what is broadly described as tradition in

Ireland provided the benchmarks along which change, in terms of family and reproduction, could be gauged and understood.

Celebrating Mothers

My initial research visit to Ireland in March 2004 coincided with two significant events on the calendar – St Patrick's celebrations and Mother's Day. These events do not always occur in such close proximity but in that year and the next, I experienced firsthand the kind of social frenzy that often accompanies the two celebrations, creating a swirl of social activities, gifting and travel. After the initial shock of the magnitude of both events, I could see the impact of consumerism and marketing on the closely held values and identity of Irish people as family oriented and as members of a Catholic nation. There seemed to be, at the heart of these events, an emphasis on sustaining 'tradition' in both the meaning of being Irish and the meaning of being a mother. More importantly, it seemed that motherhood, as an ideology, was also implicated as an integral part of tradition in these kinds of community celebrations.

St Paddy's week, as it is now celebrated, is not only a tourist draw but a huge party in which many Irish people themselves participate in a celebratory atmosphere that takes over in all communities, big and small. A 'parade' in the village of Dripsey, in County Cork, received coverage in the local press as the shortest St Patrick's parade in the country where participants emerged from the door of one pub only to 'parade' across the road to the other pub a mere 20 metres away.[2] Pubs are the central focus of St Paddy's Day celebrations and many pub windows sported hand-lettered signs that read 'No Prams Allowed in the Pub'. For someone from North America, the collision of motherhood, modernity, family and tradition implied in such signs was surprising. However, as has long been accepted practice, mothers and babies, young children and families of all sorts are welcome in the pubs and are frequent customers at some periods of the day, particularly at weekends.[3] Particular pubs are described by people as 'locals', extensions of one's intimate social and domestic space where family belongs. This proved to be an important part of my fieldwork as I conducted many interviews in pubs – a paradox in which private and intimate conversation occurred in the most public of venues.

The week of festivities around St Patrick's Day culminated, that year, with the celebration of Mother's Day at the weekend. Friends with whom I stayed in Dublin were adamant that the roads would be too busy to travel on that weekend as everyone went home to visit their mothers.

The press reported in 2005 that the average Irish man spent more money on gifts for his mother on Mother's Day than he spent on gifts for a wife or girlfriend on Valentine's Day.[4] Shops are overflowing with gift suggestions for weeks in advance as bouquets of flowers, potted plants, boxes of chocolates and other items fill the shelves and leave the store in the arms of customers bound for their natal homes and mothers' kitchens. However, on the flipside of this celebration, my participants told me that Mother's Day was an event second only to Christmas in its insidious reminder of their inability to conceive. The commercialisation of such events heightens the sense of loss for those who will never participate in an intergenerational continuity by both giving *and* receiving gifts for Mother's Day; nor will they participate in the buying of Christmas gifts for their own children.

While such material experiences may seem a shallow aspect of the celebration of either Christmas or Mother's Day, the social participation and symbolism of gifts on these occasions serve to amplify that 'presence of absence' in the lives of many. Motherhood/parenthood and family represent forms of social capital that can be exploited for marketing products, events and identities.[5] They are also absorbed into a political agenda that perpetuates longstanding gender distinctions and conservatively drawn social definitions of morality and stability through the ideal of family as part of a continuum of material and social success, perhaps never more so than in an age of marked social and economic change.

Motherhood was portrayed as the norm everywhere in the media. Television commercials for products including feminine hygiene products, fast food, cleaning products, vehicles and mobile phone plans, among others, all featured the vibrant, beautiful (if harried) young mother as the centre of their marketing strategy.[6] The image of the woman as mother, while pervasive, seemed to be largely unchallenged in the media by any counter-representation of women as other than mothers. And yet, for many women, particularly those with challenges to their ability to conceive, the essentially reproductive identity portrayed in the media is contested in day-to-day life.

The Ideology of Motherhood

Why does motherhood endure as an ideology in the wake of changing social values? The answer is partly reflected in the power of the hetero-normative assumption of a natural progression between marriage and motherhood for women in Ireland. For many of my participants the assumption was evident in the extent to which they were constantly being questioned about having children. Silence around infertility often perpetuates the public perception that people choose their childlessness and are selfish, abnormal or inadequate. The nature and details of an inability to conceive are rarely, if ever, discussed with friends or family even as the general social interest in couples' procreative lives is far from hidden.[7] For some women and their partners, the silence was a response to the perception that parents and grandparents were of a different generation and would not understand. For others it was induced by an acute awareness of lack of sensitivity on the part of siblings and friends.

The expression 'anything stirring?' came up in interviews and conversations as people described the ongoing assumption that young married couples would quickly get on with the business of having children.[8] Jane, a woman in her late thirties who was exploring her options for fertility treatment, told me how awkward the questions about children become when you are constantly replying that you do not have them. The question 'anything stirring?' locates the responsibility for fertility, conception and reproduction in women's bodies and puts a particular onus on them to answer for childlessness in a marital relationship.

> JANE: *You just don't want to say because first of all the minute you see somebody else has children you think they're just going to say something like 'oh you don't want them anyway because children are a headache'. Or 'oh jeez I envy you', all that stuff. Or then sometimes you see somebody who is expecting or they've got a small baby and you don't want them to feel uncomfortable that they've got something that you can't have and all that. You just don't go there. When you are one or two years married people say to you 'how long are you married?' and they say 'hmm, time for a family'. Then when you say I'm six years married they go 'oh'. And they don't ask. Cause it's kind of like, it's that way in Ireland. In a way maybe that's a good thing, and I have never had anybody be really insensitive or brutal. I think that has changed in Ireland. There's a lot less of the 'anything stirring?' stuff. It meant are you pregnant? The Irishisms.*

Even as she suggests things are changing, Jane points out that an assumption endures that children will follow marriage in quick succession. The incredibly high social value placed on family and motherhood contributes to assumptions about a logical or 'natural' life trajectory for women. Those who fail to enact the norms and rituals of becoming parents within a particular time period not only feel inadequate in themselves, but are questioned by others in ways that suggest that they are perceived as failing or deviating in some way.

BRIDGET: When you first start dating it's 'any news of diamond?' Then you get engaged and it's 'any news of date?' And then you're just married and it's 'any news of wee feet?'

CAROL ANNE: Do you remember my mother? It had been about two years and I had told her nothing at the time, like. And she did say to me, 'you know, you want to be thinking, Carol Anne, about having a baby.' And she actually said it and I said, 'well actually we are. We've been thinking about nothing else'. I said, 'there's obviously problems. And we have to try and get them sorted . . . But like she actually said 'because you know, people expect it . . . '
VINCE: When you get married, and people think that's it. You have your two children and that's it.
CAROL ANNE: And my neighbours used to ask and they don't ask anymore.

The assumptions reflected in the constant questioning of childless couples in Ireland is not unique, but Flo Delaney suggests it is part of the 'freemasonry of the fertile'.[9] Delaney describes the hetero-normative ideal of marriage and children in Irish society as a feature of pronatalism resulting largely from the influence of Catholicism. Pronatalism is only one facet of a political strategy sustaining the gendered and naturalised logic behind family as a symbol of the nation. Reproduction is contextualised as part of an unproblematised natural law that shapes hetero-normative marriage and conservatively proscribed sexual morality.[10] Pronatalism operates to promote the ideal woman's body as one with 'something stirring', but it is the importance of reproduction in sustaining the meaning of family in Ireland that supports the current emphasis on fertility as a norm.

Motherhood Envisioned: Conceptions of Being

While womanhood/motherhood is conflated and naturalised as a subject position in the public domain, the way this is experienced by women has shifted in response to changing social values in Ireland. The woman/mother association thus incorporates not only remnants of the past but evidence of changing moral and social ideals in Ireland's current conditions of socio-economic change. As they talk about their attempts to conceive, many women explore the meaning of motherhood in relation to and in contrast with the iconic and idealised 'traditional' family model as it is envisioned in their own past and present.

Jane describes the origins of a sense of social imperative modelled in an earlier generation. But even as she sees herself as challenging the imperative, it is evident that she also embraces the idea of motherhood. Her description also reveals the perception that those who do not conform to the ideal are social misfits.

> JANE: *Okay. So I grew up I suppose in a sort of typical Catholic family.* [. . .] *And probably what has become obvious to me in the last year is that it was always assumed that you would become a mother. It was just there. It was never questioned and the biggest thing I have recognised is I can't remember anybody ever saying there was a choice about it. It was just a fact that you understood that you would become a mother.* [. . .] *And I knew nobody growing up that ever was childless or struggling with infertility. And the only women that I did know that were childless or unmarried were considered very odd and different and living on the fringe. And some of them were considered quite mad. Extremely different and not integrated. It has only really come back to me in the last few months that* [. . .]*, that was my perception.*

Conveyed in the language of a calling from within, Jane's story evokes what Louis Althusser has described as '*interpellation* or hailing' wherein people recognise themselves as 'always-already subjects'. The relationship between ideology and subjectivity is one in which ideology 'recruits subjects' in the process of *interpellation* through which there is a shift from 'concrete individual' to 'concrete subject'.[11] Althusser refers to interpellation as a kind of 'hailing' in which someone responds to a call because they sense in themselves that they are the person being hailed. It is through this process that they become *and are* the subject of the call. Althusser points out that because of the 'always-already' nature of subjectivity there is no temporal sequence to such recognition. It is a matter of at once knowing you are the subject and being the subject.

Equally important in Jane's sense of motherhood is the emphasis on performance. Judith Butler has argued extensively for recognition of the performative aspects of gender identities – that subjectivities are about performing and about doing. In this sense *doing* is *being.* It is through the performance of an identity that we experience the processes of subjectification and enact them.[12] This sensation of performing the role for which they are cast was echoed in many of my interviews as women experienced the construction, embodiment and enactment of the norm as a powerful part of the woman/mother paradigm.

This form of subjectification employs the embodied ideals of fertility centred in women's bodies with motherhood as its ultimate representation. Jane points to the kind of oddness or pathology that was childlessness in her childhood recollections.[13] Elizabeth Throop suggests that infertility, like homosexuality, is always viewed as pitiable, deviant and suspicious in Ireland since one only becomes an adult with the birth of children.[14] Throop's description may echo a particular vision of the past but is context nonetheless for the ongoing assumption of fertility as a norm and heterosexuality as the frame in which it is enabled and enacted.

Heather Paxson describes the 'pathologization of infertility' as part of the process in which 'the social problem of childlessness is folded into nature' and the desire for motherhood is constituted as natural.[15] In Donna's story below she describes how one of her sisters felt compelled to explain her choice to forego motherhood knowing how badly Donna wanted it. A lack of 'maternal instinct' is framed here as an unnatural phenomenon and forms the basis for refusing the normative perception of a 'natural desire' for motherhood.

> DONNA: *I've a brother older than me and he lives in England and he's got two boys and then I was next to get married. And then my youngest sister was the next to get married and she met with me once, she wanted to meet with me and she said, 'I don't know how you're going to take this but I've chosen not to have children.' So I kind of looked at her and she said, 'I know that you would love to have children. But I just feel I don't have maternal instinct and there are an awful lot of children born today where the parents don't have maternal instinct and I could not do that'. And I actually respected her. I really respected the fact that she wasn't allowing society to pressurise her.*

The choice to become a parent is rarely, if ever, contested or queried, while choosing *not* to become a parent leaves one open to challenge and must be explained. Donna's sister may feel her lack of maternal instinct is also rooted in her 'nature', but she is nonetheless called to account in a way that women who want children are not. Whether women do not become mothers by choice or by fate, their childlessness is constituted as a deviation from what is expected of them as natural. I will return to the complex relationship between choice and childlessness in relation to assumptions and social norms about social responsibility later in the chapter, but the pronatalist politics in Ireland arises in a multitude of sites that produce norms – family, community, nation-state – and the social consequences of a failure to conform to the social expectations of parenthood.

While, arguably, the collision of historical and social forces in Ireland is unique, the pronatalist politics resulting in the constitution of a deviant social identity for childless women and couples is not. In her study of infertility in Vietnam, Melissa Pashigian describes this sense of abnormality experienced as forms of exclusion from an ideal promoted by state initiatives in family planning, marital responsibility and ancestral continuity.[16] Other scholars note the impact of disrupted adult identity in pronatalist contexts such as Egypt[17] and South India;[18] and disruptions in 'cultural ideologies of continuity' as part of reproductive responsibility in the US.[19] Moreover, as Lori Leonard notes, the meaning of motherhood is often what defines the extent to which infertility is deemed a problem. In Ireland, infertility represents a disruption to both social and individual identities, but on a deeper subjective level it also exposes the complex cleavage between agency and morality where the desire to be a mother is emergent. In the context of changing social norms, women in Ireland are negotiating this uncertainty by re-defining the importance of motherhood and their own autonomy in embracing it.

Donna continues by suggesting that there is a universal meaning to the ideal of family to which Irish society adheres.

> DONNA: *Yes, and Harold is my family. And my siblings are my family but it's not like . . . in the Irish society . . . I don't know about other societies but I'm sure it is worldwide that family is mother, father, children.*

Thus, even trying to redefine family as a relationship without children seems unthinkable to many couples in Ireland. People like Donna, who remain childless, have tried to imagine their marriages as constituting a family in and of themselves, against the grain of Irish social convention.[20] Jane's husband, in frustration at her sadness over not yet conceiving, asked her point blank one day, 'am I not enough for you?' This was more painful than poignant since Jane's husband has fathered two children with a previous partner. For women like Jane and Donna, being unable to perform an identity that is so important to their sense of being is also a matter of not being good at being women.[21]

A similar kind of poignancy was often conveyed in the documentary series *Making Babies*, an Irish documentary production which aired on Irish national television in October 2004. As I watched this series, described by many people as 'groundbreaking', I recall being struck by the description of an embodied sensation, evoking both subjectivity and identity, given by one of the women profiled.[22] She had told her husband during the course of IVF treatment that, for her, the idea of conceiving 'was not about something she had to do; this was something she had to be'. Most compelling, perhaps, is that these words were conveyed in the documentary by her husband as he explained coming to terms with his partner's overwhelming desire to pursue a painful, inconvenient, even dangerous medical resolution to the biological and social problem of a failure to conceive. For him, this was the moment when he understood what she felt and how deeply embodied was her desire to be a mother – the difference between doing and being.

Infertility stories and experiences highlight the social assumptions about powerful sensations of desire, instinct and desperation that are thought to coalesce in women, shaping them as mothers by nature. But at the same time, these stories also highlight the way the social role of motherhood is shaped by people's experiences in forming families, whether there are fertility problems or not. Thus while family formation is the site for affirming and continuing the paradigmatic identity of woman as mother, what has changed are the social expectations for the kind of role woman as mother must play. Change is also marked by a greater sense of autonomy within the social role in relation to past generations of women, most especially their own mothers.

Conceiving of Change: Contesting Traditional Motherhood

The conceptual challenge to the actual role of mother was more apparent as people described their own parents' marriages and family roles. In these stories people worked through the origins of meanings associated with conception, birth, motherhood and family, making sense of family relationships and reproduction by plotting them alongside the roles and experiences of their parents. This kind of comparative examination is part of a wider dialogue in contemporary Ireland in which the meaning of reproduction and the reproduction of meanings play out. Does a kind of familism endure in social and political policies and norms that press for a particular image of family? If so, how is it reflected in the shifting social roles that so many people described as they plotted their own experiences, as a means of defining social change, against the experiences of their parents? In this light, people are also making sense of reproduction in a changing context in which the family in Ireland is no longer exclusively hetero-normative or modelled on a patriarchal framework and yet continues to be defined in those terms.

It is evident in the stories of women and men that an idealised or traditional model of motherhood – a social role many people described as emblematic of Irish society – continues to animate the meaning of infertility. At the same time women often differentiated themselves from the kind of motherhood identity they believed their own mothers embodied. In her study on modern motherhood in Greece, Heather Paxson points out that it is through social practice that gender identities can be defined. She draws on Michael Herzfeld's work to point out that gender is defined more by being 'good at being' a man or a woman than 'being a good man' or a 'good woman'.[23] Being good at being a woman in Ireland is related to being a mother; it is not motherhood as a mandate that has changed in Ireland, but rather the way that mandate has been shaped by the new Ireland that is the subject of a discourse about change.

Faye Ginsburg describes these kinds of narrative alignments as 'story' and 'plot', where plot entails how the raw details are situated in relation to social meaning for particular events and then reordered in the story in a way that allows for new meanings to emerge. Looking at the relationship of life events to activism in abortion politics in one American community, for example, Ginsburg describes how particular positions 'emerge out of a confluence of generationally marked experiences and individual life-cycle events, often related to reproduction'.[24] People make sense of particular points of view as they are plotted against events in the narrative. In a similar way, people in Ireland landmark meanings associated with becoming parents against the politics of access to contraception, the politics of married women in the labour force and access to knowledge about sex and reproduction.

An extensive literature points to the significance of 'familism' and pro-family politics as a longstanding feature of Irish national identity. For example, Nicole Yeates notes that her studies on Irish public policy and 'the biopolitics of welfare' consistently 'demonstrate how familism has been upheld by the Irish State to the detriment not only of married women but of all women, whatever their marital status and how its attempts to pursue gender equality have in turn been limited by familist ideology'.[25] While there are some indications that very conservative and traditional patterns of family building and reproduction endure, particularly in the rhetoric of the Irish state, the social reality is complex and contradictory. In a recent study, researchers at University College Dublin suggest that 'marriage no longer possesses the cultural status or primacy as a gateway to family formation that it once had, since sex, childbearing and cohabitation outside of marriage now widely occur'.[26] This, of course, does not mean marriage is not still important. Fahey and Field note that, in 2006, 40% more marriages took place in Ireland than in 1995, linking this trend to a large population of people in the marriageable age range and the relatively new accessibility of second marriages following divorce.[27] Thus, in spite of changing trends in motherhood, census data from 2002 and 2006 indicate that marriage rates, in terms of the percentage of the population, have remained unchanged in Ireland.[28] What is widely acknowledged as a significant change in recent years is an increase in the number of couples who are 'cohabiting'.[29] Betty Hilliard notes that, rather than a contradiction, an increase in cohabitation and family formation outside marriage runs parallel to the steady state of marriage rates, signalling that a wider set of options now exists, rather than one form eclipsing another. In other words, people who now opt to cohabit might not have formed a family at all if marriage was their only choice.[30] In a press release about the data, compiled from the 2006 census, the Central Statistics Office (CSO) described a decline in the 'traditional family', which is still defined by marriage and children.[31] Ó Gráda suggests that although the meaning of the 'stable' family unit is expanding to include single parents, same-sex couples and other forms, the rhetorical meaning of 'traditional' is still *married* parents and their children.[32] However, it is clear that the meaning of reproduction and choice is changing, and previously unquestioned links between marriage, procreation and parenting are being challenged. Many of my participants plotted their own parents' marriages as examples of an idea they called 'traditional'. The concept of tradition was evident in three distinct plot lines and experiential motifs that seemed to dominate women's lives; the domestic, moral and parental role, the social and economic role and the marital and sexual role.

In the following narrative Lara suggests that her family was an exemplar of this notion of 'tradition' even as she points out that the usual roles associated with such meanings of tradition were reversed: her father was the dominant one in the household sphere rather than her mother, whom she describes as 'submissive'. I heard frequent reference made, in both social and research encounters, to gender-based traditional roles ascribed to women/mothers in relation to an imagined domestic or 'private' sphere in Ireland.[33] Lara's story highlights assumptions about the meaning of tradition and gender-based expectations of dominance and submission, in relation to roles in her idealised view of the domestic sphere of the family home.

> LARA: *My mother was a stay-at-home mother – a very traditional situation. My father was very career oriented. He was the strong sort of controlling influence in the house; and my mother was the submissive, stay-at-home housewife. Which actually is unusual. I thought it was the norm growing up but in fact it's not. In Ireland, normally, the woman rules the roost. Yes, I come from an unusual background in the sense that I had a very strong father which . . . a lot of Irish fathers can be quite passive really. [. . .] I have a huge respect for my husband's mother because she's a tremendous woman of integrity; and in many ways she's had a very hard life. Her husband has manic depression – a very severe form of it – and she kept the eight kids and her husband on the straight.*

Lara describes her family as traditional on one hand but unusual on the other; while her mother was a conventional 'stay-at-home mother' and her father career-focused, her father also played a dominant role at home – a contrast to what Lara thought was more traditionally a domain of women's dominance. Nonetheless, she suggests that the family was a site that nurtured her own 'career focus'. She goes on to describe the seemingly opposite roles assumed by parents in her husband's family, where Paul's mother played a dominant and powerful role in both domestic and public domains as a working mother. Both women had many children and were thus examples of an ideal of motherhood espoused at the time. However, Lara also holds her husband's mother in especially high esteem for her dedication to preserving the family in spite of hardship and for maintaining strong values and faith. The strong and virtuous mother as the keeper of domestic space, morality and social values is a familiar trope that is widely discussed and sometimes contested in the literature on gender and family in Ireland in relation to power, institutional relations and nationalist symbolism.

Maureen, a teacher in her early thirties who had one child with the help of IVF and had just recently begun a second round of treatment when we met, describes how her own mother felt the weight of motherhood and domesticity imposed upon her just a generation before. For many women motherhood was a sacrifice of opportunities, especially if they were denied the option of continuing employment in their chosen field after marriage because of the marriage bar that consolidated the distinction between public and private spheres based on gender and restricted access to socio-economic independence.

> JILL: *You said you wouldn't even talk to your mother about all of this. Is she somebody who's really very supportive of the idea of being a mother? Is motherhood a very positive thing for her?*
> MAUREEN: *No. No. Because she would rather have worked. Like in Ireland years ago in my mother's time, once they got pregnant – women thirty years ago – they had to quit work. She was one of those. That was it. She was in the civil service so she was frustrated . . .*

Maureen's answer to my question about the importance of motherhood reveals how even in the face of social norms that governed the woman/mother paradigm, women have resisted the constitution of motherhood as synonymous with domesticity. Many of the women I spoke with suggested that their mothers were either directly affected by the state-imposed restrictions on access to employment in the past, or had experienced the fallout indirectly in the social expectation that women would automatically become 'stay-at-home mothers'. As Pauline Conroy notes, the restrictions on employment and the ban on contraception were linked in an effort to control women's reproduction and limit economic independence, effecting a 'political confinement' of women, through marriage and motherhood, to domestic space.[34] Women are no longer confined by the role of motherhood or an employment bar after marriage. Now motherhood resides alongside education, competition in the workplace and career development. This marks another comparative perspective on how previous generations of women/mothers experienced 'traditional' roles.

The roots of traditional motherhood are not only linked to changing social roles, but also changes in marriage relationships. Lisa draws contrasts between her own marital experiences and her parents' marriage, which she also describes as 'traditional' in its conformity to the ideal established by the Catholic Church. She describes her intention of living a life that espoused different values from those of her parents, rejecting the kind of motherhood role she felt constrained her own mother and yet establishing it as the story against which she plots her own desire to be a mother.

> LISA: *My mother is quite traditional and my parents, actually, are quite traditional and I was always very . . . whatever they did, I was the opposite. And it probably wasn't until I was about thirty maybe that the urge hit me.*
> JILL: *And so you saw your parents as having, like you say, a traditional life, married young, had children.*
> LISA: *Yeah, when they married Mum was twenty-two, Dad was a little bit older than that, and he had just got a promotion at work. They had gone out for a year – no sex before marriage – and she gave up her job when she got married. She's only talked to me about this recently, actually, because I had a miscarriage a while back and she came up to spend some time with me and I spilled my whole story. And she told me about how six months after they married she thought there was something wrong with her because she wasn't pregnant, but she didn't even know her cycles or ovulation . . . she didn't know any of that. My grandmother was even more traditional and you didn't talk about that kind of thing. So my mother would have had no sex education. In fact, I was teaching her things only recently about that kind of stuff. So she was very lacking in knowledge, so traditional in that sense. They had five kids but we were spread out. [. . .] And they wouldn't have used contraception, certainly. And partly because of what Ireland imposed on them. They couldn't get condoms or anything, you know.*

Lisa flags the issue of lack of access to contraception and any sort of sexual or reproductive knowledge as factors in her parents' traditional marriage. Traditional, in this story, is synonymous with a lack of sophistication or sexual knowledge and rigidly repressed sexual practices, something she identifies as culturally and politically *imposed* on her parents' generation. She assumes that since her parents did not use contraception and their children were spread out that perhaps abstinence might have played a role in their family planning. Lisa describes an intergenerational schism in knowledge, understanding and the meanings associated with sex and reproduction. By flagging this difference between her mother's reproductive life and her own, Lisa suggests that tradition is synonymous with having children in the absence of choice, while having children is now synonymous with being in control of life decisions around fertility – the very essence of choice. Access to information and particular kinds of reproductive knowledge were described as a feature of reproductive choice. Many women described their own mothers as ill-informed about sexuality, repro-duction and even their own bodies.

Stories about their mothers' lack of knowledge around reproduction are framed in relation to the repressive influence of the Catholic Church on access to sexual knowledge for generations of women in Ireland. Conroy points out that while there was widespread knowledge of con-traception prior to the ban in 1937, at this point such knowledge went 'underground'.[35] While Lisa describes her mother's lack of knowledge, she also highlights her mother's anticipation and anxiety that her mar-riage should produce children. A large part of the traditional role for women, as an ideal and as a marker for social change, was motherhood without sexual sophistication or understanding. In contrast, for the women in my study, experiences with infertility were opportunities to use sophisticated knowledge around reproduction to empower them-selves in a world where procreation is now understood in biological rather than social and religious terms.

The morally problematic but necessary aspect of sex was sanitised in the past, by Church discourse consigning it an unambiguous natural purpose as a procreative act. This kind of lockstep relationship supports Adrienne Rich's early feminist critique of motherhood as an institution produced through the workings of patriarchy.[36] Central to many con-tentious debates within feminism, an emphasis on women as defined by reproductive capacities creates a tension between biology as empow-ering and biology as a constraint through which patriarchy operates. This is evident particularly where an emphasis is placed on the relation-ship between 'nature' and the gendered and sexualised 'being' of women.[37] This tension also animates the way women in Ireland talk about motherhood as tradition. As a mechanism for comparing and con-trasting reproductive identities, talk of tradition creates a way to untangle the changing meaning of reproduction, as a phenomenon of nature, from the tight nexus of marriage and family that continues to infuse reproductive politics in Ireland. The new access to information, sense of sophistication and access to contraception that constitute the presumed ability to be in control of the 'nature' of one's fertility have been reconfigured and woven into the cultural narrative of modernity in Ireland in which all women are presumed to be in control of their procreative futures, even as they continue to be compelled to be mothers.

Re-conceiving Conception: Morality and Family Values in Flux

Within the complex dynamic of subjectivity, agency and morality, the generational shift in reproductive knowledge and values could be marked with respect to religious or moral attitudes towards IVF specifically. However, a broader issue was the relationship between procreation, marriage and morality condensed in the reproductive bodies of women as mothers. While people acknowledged the changing family landscape and the changing meaning of motherhood within that landscape, there is evidence that the idealism of marriage as a foundation for family endures. Historically, marriage has legitimised birth in legal and religious terms, but birth and motherhood can also be seen to legitimise marriage in the ethos of the Catholic Church. From the point of view of the church, there is a continuous thread of moral purpose drawn from marriage to sexual union to 'accepting' children; thus marriage can be understood as producing mothers while mothers produce families. As the constitutional references to motherhood suggest, such associations have been naturalised in institutional discourse of church and state.

In fact conception remains very tightly bound to marriage, as reflected in conservative views of motherhood in the changing social fabric. In response to a public lecture given on 27 January 2005 by Dr Edward Walsh, President Emeritus of the University of Limerick, Kevin Myers, a columnist for *The Irish Times*, wrote that he concurred with Dr Walsh's 'politically incorrect' position that the welfare system in Ireland was encouraging the formation of single-parent families headed primarily by young single mothers. Meyers was widely criticised in the media for his frequent reference to 'bastard children' and Dr Walsh in fact distanced himself from Kevin Myer's article a few days after it was published.[38] The concerns expressed by both Dr Walsh and Mr Myers point to the ambivalence some Irish people feel over the issue of an increasing number of single mothers and what it means for social stability, a reflection of the ongoing link between the traditional definition of family and the well-being of the state. Part of the ambivalence can be linked perhaps to the shock Irish people felt in 1984 when fifteen-year-old Ann Lovett died alone in childbirth in a grotto, having hidden her pregnancy from everyone. The obvious culture of fear that would enable such tragedy was debated widely.[39]

An intergenerational shift in attitudes toward procreation and motherhood is often cited as a sign of change in relation to the influence exerted by the Catholic Church with respect to its negative position on ART. Such plotting of changing values can be seen as an example of 'counter-discourse that has the capacity to *situate*: to relativise the authority and stability of a dominant system'.[40] As people discussed infertility treatment with their parents, acknowledging that IVF was not sanctioned by the church, they felt they were openly challenging what they assumed were the values held by their parents. Acceptance and tolerance by their parents was attributed, not to changing attitudes among their parents' generation, but rather as a sign that the value of producing children was an overriding factor that bridged the moral difficulty of IVF for religious family members.

Siobhan acknowledges that her parents were more concerned with the fact that she chose to live with her partner before marrying him. When she broached the subject of IVF with her parents, the fact that Siobhan and Sean were married seemed now to create support for having children no matter how they went about it.

> SIOBHAN: *I was already in my thirties so my parents wouldn't be the sort to say to a person in their thirties, 'don't do that'. They were a little bit concerned when I moved in with Sean. That was more of a problem against the religion and they didn't really have a problem with IVF. I kind of explained to my mother that what I was doing was totally against the Catholic faith but I guess she understood that it wasn't in the normal sense of the word. But again I'd say that things like contraception are against the Catholic faith, and I'm sure most people who have had their children practise it.*

Siobhan describes how her parents were more concerned with the importance of maintaining the ideal of marriage and children as a unified objective.[41] This plotting of the story creates a platform from which to challenge what many people saw as the paradoxical discourse on the part of the Catholic Church in which they condemn IVF on one hand while continuing to promote motherhood and having children on the other. While many people I spoke to suggested that they were the generation of change and that assisted reproduction was pushing the envelope of the moral monopoly held by the church in the past, it is often the stories of their parents' reactions to IVF treatment that reveal the shifting attitudes. While not universal, many people who revealed their use of IVF to their parents were met with an acceptance of the procreative value of assisted reproduction even among conservative and practising Catholic families. Having children was seen as the predominantly virtuous activity, regardless of how this happened.

> BETH: *Like my mum is very supportive but they'd be very religious the two of them. Well they've never said a word and I think at this point any religious issues they have would just be overridden by the fact that they would be very happy for us to have kids so I think they wouldn't mind. Just in the wider family there has been this disapproval.*

NIAMH: *Now in my life, my parents would be very religious even though they don't force it on us. But we always went to mass. For a person who would be very religious, you know, and they would be very much into the teachings of the church, it was probably her who even said it first. She'd been talking to our family doctor for generations, and the doctor had said well would they not try IVF. And Mum said it to me you know, in a way like . . . So I don't think she has issues with it like that. And if anyone was going to I could see my parents having them because, you know, they are very much followers . . . But she doesn't seem to. The way I see it is it would be a life where there wouldn't be one.*

Niamh can rationalise her mother's acceptance by situating it alongside her own perception that IVF is 'productive' and 'procreative', promoting a conception that would not otherwise happen. The productive potential to fulfil a social and moral mandate to be a mother overrides the concern arising from Catholic values. But even as these stories indicate the widespread tendency to examine and challenge the Catholic Church's position on IVF, they continue to draw on the wider social value that collapses motherhood and marriage into an ideal that is naturalised in Irish politics and social life.[42] The values of fertility and family are distilled from their religious connotations and examined, but remain largely unchallenged as norms in themselves.

Conceptions of Agency: Choice and Challenge in an Ideology of Motherhood

Questions of agency and intersubjectivity necessitate a discussion of the idea of choice in the politics of reproduction. As discussed above procreative decisions are never made in a political or social vacuum. However, the complex influences of identity and agency, biology and embodiment all confront the issue of the subject and the point at which action, decision and notions of self collide in a reproductive politics conceived as 'choice'. In many of the stories above we saw the ideology of motherhood as it shapes the sensation of presence of absence for women who are trying to conceive. At the same time the stories conveyed the depth of intersubjectivity in which we heard women, mothers, would-be mothers, daughters and partners speak in multi-layered narratives that reveal the sense of self bound to procreative endeavours. Is it possible to locate the notion of choice as concrete in relation to the multiple subject positions women occupy? Is choice, in relation to reproduction, a representation of agency or merely a narrated expression of social and institutional influence?

Feminist debates about the iterative or performative quality of narratives centre on the question of subjectivity and agency.[43] Does a narrative provide the performative space to enable agency or is it a reflection of discursive power to shape subjectivity and moral reasoning after the fact of decision-making? In other words, are narratives a product of intersubjectivity or do they produce the very subject positions that emerge as part of the stories they relate? In the case of reproductive decision-making, this question is central to the notion of agency as women and their partners describe the meaning of choice and the notion of resistance to dominant social perspectives through counter-narratives. As people spoke about reproductive choice in Ireland in relation to infertility, they drew again on the historical meanings and ideals that have shaped tradition and familism as dominant influences. At the same time, their stories contest the very idea that reproduction is in our control, that there are always options and, most important, that all efforts must be made to choose a means of building a traditional nuclear family.

From Sinning to Selfishness: Re-conceiving 'Planning a Family'

> I was listening to RTÉ radio on Saturday morning and they were playing a bit of archival footage of a comedian from the 1960s. He was talking about how he and his wife had not been able to have children. He was describing with a kind of ironic humour how people made the assumption that they were using some kind of contraceptives in spite of the legislated ban on the purchase or sale of such items in the Republic of Ireland. He joked wryly about the notion that people thought they were obviously 'sinning', having perceived childlessness as a 'choice'. So this constituted humour about childlessness in the past (Field notes in November 2004).

Even as they talk about social change and a break with tradition, every woman tells me, at the outset, of the desire to be a mother; even those that challenge the motherhood imperative in their stories eventually describe a moment where they embrace changing reproductive values as the opportunity to become mothers on their own terms. This absence of contestation also locates reproductive choice within the changing politics of reproduction in Ireland, both challenging and affirming the concept of choice as a sign of women's emancipation from the rigours of uncontrolled reproduction associated with structural inequality for women in the past.

Such narration can signal the 'plotting' of ideals and norms as the backdrop to disruption or 'dissonance' as people constitute meanings and situate their own circumstances, in comparison with or in contrast to dominant values.[44] Women often described their desire for and exploitation of reproductive choice as the reflection of a break from tradition – a dissonance plotted against values of the past even as the value placed on procreation itself endures in the present.

For many people in Ireland, reproductive choice is a concept laden with a range of social and moral associations. As an example of Herzfeld's 'cultural intimacy' people's references to reproductive choice were infused with a sense of collective insider understanding and a hint of embarrassment about the lack of choice that had been the norm well into the twentieth century. Choice in planning a family is perceived as a new ideal aligned with materialism, economic success and professional or vocational pursuits rather than a feminist or rights discourse. Choice underscores conversations about being socially ready, financially prepared and able to provide as a responsible and logical element in family formation. Moreover, people move along a continuum of success and achievement in which parenthood seems to be the next logical step.[45] Successful middle-class men like Louise's husband James, having participated in four attempts at IVF, said, 'what's the point in having the house and all this, if there's no one to leave it to? What's it all for?' The longstanding cultural perception of family as continuity, economic containment and security and the site of property transmission means that the absence of children is also experienced as a lack of heirs, contributing to a sense of disruption that steals some of life's purpose for people like James.

In the context of social change in Ireland, the access to contraception has created social conditions that shape experiences for infertile women and their partners. The stories above often pointed to the ability to control fertility as a sign of a break with tradition described as choice, sophistication and greater access to knowledge in matters of reproduction. However, as I noted above, challenges to the moral authority that limited reproductive choice in the past did not necessarily reflect challenges to the ideal of having children. The powerful ideology of motherhood also resonates for infertile women whose struggles for reproductive 'choice' run against the grain of popular understandings. Feminist critiques of assisted reproduction point to the complexity of the idea of choice when infertile women are made to feel they must avail of such technologies as part of an imperative to do everything possible to conceive a child.[46] The very idea of a truly autonomous context for reproductive decision making is contested, since such decisions are never made in total isolation from social, institutional and political interactions.[47] Similarly, Paxson has described the contradictory elements at work in present-day Greece, where women are expected to incorporate reproductive choice as both a feature of modern urban life and as an exercise of ethics in the performance of womanhood through motherhood. In this light, the impact of modernity means choice is still largely about *when*, rather than *if*, women will have children.[48]

Talk about reproductive choice refers almost exclusively to suppressing fertility and preventing or terminating pregnancy. The dominant perception is that choice refers to 'choosing to conceive' or no longer 'choosing' to control fertility. Women trying to conceive feel the weight of the predominant assumptions that fertility and fertility control are the normative basis of reproductive choice. For women who are without partners or in same sex relationships, the exclusion is almost absolute.

This dominant ideal of choosing one's reproductive path and planning a family leads to assumptions about couples' intentions in not having children. For many couples the assumptions carry implicit (and occasionally explicit) accusations that they are deliberately and selfishly avoiding the hassle of having a family.

> CAROL ANNE: *And unfortunately what they assume in society is that you don't want children. They don't know . . .*
> VINCE: *Yeah, yeah, exactly yeah. They assume you don't want children.*
> CAROL ANNE: *We go on holiday maybe once a year, or we might go away for a long weekend, and my sister-in-law is always saying to me 'you lucky things, you've no kids, you can go off whenever . . .' And I say to her, 'Terry, I would swap every bit of that to be in your position'. They just assume we have a great life, you know, a house, no children, nobody to worry about. They don't know the half of it. They envy us!!! And we'd be saying if only they knew how we envy them.*

> ELSA: *And to me to be outside and to not really fit into the scheme, and by that also, people looking at you as being very selfish. But one thing that definitely always comes up is 'oh you're so lucky. You can do this and you can do that and you don't have to worry. And you can go on holidays and . . .' And to some . . . you know with some people I would just say 'do you want to swap?' And they don't see the heartbreak.*

> BREDA: *No, I get annoyed and I'm not completely immune to it. John's sister always says, when she rings, 'oh did I get you out of bed?' if she rings on a Saturday or a Sunday and she always says it must be lovely to have a sleep in. And I feel like saying, Faith would you ever just process the fact that this isn't what we wanted.*

Couples who desire to conceive but have been unsuccessful under 'conventional' circumstances are often caught in this web of assumptions around the reasons for their childlessness, facilitated by the new virtue of choice that had constituted them as selfish.[49] Choice, as a product of modernity and changing social values, is aligned with the new sophistication and knowledge of family planning that enables women to make positive choices about when to be a mother. However, choice is not supported as a means of foreclosing motherhood. Women remain the moral gatekeepers as old values are reconfigured and they feel bound to 'choose' motherhood. Again, Paxson's work in Greece provides an interesting parallel where the meanings associated with planning a family and exercising responsibility retain the old ideas of motherhood as an identity – that which is natural and 'completes' a woman. But at the same time, '[u]nder an emergent ethic of choice, women's virtues of service and sacrifice are weighted against newly available virtues of self-determination and autonomy'.[50] The meaning of motherhood has shifted somewhat in response to change in Ireland but nonetheless remains locked in an ethical domain of duty or social responsibility.

Assumptions about choice and childlessness are not new but they continue to resonate for infertile couples in Ireland in the present.

> MAEVE: *But then there was a conversation and my Mum was sayin' about another cousin 'oh she's not sterile . . . she just doesn't want kids'. Well I said, 'jesus that's a terrible assumption to make. You know you don't know what people's circumstances are and maybe they are saying that about me.' It's the only time I ever touched on it with her but it was enough of a ring for her to know.*

> KRISTEN: *Well my mum actually said to me, when she'd had two of her children, she said there was this woman down the road and she always thought, 'isn't she so selfish not having children and going out having a good time'? And then my Mum realised when she actually adopted. But she said that was the assumption back then, that if you didn't pop them out straight afterwards, then the assumption was like, 'oh she's selfish now, she's minding herself'.*

Citing a 1969 study by Humphreys, Conway contends that childlessness has always been presumed to be a choice in Ireland.[51] What has changed is the perception of what the choice means in terms of deviating from norms. As I noted above, the women I spoke with in 2004 and 2005 about infertility were of a generation who had access to contraception in a way that their own mothers did not, creating a social context for defining the meaning of reproduction and the social role of motherhood in different ways. However, there is continuity in the kind of moral responsibility that underpins the negative perceptions of childlessness as socially irresponsible, now framed as having the wrong priorities.

> JANE: *I would occasionally get that . . . you're very career driven. You know that perception.*

> MAEVE: *There's all these ideas like. [. . .] And to hear it third hand is worse. Like you know, we've heard back from people saying oh we're having too good a time or we've got too good a social life or . . .*

In this light, access to contraception has been absorbed into the Irish ideal of the family as part of the discourse of social responsibility and material security. In contrast to stories of a time past, where multiple children and stretched material resources were common, the couples I spoke to all 'planned' their approach to having a family around a point in which they felt they could provide materially and economically for children. Many lamented having fretted over contraception and trying *not* to get pregnant for years prior to marriage or perhaps waiting for the well-established and materially comfortable point they had now reached. For nearly everyone the inability to conceive easily and quickly, once they planned it, came as a shock to the perception of order in their own lives. In an era of new economic promise and prosperity that gripped Ireland at the turn of the twenty-first century, people located their projects of conception and family-building within the building of material conformity evidenced by the shiny new kitchens full of appliances where I heard many infertility stories during my research.

Reproductive choice, as an issue of women's rights, has been at the forefront of many feminist debates in Ireland and elsewhere, but there is a flip side for women struggling to conceive. The emphasis on emancipation associated with women's fertility control, as an issue for women, perpetuates the misconception that they are responsible for a failure to conceive.

> GAIL: *My husband couldn't knock me up with a bat. There are people who already know there is male factor because Martin is very honest about the fact. Because I know a lot of couples where the woman just . . . it's not said that there's male factor and she accepts whatever 'what's up with you love?' comments that come.*
>
> MARTIN: *People do assume it is the woman.*
>
> GAIL: *And certainly people would look at me then and say, 'oh she's overweight'.*

Infertility thus complicates the meaning of reproductive choice in a number of ways. In particular, reproductive technologies themselves are now constituted as an accessible reproductive choice. Many couples spoke about the frustration of people saying, 'would you not just do IVF then?' The idea that this is easily accessible is frustrating to many who struggle not only with the cost, the physical and emotional challenges and the time commitment, but also ethical and moral difficulties.

ELSA: And it is an issue that keeps coming up and it really annoys me. They still say, 'well if they really wanted to they could adopt'. It is the same with IVF. Obviously we are not trying hard enough because we didn't do IVF. Thirty years ago it was accepted – there was always some-body who didn't have children and that was a fact. But nowadays the pressure because of technology and the stories you read and it comes across that if somebody wants a child they can just do it and it will work.

BREDA: John told his sister on the phone one night just because she was being such a pain. So he told her and I think she actually said, 'well, would you not try IVF?' and we said, 'well, we have but it didn't work'. But she hasn't brought it up since.

LYDIA: And our names had come up for the adoption and we decided we were going to be truthful here. If we had to tell them we were about to start an IVF – this is the third one – we'd waited the year for the adoption and if they say we're going back on the end of the list we won't do the IVF. But if they say, look, do your IVF and if that doesn't work you'll come back on, we'll go with it. So that's what they said, so we decided to put the adoption there and we'd do the IVF. And then we did the fourth one.

Lydia notes that she and her partner had put their names down for adoption while still going for treatment. They were relieved that while they were told their application would be put on hold, they would not lose their place in the queue for an adoption assessment if the treatment failed and they wanted to continue with the process of adoption. This suggests there is some flexibility in the system. They did ultimately adopt a child after the fourth course of IVF did not result in a successful pregnancy.

The opportunities for producing a family become stratified in a hier-archy of choice. As these stories suggest, for people who can afford to explore ART as an option, they are encouraged to 'close the door' on the idea of biological reproduction in order to explore adoption. Adoption is thus constructed as 'alternative' rather than one of several possibilities for producing a family. For many people the idea of adoption is only a conceivable option once they have ascertained that they cannot conceive a child themselves.

Choice is now absorbed into the social expectation that people must try all available opportunities to become parents, particularly biological or technological ones that enable them to conceive and give birth. Franklin notes that the idea of ART as a 'choice' incorporates not only the means of overcoming 'disruptions' to life stories but also an ongoing need to make choices as part of the course of IVF itself.[52] It is now a matter of being medically responsible to seek medical care for even the most normal and unproblematised reproductive events.[53] Medicine increasingly exerts power over bodies by shaping the day-to-day events of sexual reproduction and pregnancy as site for surveillance and the failure to participate in this process as irresponsible and reckless.

Infertility and ART have been drawn into the medicalisation of reproduction as part of the powerful normalisation and self-perpetuation of structures and institutions.[54] The primary discourse is around the management of risk, something that is increasingly a factor with respect to infertility; women are constantly reminded in the media that advancing maternal age associated with waiting to conceive is a risk to successful fertility projects. This is, of course, another issue for women as they are now held to account for the results of exercising reproductive choice wherein they might not be able to exercise their responsibility to procreate. The financial cost of treatment raises the issue of economic status on both the meaning of infertility and the notion of choice. The economic wherewithal to access IVF is another aspect of 'the links between stratified reproduction and the reproduction of stratification [that] position women differently and entail diverse experiences of biocultural processes'.[55] The fact that tremendous financial resources are needed to pursue any level of diagnosis or treatment has tended to exclude people in a low-income bracket or dependent on state income support. While the HARI (Human Assisted Reproduction Ireland) Unit at the Rotunda Hospital in Dublin does provide services to a limited number of people classed as 'public patients', no numbers are available for how many and what criteria might be used for their selection. The HARI Unit claims to charge its largely fee-paying clientele a slightly higher fee in order to offset this cost. But for the majority of people who cannot afford the €3,000–€4,000 average cost for a single treatment there is no recourse to ART as a means of dealing with infertility.

Certainly all the people I met in my study were decidedly middle or upper middle class with comfortable and financially secure lives. As I noted in the Introduction, none of my participants were in lower-income situations in which assisted reproduction technology or international adoption would have been totally out of the question.[56] Many of the people I spoke to, like Breda, acknowledged that the cost would be a restricting factor for some.

> BREDA: *I think everybody should . . . I suppose maybe on the financial side I think from society's point of view it should be available to more people. I think, say, what they charge in Cork, €2,700, is not out of the reach of any middle-class people. I think most people can get a hold of that kind of money once or maybe even twice. But I think for working-class people or people who maybe have other big commitments or financially, maybe looking after a lot of other people, it can be out of people's reach.*

For the majority of women who are dealing with infertility, the notion that they are in control of reproductive events is one of the most important myths to be challenged. Through narratives of infertility experiences, women contest the fallacy of reproductive choice on many levels, from the constitution of subjectivity and the 'always-already' to the assumption that everyone has reproductive choices on a continuum from nature to technology to adoption.

Conclusion

The endurance of an ideology of motherhood in the midst of a perceived social and moral sea change in Ireland is evidence of the inconsistent and incomplete nature of shifting values over time. Women, in particular, narrate changing social roles that are still evocative of the dominant social values of the past. Moreover, having a choice about one's reproductive destiny, particularly for women, is idiomatic as a marker of a changed Ireland and a clear sign of generational difference. At the same time, however, these narratives serve as a means through which people reaffirm the meaning of fertility and hetero-norms as these are linked to ideas of tradition associated with Ireland's past.

In the stories about the social imperative to achieve motherhood, we see both the contingency and the resilience of the institutional and political naturalisation and normalisation of fertility and motherhood in Ireland. Women who embrace the idea of motherhood also see themselves as agents of resistance and challenge to assumptions and norms. Even as they represent themselves as the generation of changing ideals, their stories reveal their own parents' understanding or willingness to challenge the status quo and the politics of reproduction. Change and shifting social values thus move along a continuum but not necessarily at a consistent pace. At the same time, values from the past are not necessarily shed along the way but have, rather, become part of the structure of possibilities and ideas even for those who have built their families and value systems on different platforms. The changing social conditions in which motherhood and family are defined in Ireland on one hand support new ideals in procreation and reproductive choice while, on the other hand, sustaining old value systems that exploit new meanings as part of the motherhood imperative.

As some of these stories highlight, assumptions that one is 'always-already' a mother (or mother-to-be) by virtue of being a woman and that reproduction is something that is always within one's control can be painful for women and their partners. In these stories 'tradition' and 'choice' become cultural idioms that convey complex meanings that draw upon family and reproductive politics from Ireland's past. The contested meanings associated with these concepts highlight the significance of infertility as part of the challenge to redefine not only the meaning of procreation but the meaning of motherhood and family. Stories about infertility thus expose the disjuncture between choice as an opportunity and choice as an idiom for conformity in the interest of sustaining family and motherhood as symbols of stability in Ireland.

3. Conceiving Nonconformity:
Challenging Hetero-normative Meanings
of (in)Fertility

Many of the stories above have explored how women see their own journeys towards motherhood as part of a resistance to the institutional operations of power that have shaped the meaning of motherhood in a number of ways. Through these stories women speak about the agency with which they harness the meanings of reproduction, viewing their potential role not as a biological burden but rather as a positive experience that also shapes the meanings through which power is exercised. In fact, the reproductive experiences of many of the women in my study lie outside of and pose challenges to, the hetero-normative ideal based on marriage and family politics in Ireland.[1] Their fertility challenges are thus often part of a complex set of relations described by one woman as 'infertility by association' – cases where it is a partner, same-sex partner or lack of partner that influences the course of their reproductive story. Engaging with fertility and motherhood outside of the normative definition of family provides a glimpse into the processes of social change that are happening in Ireland, exposing where inconsistencies and challenges are factors of enduing social values and definitions from the past. At the same time, we see the shifting meaning of family in relation to such issues as international adoption, marriage and sexuality and even maternal age and biology as markers of 'natural' fertility. I use (in)fertility as a rhetorical reflection of the tenuous and contingent meanings of both infertility and fertility.

Women who seek the means to embody and enact motherhood outside the conventional and normative definition linked to heterosexual marriage invite us to explore more fully the contradictions of agency and power in shaping subjectivity. Saba Mahmood calls for 'uncoupling the analytical notion of agency from the politically proscriptive project of feminism', looking instead at 'other modalities of agency whose meaning and effect are not captured within the logic of subversion and resignification of hegemonic terms of discourse'.[2] In other words, agency can be exercised from within the very dimensions of social life – in this case marriage and motherhood – that would seem to be the means of women's subjugation. Women's decisions to undertake forms of biological and/or social motherhood are often exercised within the social structures that constitute the woman/mother paradigm. However, their decisions are no less examples of agency even as they enact the roles that would seem to exemplify the hegemony that has produced such paradigmatic social roles. Here we confront the feminist dilemma of 'nature' and reproduction head on by looking at four women who refute the idea that reproduction is an imposition of patriarchy and embrace instead the powerful satisfaction of fulfiling a desire to become mothers on their own terms.[3] But they must do it by confronting the issue of (in)fertility, redefining it and claiming for themselves the legitimate access to a means to becoming a mother.

As noted in the last chapter, the Irish Constitution leans heavily on naturalised associations between the composition of family, procreative relationships and gender roles. The historical production of an ideology of motherhood as a linchpin in this constitution of family and marriage underscores the predominant view that infertility is defined by its occurrence within a marriage but not acknowledged outside of one. Despite the emphasis on tradition among couples who conform to normative definitions of the idealised family, there are women who challenge the hegemony of heterosexual marriage as central to the formation of family. Their stories highlight more clearly the other apparent cracks in the marriage–procreation nexus such as increasing numbers of children born outside marriage and higher numbers of cohabiting couples that has become a reality in twenty-first-century Ireland.

I turn now to an exploration of the ways some women also challenge the hetero-normative ideal of marriage and family, while nonetheless choosing to pursue motherhood, exercising a kind of agency that encourages an even deeper exploration of the relationship between subjectivity, agency and morality. These women are not victims of biology who must be rescued in a feminist analysis of their subjection; but neither are they actively resisting the idea of motherhood as fulfilment of an identity for women. Their desire to be mothers seems to be less a need to be 'good at being women' and more of a desire to fulfil an embodied potential and exercise a social and biological power associated with sex/gender difference.

To move into other such modalities of agency I begin with the story of one woman who exemplifies the extremes of this revision, alternately resisting and embracing a motherhood identity in a variety of ways. She embodies a particular kind of contested motherhood – a postmodern challenge in which infertility itself is redefined even as it defies a number of cultural logics and categorical relationships. These logics include the relationship between sex and procreation; procreation and marriage; the limitations of a biological clock; and assumptions about impermeable biological, cultural and nation-state borderlines.

Sarah's Story[4]

And God said unto Abraham, As for Sarai thy wife, thou shalt not call her name Sarai, but Sarah shall her name be. And I will bless her, and give thee a son also of her: yea, I will bless her, and she shall be a mother of nations; kings of people shall be of her. Then Abraham fell upon his face, and laughed, and said in his heart, Shall a child be born unto him that is an hundred years old? And shall Sarah, that is ninety years old, bear? And Abraham said unto God, O that Ishmael might live before thee! And God said, Sarah thy wife shall bear thee a son indeed; and thou shalt call his name Isaac: and I will establish my covenant with him for an everlasting covenant, and with his seed after him.

(Book of Genesis, Chapter 17: 15–19)

I met Sarah in her home in a mid-sized urban centre where she was employed in education. I found myself wandering through a suburban neighbourhood with well-tended lawns and cul-de-sacs. These would be filled with children playing street hockey in Canada but in Ireland soccer is the road game of choice, and nets and balls remained on the roadsides in the twilight long after the children had gone in for their evening meals. This was a conventional, comfortable, middle-class family neighbourhood that could have been situated anywhere in Europe or North America. But Sarah's family was not exactly conventional and neither was her road to motherhood. Even her experience with infertility challenged the socially constituted meanings derived from biological conventions. She welcomed me at the door and I realised her child was asleep but very much present as toys and paraphernalia of childhood were evident around the house. Sarah offered me tea and homemade cake and we settled in the kitchen for our conversation. Bright, articulate and confident, she was the only participant in my study to ask me what theoretical leanings might underwrite my project – a testament to her own academic and reflexive analysis of her circumstances.

Sarah had been born and raised in Ireland and was nearly fifty years old when I met her. She described having had a very tense relationship with her own mother, which she attributed to the reproductive challenges her mother had faced. She felt she had been 'wrapped in cotton wool' her whole childhood and was smothered by her mother's attention and concern. At the same time she felt that she never quite met her mother's expectations. Sarah approached a professional career thinking that she would work with children but not have any herself.

JILL: *Can you tell me a little bit about yourself growing up and how that influenced your feelings about motherhood or becoming a mother?*
SARAH: *It probably influenced me quite a lot. I grew up in Dublin, I was the eldest of three children. I was the first child after three miscarriages and I was the 'survivor'. My mother and I had . . . it's hard to describe it . . . it was stormy. My mother had a lot of difficulties herself. She felt that she was never wanted as a child by her mother. She felt that she cramped her mother's social life and she was very close to her father. Me being the oldest child and a very precious child, I felt almost suffocated. And because of that relationship I never really wanted to have children myself. I just felt . . . it's hard to describe it. I felt my own self-esteem wasn't that great and I just felt that I would actually produce a monster child. [. . .] I worked with children, I always had children around me. [. . .] I loved children. It was just like one of my own . . . it would be too much of me in it. It sounds stupid but . . .*

Sarah married a man five years younger than herself and, while she was aware that he wanted to have children, she felt that he knew her feelings at the outset so should not have been surprised at her refusal to embrace motherhood. Their relationship grew tumultuous and he left to pursue a short-term contract abroad, suggesting that she could either follow him or wait for his return. She chose the latter but after many extensions it became apparent he was not going to come back. She left her job and followed him, prepared to try to recover her marriage. She discovered after some time that her husband was in a new relationship. Sadly for Sarah, she had at this point decided that she was ready to be a mother. Folding guilt into the ideal of the woman/mother, her ex-husband said that if she had only been willing to embrace this identity sooner their marriage might not have failed.

SARAH: *I was never able to explain it to him. I found it difficult getting close to him and again like how I always found it difficult to get close to my mother. I would lose all sense of myself and I couldn't risk that. I couldn't risk losing what felt like my autonomy and it felt the same thing having a child. [. . .] I sort of realised shortly after he went over there that I really wanted to have a child. And we talked about it over the phone and so the relationship hadn't completely dissolved and there were dreams on my part of being with him and being pregnant and us having a family. And at this stage I was getting on a bit, I was forty-three at the time. I was working towards it and I really wanted it to happen and it wasn't happening. He didn't want it.*

Sarah described feeling compelled to stay on in her new situation and make a life close to her ex-husband. She decided to embark on the road to motherhood without her husband (or any husband for that matter), investigating local fertility clinics as a means of overcoming her age and peri-menopausal limitations to conceiving. Sarah was prepared to undergo IVF with donor eggs in order to conceive, even though this meant a very heavy regime of hormones and drugs to achieve the results. She described how she fantasised about her former husband being the sperm donor so she could have the child she now longed for 'with' him. Meanwhile her ex-husband and his new wife were expecting a child of their own.

> SARAH: *I still wanted very much to have a child in my life and part of the process of that was realising I could do it myself and that's when I decided I'd … I was cutting it a bit fine but I would start a fertility programme. And I started that where I was living and because of my age, I was 46 at the time, the gynaecologist told me the risk factors and the possibility of twins. They took FSH[5] levels and they were quite elevated so I was borderline and the options that were presented to me but it was getting pretty tight. I never actually went for insemination and at that stage there was consideration of egg donation as well. And I was sort of weighing up all the possibilities and I actually started to think this isn't going to work. And so I thought maybe I should just go ahead and adopt.*

Sarah described how impending parenthood was a means of sustaining the relationship with her former husband as she relied on him for rides to medical appointments and shared with him her plan to conceive a child. Sarah's plan to conceive through IVF was eventually undone by the discovery of an unrelated medical condition which required treatment. Although the problem posed no direct threat to IVF success, she described how she began to re-think the issue from the perspective of her own health and well-being and the risk of becoming pregnant in her late forties. She turned her attention to the possibility of adoption. While hardly a straightforward path either, Sarah was able to legally adopt a little girl she had formed a relationship with through her work in the community. She again engaged her ex-husband in a relationship around parenthood by asking for advice for purchasing baby items. Caught somewhat by surprise, she had only three days to prepare for the arrival of her child and she turned to him for support.[6]

> SARAH: *Philip, who had been my husband but, at that stage, was somebody else's husband, was looking around Baby City with me because they had a little girl. He said, 'look you need one of these and one of that'. And I said 'so fill the trolley; what else do I need?' And I was in total shock. So we got a trolley load of stuff.*
> JILL: *How did that feel, having your ex-husband take you around shopping for baby things? Is there a sort of irony in that?*
> SARAH: *Yeah, there is. Well I just felt that he's a super father so he must know. He must know what's good for babies, and what is good for his baby must be good for . . . (voice trails off without finishing). I felt he was sort of an expert father. Of course his wife probably wasn't too pleased about it all.*

But no, it was kind of like he took me around and we . . . because he was one of the first people I called just to say, 'look I'm getting a baby'.

Sarah had recently returned to Ireland from Africa and was in the process of adopting a second child from abroad. Her story is one of both resistance to the imagined ideals of motherhood in Ireland and at the same time one that reveals the social and familial influences that have shaped the identity, the subjectivity and the ideal. Sarah is anything but a typical mother since she is single, older than most mothers of toddlers and her child is clearly adopted. And yet her own agency in embracing an identity that was previously unappealing to her is linked to an ideology of motherhood that has helped define womanhood in Ireland. Her story also betrays the tension and expectation of performance of an ideal, since her initial rejection of the idea was rooted in her sense of inadequacy and inability to be a mother and to perform motherhood. Her decision to adopt provides a solution, not only to the obvious limitations to fertility posed by her age, but for her concern with having too much of herself in a genetic or biological child of her own. The ideal of motherhood prevails in this reconfiguration as she works through the filling of a need for herself as part of an identity.

JILL: *What about people here in the community since you have come back? The assumption will obviously be that you adopted her.*
SARAH: *It's very obvious . . . [laughing].*
JILL: *Do you think that makes it any easier for people when they think that you have chosen this child and to accept you as a single mother?*
SARAH: *Oh yes, I think so. The benevolent 'oh you're a saint' kind of thing is working both ways. They don't see adoption as being a mutually beneficial thing. They see it as benefiting a child as opposed to actually filling a space in me. It's not just providing a mother for a child, it's actually filling a need for both of us. I also think the fact that it's so obvious that we're not genetically related and the old patriarchal missions and Ireland was a great missionary country, sending missions to Africa . . . You get that aspect of it. Oh look, aren't you great. Oh look at the little ... they think of her as a boy . . . look at the little black boy . . . There's a certain, I want to say, novelty factor.*

Sarah sees her new family as both shaped by and a challenge to Ireland's past perceptions of racial difference and intolerance to single motherhood. Her ability to challenge these perceptions is not so much rooted in social change as in the merging of the two issues in which the benevolence of rescuing a 'black baby' who needs a mother offsets the judgemental attitudes that are sometimes still associated with single parenthood. The concept of reproductive choice and planning a family is dissolved into the ideal of missions and rescue.[7] Adoption from overseas is increasingly popular as an option for single people to become parents in Ireland. In fact, in 2008 the International Adoption Association (IAA) estimated that single adoptive parents or those trying to become single adoptive parents constitute about a fifth of their membership and the majority are women in their thirties and forties.[8]

Sarah's story also traces several generations of discordance with the imaginary social ideal of motherhood. Her own mother had a difficult time as an only child of a mother who seemed to have little to offer her emotionally and socially. Her mother's subsequent fertility challenges, evidenced by multiple miscarriages, played into an overprotective response to Sarah as an individual, quashing her autonomy and self-esteem. Here are three generations of women who represent multiple contestations of the dominant narrative of the fertile, self-sacrificing woman who marries and rapidly produces multiple children. Sarah embarks on a journey towards motherhood acknowledging, to herself, that it was the failure to embody this ideal that resulted in the loss of her husband.

Like the biblical story, Sarah defied the biological clock, but rather than a miraculous intercession from God, Sarah was prepared to engage in the miraculous interventions of medical science in order to have a child.[9] We might also liken Sarah to her biblical 'namesake' in that clearly the identity of biblical Sarah as a mother was bound largely to the need to make her husband a father. Abraham needed heirs. The Sarah in this story describes how her need to be a mother emerged as part of a missing element in her marriage, a social contract still bound to a procreative purpose for many people in Ireland. She takes on the challenge outside of the institutional structures that have shaped motherhood and even develops a unique kind of parenting and 'procreative' relationship with her former husband. For some women I spoke with in Ireland, the desire is more about fulfiling a partner's project of conception and parenthood than a need to fulfil their own parenting desires.[10] But Sarah's desire for motherhood represents an inversion of this since she wanted her ex-husband's child for herself, rather than for him. Her aspiration shifted from having *his* child – even through an imaginary scenario that would substitute technology for sex in the procreative relationship – to eventually sharing the social experience of parenting, drawing on his social 'fatherhood' role as a friend and supporter.

Women like Sarah, who pursue motherhood as single individuals, still stand in sharp relief against the idiomatic association between fertility and heterosexual partnership – mainly, although not exclusively, defined as marriage. Sarah's single motherhood was made less socially problematic by her decision to adopt a child from an African country – a fact marked by their lack of resemblance (skin colour). But single women who pursue motherhood through assisted reproduction outside marriage experience a sense of illegitimacy as a result of their nonconformity and challenges to social conventions. Single women are not necessarily viewed as 'infertile' even though the barrier to their ability to conceive might be parallel to that of a woman whose husband has no sperm, for example.

Joan Marie's Story

Like Sarah, Joan Marie is a single woman pursuing motherhood on her own. At thirty-seven years old, she had her own business in media consulting. As a product of a very conservative family and strict Catholic upbringing, Joan Marie felt certain her family would not approve of her decision to pursue motherhood on her own after the dissolution of a long-term relationship and terminated engagement. She was the only woman in my study who refused to have her interview recorded, although she met with me twice and corresponded regularly by phone and email. Some of her reticence to be recorded related to her concern about confidentiality, particularly with respect to members of her family. She also wrote me long and detailed letters. What follows is an excerpt from one of these letters in which she explains her sadness when her fiancé ended their long-term relationship.

> JOAN MARIE: *That left me not only bereft of a 'husband' but also with the prospect of motherhood now gone too. I hit a desperate low point in my life. I was devastated, felt wronged, cheated, hard-done-by, robbed of my right, bitter, full of anger, terrified, alone, isolated, empty, without purpose in my life, every feeling and emotion imaginable. And when I analysed it I realised that not only was I grieving the loss of my 'marriage' but also the loss of the child that I was now possibly never going to have, given my age and the fact that that relationship was possibly [probably] my last chance at having the traditional type of lifestyle to which I aspired, i.e. that of marriage and kids – in that order! Being single at my stage was hard enough, but not ever having the possibility of motherhood was more than I could bear. I started to question whether the loss of my dream of marriage had to necessarily mean the loss of my dream to be a mother. And I decided that, for me, this did not have to be the case. The relief, excitement and hope I started feeling with this realisation was immense. I am an independent, well-educated, balanced, healthy and financially secure woman with a deep desire to fulfil what, for me, amounts to my life purpose, i.e. that of motherhood.* (Letter from Joan Marie in November of 2004.)

Joan Marie's first encounter with the clinical aspects of conceiving as a single woman took her to Belfast, since no clinic in the Republic would provide ART to a single woman at that time.[11] She found several options for acquiring sperm but needed a clinic to provide the technical support and actual procedure for getting the gametes together, in her case a less invasive procedure called inter-uterine insemination (IUI).[12]

Discrimination is evident in the way clinics in Ireland determine who can access their services. Only heterosexual couples in stable relationships were deemed eligible for treatment by individual clinics in Ireland, and single women and gay/lesbian couples were, until recently, excluded. The CAHR report notes that there is no current regulation that prohibits clinics from providing service to single women and couples who are not married, noting also that the Medical Council guidelines no longer stipulate marriage as a requirement. However, the CAHR acknowledges that providing assisted reproduction to unmarried people might violate the state's constitutional duty to 'guard with special care the institution of Marriage, on which the Family is founded and to protect it against attack'.[13] Since, as I suggest above, marriage produces mothers and mothers produce families, some conservative foundations are shaken in the potential paradigm shift when single women seek to make themselves mothers.

Joan Marie went to Belfast to a popular clinic dedicated to women's reproductive health and saw two different consultants. She described them both as kind but somewhat 'patriarchal, condescending and not very supportive'. They both told her several times that she might 'find a man in the next year and regret what she was doing'. Joan Marie said she was not moved by these sentiments and felt that if she took a risk and waited for 'Mr Right' she might find herself at forty-five without a child or a partner. She found the lectures by these doctors to be 'demeaning' and the visits were negative experiences and very 'uncomfortable'. She did not want her interest in motherhood to be completely shaped by the hegemony of marriage as a necessity. Joan Marie's search led her to a clinic in London which she described as very accessible and welcoming, particularly since the waiting room was full of other women who were not accompanied by partners.

Joan Marie described to me how her struggle to sustain a failing long-term relationship was really about 'trying to please everybody else' and 'do the white picket fence thing'. Joan Marie described her own mother as 'being in bits about it all' when the relationship failed. She also realised that the relationship was really about creating a legitimate space for parenthood rather than the relationship itself. She noted in a letter that she felt less urgency to pursue another relationship since she was no longer thinking about it as a vehicle to motherhood.

Some of the women on websites have, in the process of arriving at their decision, discovered that 'dating' is now such a pleasurable and relaxed experience as they are no longer looking at every man as potential husband and father material who they have to chase up the aisle ASAP while their biological clock is still ticking. Some realise that their desire [sometimes desperation!] to find a husband was really only a vehicle so that their need for motherhood could be achieved, meaning that the MOST important role for them is actually being a mother over and above being a wife. Of course the ideal for the majority of us is still the traditional way i.e. marriage and children. (Correspondence from Joan Marie – 9 November 2004).

In an interview later, Joan Marie described how she could now 'date like a man'. Her perception that dating objectives differ based on what women and men want from the relationship highlights the power of discourses on biological limitations and reproductive windows in shaping the life narratives and ideals in relationships, procreation or parenthood. Joan Marie's story, like Sarah's, highlights a different meaning for both fertility and infertility as both women challenge the marriage and motherhood model directly. As Mahmood argues, agency is not always about politically or socially subversive actions. Women like Joan Marie and Sarah resist the current ideology of motherhood as locked into a marriage and family paradigm. But their interest in achieving motherhood is a product of the same social and political discourses, evident in their stories of the desire to perform an 'always-already' subjectivity as another facet of the dominant ideology.

Cara and Aoife: A Tale of Two Mums

A similar kind of agency is at work in the relationships of lesbian women who become mothers with same-sex partners. I met Cara and Aoife at their home in a tiny community outside a larger city. I met Aoife through a number of shared interests; she was also pursuing graduate studies at the time and we became friends. She offered to share her story about overcoming the fertility challenges posed by a lesbian relationship as she and her partner were using assisted reproduction to conceive a child of their own. Aoife recounted a childhood filled with baby dolls and babysitting, culminating in an early marriage and pregnancy in her late teens. While that first pregnancy ended in miscarriage, she went on to have two sons with the man she married and later divorced. She said little about her own mother but described a feeling of 'being expected to be a mother and expected to have children'. Aoife also noted that neither of her sisters was very 'maternal' but both have gone on to have children. Cara described a very different relationship between motherhood and family life in which her mother was actively pursuing a career.

> CARA: *She wasn't a motherly mother in that way. She wasn't there, you know I used to give out to her so much when I was a teenager – 'you never made my lunch and you never made my breakfast . . .' Everyone else had a lunch box and I didn't. It's curious now but I'm a councillor and one of my clients is in his early twenties and came to a big moment one time by saying . . . 'and she never gave me a packed lunch . . .' and this was a defining thing about the lack of mothering. And I had to laugh because that was exactly what I used to throw at my own mother. It wasn't my experience and I didn't grow up thinking that or even assuming the responsibility of having my life mapped out. It was much more to do with professionalism and getting your qualifications and getting a job.*
>
> JILL: *Making a mark in the world. So at what point did you decide you wanted to be a mother?*
>
> CARA: *I don't know. It kind of crept up on me. I remember having a conversation with Aoife about it just literally the week before we got together. Something had happened in me that I really wanted a child at that moment and I was about twenty-seven. And I don't know what came up that precipitated that or sort of put me in mind of it. It was a big, big period of transition in my life. I had previously entered into a five-year relationship with a man that I had been with and I would have married and would have had children. But he didn't have the slightest bit of interest in doing that really. He was a vehicle to having a child basically. I was happy to do that on my own if I needed to. But it just kind of appeared as a growing process that had been going on for a year or two before that. It was a bit of a surprise to me, I think. It's odd looking back on it. I don't have this big long . . . normally you might have a kind of 'then this and then this and then this'. I have nothing. It was just a moment when then it was just there.*

Cara identifies the absence of such symbols of the 'traditional stay at home mum' as a packed lunch as formative in her own decision that motherhood could take a different shape. Her realisation that re-entering an unsatisfactory relationship with a man was only a means to becoming a mother again points out the powerful normative construct between heterosexual marriage and motherhood. Cara and Aoife began a long journey into the maze that assisted conception presents to lesbian couples in Ireland. This has been described as involving 'train rails, jet trails and emails' in a constant search for treatment options.[14] The pursuit of motherhood through assisted conception in a lesbian relationship is just as challenging as that faced by single women.

They began with a sperm bank in California but hit their first hurdle when seeking a clinic to provide the service.

> AIOFE: *So that appealed to us, the fact that we could do it here in our community, we thought . . . wrongly. Because we thought it was the donor*

sperm that they didn't want to give us. But it didn't turn out to be that. It turned out that they didn't want to actually do any insemination even if you provided your own sperm. They didn't want to come near it. It was just a hot potato. [. . .] Well it's because there is no legislation so the old legislation said married couples and the new one didn't say anything except one of them said a stable relationship. But everybody is too scared to touch us and they didn't want to get their hands dirty. They didn't want to be the person in the Sunday Mirror *or the* Daily Star *or something that said, 'Doctor performs miracle birth' or you know.*

CARA: *Starting it again, if we were four years ago now and I knew what the experience of being inseminated was like and what you actually need I'd bloody do it myself. I'd get a syringe and catheter and figure out how to use it.*

AOIFE: *I'd written to people and we'd gotten very clear answers back saying we do not treat lesbian couples.*

CARA: *I think the doctor in the clinic here did say it to me. I know he did. He just said no, we can't. It's not regulated and there's this commission and we're hoping it will be regulated and in the meantime we'll do whatever we can. And in fairness to him and his clinic, they're really, really supportive. I clog up their books. I ring them up at a moment's notice looking for a scan, sometimes on a Sunday and all they get is €70 out of me. They do all my prescriptions, fax back and forth and make endless phone calls and allow me to use their pharmacy to get my drugs. They have facilitated me in all of that and have been very supportive around wishing they could offer me this service but when it is unregulated . . .*

AOIFE: *On the issue of sex and reproduction, doing the insemination in London is odd because I haven't actually been there for any of the inseminations. I've been here looking after the children and the animals and I actually miss that. I really do. I do miss it being a sexual thing. I think that would be nice but there's my bit of Irish consciousness. I really miss being there. I hate that aspect of it.*

In spite of the support described in this story, there are significantly fewer services offered in Ireland to couples or women outside of heterosexual relationships, and most clinics will not provide fertility treatment. Their fertility challenges, or (in)fertility, belong outside the conventions defined by and naturalised in the social and political relations of reproduction. Given that the terms for access to ART are defined by an absence rather than the existence of regulation, the irony deepens. As Conrad argues, homosexuality threatens the ideal of the heterosexual family precisely because it is assumed that gay and lesbian couples do procreate thus challenging 'the inevitability and the security of the notion of the family cell as the only "natural" and fundamental unit group of society'.[15] Women like Aoife and Cara will force a rethinking of the basis for such debates since they are a stable, procreative unit and family in every sense save *hetero*-normative.

Of course the issue of political rights for people in the gay and lesbian community in Ireland has long been controversial more for its tendency to expose the social, cultural and political contingency of meanings accorded to sexuality.[16] In its discussion on the provision of services to people who are not married, the CAHR report also describes the issues related to the Equal Status Acts 2000 to 2004. The issue again revolves around whether any state support for the provision of ART to gay and lesbian couples represents an attack on marriage. The commission report notes that since ART is provided in private clinics, the state cannot be held to account as abrogating its responsibility to uphold marriage, even if representatives of the state and the public at large believe that such provision undermines the family unit.[17] The argument really centres on the issue of whether the state should compel clinics to provide such services based on the requirements of the Equality Act 2004. In a public lecture at Cork University Hospital in the spring of 2005, just prior to the release of the CAHR report, Dr Deirdre Madden, an expert in biomedical legal issues, pointed to this failure to uphold the act by clinics as an invitation for lawsuit. The clinics appeared to be unmoved at the time of writing.

When I asked some of my participants about who should be able to access ART there was unequivocal support for same-sex couples to be able to use these services to reproduce. The potential challenge to the 'nature' of family is welcomed by some who see the need to redefine the terms around which we assess stability and norms.

> BREDA: *For gay couples, yeah for gay couples I think it's great. I think, I suppose maybe some people question the gay couples and say will they always be a family but you can say that about anybody. I mean John and I, we could have an IVF baby and not stay together. I think most gay couples who get as far as having a baby are probably more committed than some who just wander into marriage because it's the time in their life to get married. I think people who go for IVF have thought more about having children than anybody else [laughter]. So they are sort of self-selecting in a way, you know. They are very motivated and know they want to be parents.*

> TARA: *Our daughter has a friend at school and her parents are lesbians and they love the kids and they are really nice people. They are funny you know, one of the mothers stays at home and the other goes to work and sometimes she'll make comments, like.*
> KELLY: *Comparing Les (her partner) to me.*
> TARA: *Yeah I'll say Kelly did whatever, and she'll say 'oh Les is the same you know. And it is like it's the same. Of course this is the friend our daughter made in school and she says 'why has she got two mummies?'*
> KELLY: *Because her daddy's a lucky guy!!! [laughing].*
> TARA: *I just said some people have two mummies and some people have two*

daddies and she was okay. I don't know her well enough to know the circumstances of their birth.

Aoife and Cara relate a similar experience in which someone asked them at daycare what their adopted son calls them. When they replied, 'he calls us Mum' the person was clearly shocked at the very idea that a child could identify two people as Mum at the same time. Tara's narrative 'normalises' the relationship of the two women she knows as being just like her own 'conventional' marriage. Kelly's joking, on the other hand, normalises it in a different way as it sexualises the 'two mummies' in the realm of a non-conforming but nonetheless hetero-normative frame as he conjures an image in which there is still a man in the picture – a man having a good time. He is unable to separate an identity as 'mother' from the heterosexual image of woman/mother through which motherhood itself is still defined, at least for many people in Ireland.

Conclusion

The marriage and motherhood continuum for women in Ireland is and has been a contested reality for many. The four women in the stories above all struggled with and ultimately embraced the idea of motherhood in a way that goes against the grain of conventional assumptions. Their stories contrast with foundational ideas of marriage and time lines that are deeply embedded in the politics of reproduction and the meanings of motherhood, family and fertility in Ireland. The ongoing dependence on a symbolic value of family as the source of stability is obvious in the state and institutional concern for undermining the institution of marriage. In this light, women will continue to have their reproductive capacities constrained by relations of power that favour the status quo. At the same time, obstacles to conceiving a child and becoming a mother – both biological and social – are also experiences through which old paradigms and discursively constituted gender roles are being challenged and reconceived. The procreative foundations that naturalise the arrangement between motherhood, family and heterosexual marriage are challenged by both infertility and the desire to enable one's fertility outside of the norm. The experiences of enabling fertility provide an opportunity for some women to challenge the link between fertility and the hetero-normative performance of the motherhood role. The next chapter turns to the stories of women who deeply embody this woman/mother subjectivity and must work through the social constitution of failure in the absence of conception, birth and motherhood.

4. Conceiving of Grieving

I covet their children; wardrobes
Stocked with blue and pink
Waters petrified by spittled winds:
Little fish will not swim here
Maddened by
Lunar crumblings, the false prophecy
Of tingling breasts, the turgid abdomen . . . blood seeps again.

Mary O'Donnell ('Antarctica', in
Reading the Sunflowers in September)

Mary O'Donnell's words above convey not only a sense of emptiness but the cyclical nature of grief that comes with the body's betrayal each time there is a failure to conceive. The last two chapters located the meanings of conception and motherhood within particular normative contexts in Ireland, as both products of and productive of particular meanings in politics, history and institutional relationships. These normative contexts include marriage, the production of family and the sustaining of a social and moral hegemony of gender difference and patriarchy. We saw how the meanings of motherhood and (in)fertility are being redefined by women who, in their bid to become mothers, challenge the social, institutional and political structures and discourses that constitute and perpetuate the social norms. In this chapter I focus on the way these same contexts and meanings are embodied by women who do not conceive, at least in a physical or biological sense. As we have seen, the powerful ideology of motherhood that dictates what it means to be 'good at being a woman' constitutes childless women in Ireland as lucky, selfish or in control. Such assumptions leave little room for acknowledging the frustration of women who have embraced the desire and the identity, and sense themselves to be mothers.

Many childless women and their partners frequently described the need to redefine a 'failure to conceive' in order to express adequately the meaning of what they were experiencing. Some women struggle to reconcile the loss of part of their identity as women. For others there is a need to appropriate and maintain a motherhood identity in the absence

71

of conception. Many sought ways to legitimate their emotions and make tangible a loss that seemed invisible to others, suggesting an order of magnitude akin to the death of loved ones. Through narratives that constitute and reconstitute selves and meanings, women enact a kind of agency. Grief and the performance of grieving serve as a means of acknowledging and addressing infertility as both continuity and disruption to life plans. At the same time it reconfirms the dominant social values inherent in those life plans.

In this chapter women describe how childlessness is articulated with the embodiment of an ideal of motherhood, constituting the 'presence of absence' as a resistance to the identity of 'other than mother'.[1] Through careful attention to their sensations of grief, women simultaneously challenge and reaffirm the social convention that all women will be made mothers by a biological process of conception. In many of these stories, grief becomes a frame for making sense of the losses that accompany infertility. At the same time, grief enables women to break through silence, to make legitimate claims to the everyday experiences of motherhood and, perhaps most importantly, to resist the perception that they have failed as women.

Motherhood and (Re)Conceptions of Loss: Narrating the Presence of Absence

Catherine's story introduced me to the idea that conception was not always about biology when she spoke about 'conceiving in the heart'. I met Catherine many times throughout the course of my field work. After I had known her for some months, I approached her about doing a formal interview and we met in a large pub not far from where she worked. Although I heard similar stories, Catherine's exemplifies best the experience of being childless while embodying what seemed to be a motherhood identity. She describes the puzzle of grieving for something that is not – something that may never have existed materially but seems real nonetheless. Catherine faced the challenges of an inability to conceive in conjunction with a long medical history that began with a back problem when she was a child. The result was chronic pain as an adult – something she links to her difficulty in conceiving. She and her partner were raised in devout, practising Catholic families and Catherine was unable to reconcile the use of IVF with her religious values.

For many years Catherine struggled with what felt, to her, like a contradiction in her identity – an identity in which she felt she was a childless mother. Eventually she asked her parish priest to hold a mass for the children she had not physically conceived. Catherine felt that, in fact, she had two children – a boy and a girl – whom she had named and wanted to 'introduce' to her family and friends in order to make her loss tangible for others to share.

> CATHERINE: *The priest was saying the mass and I felt perhaps maybe that they don't understand me and don't understand that there might be people like me in the congregation. Missing something. Because they don't understand that you would have had a loss.*
>
> JILL: *It's a hard thing for people to conceptualise a loss . . .*
>
> CATHERINE: *. . . Of something that hasn't ever been. Yeah, yeah, even though in one's heart you would have conceived them. That's what Father J. said to me. You know, he said they were all conceived in your heart. They were conceived. I decided to hold a mass because I felt where am I to grieve? [. . .] I'd like to have a mass for my unforgotten dreams and for all the unforgotten dreams in my family. [. . .] It was just absolutely amazing. And that became more important to me. And then at the mass we were singing and I had picked out all the hymns and it was just beautiful.*
>
> JILL: *How many people came?*
>
> CATHERINE: *Eighty something. I dropped them all an invitation. Two hundred and some people. They probably all thought I was mad. I didn't care. I felt that they deserved . . . my children deserved to be known by their names. The fact that they [the children] didn't come didn't mean that they weren't wanted. So everybody who was important to me knows their names now.*

Catherine uses a familiar religious ritual to expose her hidden sorrow. Her use of this ritual exemplifies a kind of agency through which some women constitute themselves as mothers in the absence of children when she talks about conceiving children, not in conventional terms, but rather in her heart. In the commemorative mass her 'conceived of' children were materialised and symbolically embodied as if conceived biologically. Moreover, in her narrative she locates herself in relation to familiar discourses that have shaped her as moral and socially conforming by allowing her to embrace the values of the church, the family and the community. Even as there is agency in the creative resignification of failure as loss, the powerful discursive elements of the ideology of motherhood are unchallenged.

> CATHERINE: *Coming to terms, or whichever you'd call it. I'm not comfortable with the word 'terms' because I do live with it. And they are within me. You know the children that didn't come. The love is still contained within me. So it was kind of realised and forgiven, and resolved. Within myself, you know, letting them go. Letting them be free. Saying to my children, you know, at the end it's okay. I forgive ye . . . It's a pity you didn't come but it's alright. I'm alright now.*

The need to forgive the children for not coming imparts to them a measure of personhood and draws them from the shadows of the imaginary into the reality of Catherine's daily life. It was a way of reconciling the duality of grief in infertility, providing a space where the absence of motherhood was recontextualised by the presence of children as 'unforgotten dreams' – material recognition of what had been the intangible. Linda Layne describes a similar process in the making of memories in the context of pregnancy loss and miscarriage in the US. She notes that this kind of 'memory making is pro-active' in the context of consumer culture and suggests that memories, in this case, are constructions rather than reconstructions.[2] Even as she talks about letting go, her narrative is about sustaining an identity as much as it is about moving on from an interruption in her imagined life course. Pointing out the inadequacy of a phrase like 'coming to terms', Catherine resists the idea that she must relinquish her sense of self as a mother. For women like Catherine, who do not manage to conceive or adopt children, motherhood lingers as a presence of absence in their identities. Their narratives reveal a subject position of 'failed woman' even as they convey the irreconcilable elements of the recruited subject position of 'mother'.

Catherine's story thus raises questions about the relationship between subjectivity, embodiment and reproduction. Clearly Catherine's sense of being a mother was deeply embodied in a way that necessitated reconciliation with a body that did not produce children. Here again we see the subject position where, more than that of being hailed and thus 'recruited' as a subject,[3] there is an actual performance of an identity like motherhood that Judith Butler has described as part of the subjectification.[4] More complex still is the element of agency wherein Catherine's subject position is both a product of her social circumstances and her own conceptions of how she can be a mother. Her claims to motherhood are thus at once socially constituted and performative while situated within a normative frame of loss and grief.

Gayle Letherby argues that a distinction often drawn between the 'biological condition of infertility and the social condition of involuntary childlessness' is inadequate to the task of describing the range of experiences associated with an inability to conceive.[5] The experience of infertility, as an embodied phenomenon, challenges the unified subject of woman as mother. These narratives thus produce subjects who are counter to the norm. But these are not only counter-narratives of resistance but also stories of affirmation rooted in the dominant motherhood ideology. Women like Catherine highlight the importance of finding creative ways to give their grief and loss legitimacy in a social context where they perceive their own exclusion by virtue of the very definition of what constitutes the ideal family.

> ELSA: *I think it was at a NISIG meeting and we were comparing it with grieving and the grieving process that you go through. And it was really kind of important to me that we could grieve for the children that weren't born. I think that did help a lot and I did let the process go on and there was a real anger and there was depression and the stages that you go through when somebody dies and I think that's where I'm at now. I mean my children haven't been born or died for whatever reason but I feel they are still very much there. And so how can it be? I think that makes a lot of people think . . .*[6]

Like Catherine's story at the beginning of this chapter, Elsa describes the continuity of the sensation of the presence of absence when she talks about grieving for children who were not conceived but are still very much a part of her lived reality. Grieving then is more about continuity and maintaining a connection to a motherhood identity than it is about acknowledging an end. The embodied sensation of being a mother is made clear when Elsa and Catherine point out that accepting childless-ness is not the same as accepting that they are not mothers. But in addition to the significance of maintaining a motherhood identity, there is also the need to configure what is lost. Marcia Inhorn describes how childless women in Egypt forestall notions of social failure by remaining liminal, 'searching' for the children who have not yet come.[7] Among the women I spoke with in Ireland, it is not liminality but rather a recogni-tion that they have performed or achieved as women. Similarly, Paxson found that there was an emphasis on motherhood as completing a woman's identity in her work in Greece.[8]

The sense of being 'complete' as a woman in Ireland resides in the claim to an ongoing motherhood identity as they reconfigure themselves as *having* children who did not come. In so doing, they resist the stereo-typical stigma of childlessness that casts them as the 'other'.[9] Stigma around childlessness has been described as the result of a 'spoiled iden-tity',[10] and a product of the dominant or 'master status' that shapes women's lives.[11] However, grieving 'lost' children recasts their experi-ences in conformity with the social imperatives that have shaped them as women/mothers, allowing them to claim to be mothers in the same way that women who have lost a child can maintain a claim to motherhood.

There is a deeper expression of sensibility here – one in which women cannot find that moment when they were and then were not mothers and when the disruption occurred. The importance of death as a metaphor or analogy helps to construct the moment of disruption in an experience that might otherwise be unmarked by particular moments of loss. The significance of language in constituting and reconstituting subjects, or as Butler argues, resignifying, is evident if we consider that 'discourse is the horizon of agency, but also performativity is to be rethought as resignification'.[12] The performance and iteration of infertility in terms of motherhood realised in sorrow creates the space for agency in the appropriation of meanings. Subjectivity is shaped as much by intention, narrative and sensation as it is by discourse and social and political relations of power.

Narratives often employ powerful tropes that hinge on the meaning of presence of absence. Other tropes such as metaphors can be employed in the narrative plotting of fertility events as a means of making meaning or reordering experiences of disruption in life narratives.[13] Below Anne describes how she used an analogy once in response to someone who she felt misunderstood her situation. The metaphor of violence in her story highlights the depth of her feelings of loss as surely nothing could be more painful than the brutality her story suggests. Her need to establish the legitimacy of loss and grief is equally palpable as she struggles with what she perceives as the failure of others to acknowledge the meaning of an inability to conceive as not only a loss of identity but a loss of imagined children as well.

> ANNE: *Well I had somebody say to me once, 'why don't you just adopt and don't do the IVF? You've been through enough.' And that person had three kids. And I said I'm going to take away your three kids and murder them and you're going to have that heartache and that grief. That all consuming . . . [pausing] I can't even explain it. That horror inside you. That pain. I'm going to leave you with that. How would you feel now? Wouldn't you want your kids back? She said yes and I said that's how I feel every day and that's how my husband feels. That's the only way to explain it. It's not just the loss of your dream. It's a sorrow that won't go away. It's an emptiness as if you've this perfect family – yourself and your husband. You have the best relationship you could ever hope. And the one thing you're missing is a child. And that's the heartbreak.*

For women like Anne and Elsa, their sense of loss is as tangible as death but the fact that children never came makes the grief difficult for people to understand. It is this lack of understanding that Anne, Catherine and Elsa resist when they talk about sustaining the meaning of loss rather than 'moving on', 'coming to terms' or 'getting over it'. In contrast to Becker's work, which focuses on the ways people strive to reshape and reclaim a sense of continuity after chaos or disruption to their lives, many of the women I spoke with in Ireland were clinging to the disruption as part of their lives and had resignified failure as loss in order to sustain the connection to the motherhood identity they claim.

The rupture in the imagined life narrative is reconfigured and they grieve lost children, not lost fertility or lost motherhood. Disruption here was not chaotic but rather, the basis of their identity as childless mothers.

In another narrative rich in powerful tropes Lydia constitutes tangibility and identity as she shapes her ectopic pregnancy and resulting loss in the context of death in her personification of her embryo. [14]

> LYDIA: *And that's what I was told. So he took my tube and [crying] . . . I went down that evening and I had an ectopic pregnancy in the left tube and it had . . . when I eventually asked, it had . . . it was in the open end of the tube. It had eaten into . . . I say eaten but however it is said, but it had actually . . . I know you don't use that word.*
> JILL: *I know what you mean.*
> LYDIA: *It was my baby, you know. But it had grown and used the resources at that end of the tube, and had possibly died on the Sunday night when I had that huge pain. Because the baby, and I still refer to it as a baby, and that is the huge thing with infertility, you know it [an embryo] is your baby.*

During this interview we started and stopped the recorder numerous times to allow her to regain her composure. At Lydia's insistence, the interview continued for several hours, her tears rendering a plate of scones inedible and our cups of tea going cold in spite of the old adage about its potential to soothe. Lydia built a scenario to conceptualise her 'baby', normalising the events with a metaphorical description of the embryo feeding on her maternal body until it 'died', reshaping her grief for the loss of her fertility as a way of making sense of and reordering the experience. Her metaphor draws on the image of nurturing and suggests order can be constituted from the chaos of an ectopic pregnancy. She also actively constructs a memorial for herself that enables the material connection of a baby to remain relevant.

The context of a death provides a way of making sense of people's lack of understanding of the impact of infertility loss.

> LORNA: *People who have experienced a mother or father or brother or sister death know what that is like but this is a very different type of death and I always feel angry when I hear people say they've lost a child and sure she has other children. I am absolutely so angry when I hear people say that. And they do, they do. I always feel very angry; that is your child. You wanted that child equally as much as you wanted the ones that came before, the ones that came after. That child is a huge loss. That huge sense of loss will be there for ages and ages.*

Lorna also describes the end of an IVF cycle without a conception as a kind of death. Her analogy with people's lack of understanding about what it is like to lose a child draws on the social or cultural notions about what constitutes legitimate forms of grief in relation to an imagined hierarchy of experiences of loss. Lorna suggests that people misunderstand the impact of fertility loss by describing how a woman who has other children might be expected to grieve less for the loss of one because she has others. Like Anne's story above, Lorna narrates a lack of faith in people's capacity to understand the equation of absence with loss. All of the stories above employ powerful metaphors that draw on the social meaning of the death of a child in order to convey the emotions necessary to legitimate grief.

Narrating Contradiction: Inclusion/Exclusion, Disruption/Continuity

As described in the preceding chapters, an ideology of motherhood in Ireland is embedded in and sustains both a nationalist identity and a patriarchal norm as the basis for both family and state structures. This goes hand in hand with what many describe as an ideology of familism in which there seems to be little opportunity for alternatives to hetero-normative identities.[15] The sense of oneself as 'always-already' a mother even in the absence of children is at the core of the experience of presence of absence, as described in Chapter 2. We are called and at the same time recognise ourselves as subjects. Women, by virtue of recognising themselves as such, are thus already constituted as mothers.

Women who are asked about children, or reminded of their childlessness, are thus shaped not as having *lost* something but as missing something. What they experience, however, is very much a sense of loss, emphasised most directly by an accompanying sense of exclusion from participation in many aspects of society.

> ELSA: *I do sometimes think 'what would I have been like as a mother?' I kind of think I would have been really good as a mother. When I am with other [people's] children I am wondering what my kids would be like. Just something that . . . Sometimes it's still complete and utter disbelief that . . . [laughing] that it's really not going to happen. I mean, I'm forty-one now, and it's something that . . . Sometimes I just still don't believe it. I just kind of think it's still . . . it can't be real. You know sometimes I actually don't want to accept it but I think the one part, the one big part is that I feel excluded. You know I don't really belong, I'm not part of this society and I don't have anything to talk about the general experience – women's experience, I don't have and I never will. And that's something that is kind of . . . comes to my mind about it all.*

This disrupted life story incorporates the vividness of the imagined social relationship. Elsa speaks of her own disbelief when she imagines herself as a mother. Social exclusion as a result of the absence of children in day-to-day life is bound to the imagination of a life narrative and the dismay at the actuality of this disruption. Becker describes how a sense of normality is sought when 'the life story must be reconstructed to fit a set of life circumstances different from those originally anticipated'.[16] In narratives like Elsa's when she speaks of imagined children, her life story is reconstructed in a kind of dual mode; her new life story incorporates the imagined continuity of the old life story which included her identity as a mother. But even more remarkable is Elsa's description of feeling doubly excluded because she has no children and has not had the experiences of becoming a mother that seem vital to *being* a woman.

The dominant values that produce the life narrative also underpin the more subtle dynamic that operates to confirm the relationship between motherhood and marriage in the way questions are employed.

> CATHERINE: *Actually a very good friend of mine who would have been in a relationship for nearly twenty, twenty-five years, I think. And would have been trying to conceive for years and years and years, never was expected to be announcing that she was pregnant because they weren't married. So she had the freedom.*
> JILL: *Okay, so there was a sense there that she wasn't expected to want a baby . . . That's interesting*
> CATHERINE: *She was never asked even though she wanted them. I thought that was interesting. No one expected her to be pregnant because she wasn't married. Even though, I suppose if she did become pregnant, you know, every other person would accept it. But because she never once was asked are you pregnant. But because you are married you're asked.*

> JILL: *So you were married for a few years before you started?*
> BREDA: *Oh no, just the opposite. We were trying for a few years before we married [laughing]. No, as I say, we got together when we were about twenty-four and then we bought our first house together when we were twenty-nine and it was then we started trying but we didn't get married until we were about thirty-two. It took us a lot longer to get our heads around that [laughing]. [. . .] I suppose in a sense there was no pressure on us for the first couple of years because nobody would have guessed that we were trying and certainly no pressure on myself either. But then I suppose once you do get married then there is that society pressure.*

The marriage and children paradigm thus has both temporal and social elements that must follow in a normative sequence – first marriage and then motherhood. The naturalisation of conception and motherhood as part of marriage is apparent as Catherine and Breda both point out that questions and assumptions about children are rarely visited on those who do not conform to the hetero-normative ideal. While it is widely acknowledged that children are born outside of marriage in increasing numbers in Ireland, an inability to conceive is only perceived as problematic within the institution of marriage.

Leah's story also highlights how an inability to conceive becomes the point of rupture between her imagined life narrative and the one she now relates to me.

> JILL: *So tell me about the infertility experience. When did you first realise there was a problem?*
> LEAH: *Um, it took a long time really considering we were together for so long. But like that's because we weren't trying to have a baby because we weren't married and we were trying to wait. So as soon as we got married I said right, that's it, you know. Let's have babies, and kind of took off any pre-cautions or whatever and relaxed and nothing was happening. And it was about two years and we moved house and had this nice house and this bedroom and had a nice happy job and it was like okay, come on, where's the family? And it's like everything for me was focusing around the family issue and having a baby and expecting it to happen.*

An inability to conceive is only perceived as disruption and under-stood in wider networks of family and friends once the ideal of marriage is accomplished. Infertility is rarely interpreted by family, friends and acquaintances as a disruption to the life narrative in a context outside marriage. The space for legitimate sadness and grief over an inability to conceive is foreclosed by the assumptions that infertility is defined and/or recognised as a problem largely (perhaps exclusively) within the social context of marriage in Ireland.

Grief, however, can also make room for alternative forms of emo-tional legitimacy even in the absence of wider social recognition of loss. For some people grief forestalls or mediates the sensation of failure. At the same time, however, grieving shapes a kind of resistance to societal perceptions that women who do not conceive have failed to embrace the values of parenthood, family and generational continuity that are hall-marks of Irish social life.

Embodied (In)Fertility

The lived body furnishes additional grounds for experiencing loss and grief in the quest to conceive. The finality of death is a counterpoint to the kind of indeterminate status of one's fertility at certain points in the journey. The whole cyclical nature of women's fertility furnishes bodily reminders and sites for grieving loss on a regular basis. This loss is then countered emotionally with a renewed possibility of 'next month'. Elsa also describes how the experience of the disruption in one's reproduc-tive life story is often seemingly tentative and incomplete.

> ELSA: *I mean we're still not using any contraceptives. There's stories of when women are coming to menopause and they suddenly become*

pregnant. I hope this doesn't happen and you know if I really had a choice now and somebody would give me a child and say here, do you want it or not . . . I don't think I want it, to be honest. I mean we've been living together for so long, you get used to your life. To be forty-one and for years I always did what I wanted. So it would be tough. But then, like I say, we're not using any contraceptive and if I was able to get pregnant we'd be delighted and I'd find ways to cope with it.

In her work on disruption, Becker aligns the experiences of infertility with other kinds of disruption such as political persecution or disabling or debilitating illness. With infertility there is also a repetative and ongoing engagement with the possibility of conception well into menopause as couples continue to think in terms of hope or at least possibility even after treatment is no longer an option. In this sense, the disruption is not final but cyclical.[17] This indeterminacy or absence of finality carries over to the experience of IVF as well, as part of the motif of possibility or 'liminality' in a precarious state of uncertainty, or possibility as a catalyst for hope and proactive 'persistence' in trying to manage disruption.[18] The cycles of hope and loss are repetitive and indefinite. While many women spoke of the sense of hopefulness they felt with each unsuccessful treatment, they also describe the role of loss in jading their views about subsequent treatments. Subjectivity and a sense of motherhood as imminent during treatment create conflicted emotions as women try to make sense of how and what to grieve.

NIAMH: Well, it's before . . . Well you see the first time you do it you think it's going to work. That's the problem. You think this is it now, we've done everything else so this has to work. So the first time I knew, you see I knew. Because I felt my period coming every time before the two weeks were up. I just knew. [. . .] So it wasn't a total disappointment because I knew. But this time I am just a bit more blasé about it probably. I'm a bit more . . . I'm looking forward to the adoption. That's what I'm looking forward to. And if this works great but I'm trying not to think about it. Because it's just too hard on your head to be thinking about it.

ANNE: The same way I'm taking a bit of control. I'm going to find out the information. I'm going to ask questions. You start getting your identity back. But it takes a couple of years before you get the courage to do that. You know what I mean. When you're a new person, you don't. You honestly think it's going to work for the first time, maybe second time at the most. But it will work.

The cycles engender anticipation even if this lessens with each attempt. It is not unusual for people to undertake three or more cycles of IVF. The constant engagement with potential and then loss complicates and forecloses the ability to make sense of the experiences, perpetuating the sensation of presence of absence.

Similarly, every menstrual cycle signals loss but at the same time generates another month of hope and possibility. Mairead has used a process that involves tracking cycles and body temperature to predict ovulation while making a decision about treatment.

> MAIREAD: *Doing something. When I'm doing something I don't mind. I find it very frustrating when I'm not and another month has gone by and you're ticking them off. And there's just been so many. I do it every month. I have a little ritual. It really is frustrating. There is a little mourning and you get over that loss and you start again. But there is, every single time. Even if it's a day over you are in hope. I find actually what's worse is a kind of . . . by the third week you start to think, I feel a little bit different. I'm feeling a little bit sick. You almost are playing a game with yourself. And I do it every month! I don't believe it but I do it!! Obviously it's a part of my psyche because I get it every month, without fail. And then I go back in and they say nope. It definitely is something that is hard. But I think the last time James said as well with the results, you felt very . . .*
> JAMES: *Disappointed. It hit me. It doesn't hit me with the same kind of mechanical regularity but it does hit at times.*

Mairead described the rituals she employed every month as part of her embodied experience of the possibility of fertility within infertility. Mourning the onset of a menstrual cycle as another loss, she described taking up hope again as she approached the next cycle. The reproductive body, from this perspective, is deeply embedded in the making of experiences, as 'the existential grounds' for the cultural interpretation of reproduction.[19] Through the cyclical nature of reproductive bodies, women are subject to the sensibilities that can become embodied as motherhood identities.

There is an irony in the fact that the absolute regularity and order of bodily processes of menstruation are often experienced as 'disorder' for those who are trying to conceive. Women are caught in emotional contradiction, often redefining this regularity as the grounds for grieving even as they also see it as the point of beginning again.

> DONNA: *And then we have reminders, I mean we have hormones and we have a womb and we have reminders every month. I mean we give out about it so many times but then when you desire to have a child you realise you know, that when you do get your period that it's just absolutely devastating. It's a huge, huge grief and every single month when you're trying to conceive.*
>
> KRISTEN: *I think it's the way it just takes over every waking moment. Calculating the minute you've got your period when your next period*

will be due and when can you do a test, and on and on. I've gone through so many early pregnancy tests. It's costing me a fortune. I think the hardest thing has been the way it's taken over my life. And the impact that it's had on our relationship because it has taken over more of my life than it has taken over my husband's.

KATHLEEN: *And anybody that is trying to conceive will tell you it takes over your life completely. Your whole month is dominated by your cycle. Okay, you're ovulating on such and such a day. And your poor husband, you know what happens there. And then you have the two-week wait until . . . then you're disappointed and you shed a few tears and then you pick yourself up again*

Kristen points out the difference between what her husband experiences and her sense of what is going on in relation to the cyclical evidence of fertility and infertility lived through her own body. Marie Claire and Gretchen also describe the added difficulty of having invested emotionally in treatment only to feel betrayed by the rhythm and regularity of one's own body once again.

MARIE CLAIRE: *Every month. Every single month. I get a blast of energy and I'd say here we go, the injections are over and now we've got this . . . Until the end of the month and then obviously disappointment again. More tears. Tears and tantrums. Very disappointed. Very tough . . .*

GRETCHEN: *It is so hard to focus on anything else. You are so scared that you might miss out on that window of opportunity. After treatment . . . When you get your period. You have no other choice but to cry your eyes out. For me it is more important that you are healthy and well.*

For many women there is the broad issue of the constraints of a biological clock – in terms of fertile years. But for women who are challenged by infertility there is another intrinsic or internal clock that keeps ticking every month, reminding them when they are potentially fertile and definitively unsuccessful in conceiving for yet another month. With every monthly menstrual period comes a sense of loss, grief and anxiety as women now have to wait another two weeks for ovulation once again. Leah told me that now that she has given up trying to conceive, she has dispensed with her cycles altogether. She uses the birth control pill in a continuous cycle to refuse her periods. She no longer wants the monthly reminder. Her narrative begins with telling me how she felt compelled to try IVF. For Leah, as with many women in my study, this compulsion is part of the socially driven need to do everything possible. She and her partner made the decision to stop IVF after four treatment cycles even though the clinic was encouraging them to try again. Having come to the realisation that she had done everything she could to conceive, she no longer needs or wants any awareness or reminders of the physiology of reproduction.

> LEAH: *I thought maybe I would feel that you didn't give it your all, you didn't give it your last shot but no regrets whatsoever. I really feel that was the thing to do and I feel comfortable. I don't have a period anymore because I'm on the pill. I put up with so much prodding around with my body and maybe that's why I feel maybe because I'm not menstruating that I don't feel the loss as much psychologically. That's nature's way and that's what it's all about. That's what you have a period for. I thought maybe eliminating that in my own body, for me it's a good thing.*

Redefining the meaning of loss in relation to the experience of infertility treatment is often even more complex. When there is no conception after IVF, medical practitioners sometimes left women feeling that it was not the treatment that had failed, but rather the women themselves. This is especially difficult if the infertility resides with the male partner and successful conception still depends on the rigours of IVF for women.

> LEAH: *We couldn't understand if they're telling me I'm fine, they're telling me my womb was fine, they're telling me I should have no problem conceiving, and yet they're doing the job themselves with the little sperm. They're telling me that the cells, the division, is happening, they're putting it back inside me after the divisions have happened. So I was like, 'what's going wrong?' And their explanation to that was there's a huge amount of it goes on and the sperm is still very involved, that he's other roles to play and genetically he may not be able to play those roles. And other things in a woman's body that they really don't know about, why nature decides to expel it. And they basically really never gave me an answer except to say there really isn't an answer. But I know statistically, I know biologically it isn't . . . it's there, you can look at the stats.*

Leah's treatment failure is framed in the discourse of statistics and science, but in the end she holds 'nature' to account as that which expels or fails to do its part. This merging of nature and science in the discourse of assisted reproduction is part of the narrative of hope. In her work with women who were undertaking treatment with IVF, Franklin describes how infertility treatment operates to sustain the possibility of fulfilling the life narrative, forestalling the acknowledgment of disruption.[20] This is achieved, in part, through rhetoric that suggests science can overcome the inconsistencies and flaws of nature. Moreover, it participates in the redefining of what is culturally constituted as natural. For couples who seek refuge in a medicalised explanation for their infertility, a failure that is situated and then reiterated in women's bodies does little to validate an identity so firmly attached to motherhood. In fact, some women refer to themselves immediately after IVF as 'pregnant until proven otherwise', in an attempt to experience, however briefly, the sensation of being a mother, seeking the needed validation of that identity. The experience of having embryos inside their bodies is often balanced against the weight of grief after the embryos are deemed to be lost at the end of what is described by many as the longest two weeks of their lives – the two weeks between embryo transfer and the onset of a period or negative pregnancy test.

> CAROL ANNE: *I suppose the first two times the treatment failed, I was feeling a failure as a woman. That you can't, a) have children naturally, and b) that you tried treatment and that even then you still failed to, you know, the embryo failed to implant.[. . .] Because if you believe in conception being the beginning of life then you have a life within you. A woman, normally, the only way they know they're pregnant is if they miss a period or they start feeling sick. Whereas you know from the very beginning that there's an embryo in there that could turn into a human being and you feel like you're pregnant right from the start. So that when it fails it's like having a miscarriage because you feel there was something in there that was growing and it just died. So it's like bereavement.*

Carol Anne describes succinctly the convergent losses of both her embryo and her identity as a woman. She carefully redefines her grief as the same as a miscarriage since with IVF women know there is an embryo placed into the uterus. The sheer visibility and materiality of embryo transfer constitutes a sensation of pregnancy.[21] The very idea of when pregnancy begins and how treatment is viewed in the context of success or failure is now redefined in conjunction with the progressive successes involved in an IVF conception.

Alexis describes her desire to just experience the sensation of a kind of material conception in order to have something on which to base both a feeling of motherhood and the grief of losing it.

> ALEXIS: *What happens with us . . . what seems to be happening is the eggs look fine and the sperm looks fine and they do the ICSI [intracytoplasmic sperm injection] and they look fine on day one. But then through day two they all died off. They didn't last until day three for the transfer. I've never had the embryos back. I've had the egg collection but I've never had the transfer. [. . .] They always do the day three transfer for ICSI and I was saying, 'should we not do day two when they look so well on day two?' And they were saying, 'well, your chances are pretty slim, like, because if they're going to die in the lab on day two the same is going to happen inside you'. But psychologically I'm expecting a miracle by having them inside me, whereas I've never had them inside me and I'm missing out on that bit. I know some of the girls would be on the IVF websites saying something about their embryos and I would be thinking God, you're so lucky to even have them inside. Like what do you feel like or do you feel anything? In some ways*

it's silly because there's nothing and I'm probably better off waiting the three days and then if they are gone, they're gone instead of waiting the two weeks. But the embryologist said if he had his way everybody would be a day three. You wouldn't have to wait the two weeks then because you'll know. And I was saying, 'surely, the best place for the embryos is your womb', and he said, 'no, the conditions in the lab are just as good, if not better.'

Alexis found the sadness of never even contemplating the presence of embryos difficult to deal with emotionally. She tried to imagine the sensation of performing motherhood by housing and nurturing an embryo herself, however briefly. The embryologist assumed he was foreclosing grief for women by insisting that only embryos that survive *in vitro* until the third day get transferred to the womb of the mother. However, this also fails to acknowledge the significance of embodied motherhood as both subjectivity and a social ideal.[22] The embryologist here dissociates the powerful subjective experience of nurturing in motherhood from the bodily function of providing an environment for an embryo when he suggests that the laboratory might be a better place for this process than the body of a woman/mother.

Feminist theorists have directed our attention to such accounts in which 'scientific discourses have come to articulate the authoritative social theories of the feminine body'.[23] As Foucault has argued, discourse facilitates the power of clinicians to name the conditions of deviance and illness and to shape normative practice as well as what constitutes legitimate knowledge. This results in an often contradictory and variable meaning attached to 'achieved conception' in assisted reproduction as medical practitioners have a differing view of achievement than the women receiving the biomedical interventions.[24] For women, the meaning of achieving conception is embedded in the significance of becoming a mother. For practitioners, however, it is the scientific and biological accomplishment of having fertilisation and implantation occur through the *craft* of medicine – an achievement in and of itself, distilled from the social meaning of conceiving a child. The scientific measure of success or failure can leave women feeling external to the process of their own procreative events when they embody the social role without being able to embody the biology as well. This leaves them not only bereft but somehow unable to situate their grief.

Treatment failure, and the grief that accompanies it, can be difficult for some women to try to put into a context that friends and family members will understand. For them, it is perhaps seen as a failure of process or even an example of nature triumphing over technology. Neither of these creates the kind of context for emotional support that women need after treatment does not result in conception.

DONNA: *After my last embryo transfer . . . and it didn't work, and I had said to my siblings and quite a few close friends of mine that I'd been for infertility treatment. And when I said that it had failed, I didn't get much empathy from them. It was like it really didn't matter. Well I rang the Miscarriage Association and I asked their permission to say . . . could I say I had a miscarriage because then my needs might be taken care of if I did say it. And I felt the recognition of my baby would be . . . And they were absolutely brilliant [emphatic]. They said 'of course you can, of course you can, because you did have embryos inside you and you don't know, they might have implanted for a few days. You don't know. Of course you can say it but we do have to warn you about something'. And they said, 'number one, the female is always to blame and number two, they will ask you how many weeks you were'. I said I didn't care. I went home to my hometown and I told my siblings and they got up and they hugged me and they cried. But I thought that was very sad that the grief of infertility was not . . . that I had to say I'd had a miscarriage to get my needs met.*

Donna redefines her experience as a miscarriage thus discursively creating the dimension of loss in which people could empathise with her. However, Donna did not feel entitled to claim for herself the right to experience a miscarriage until she was given permission to call it a miscarriage by the appropriate support network. An alternative, but authoritative, medicalised definition of what happened allows Donna to shift the meaning from a domain of failure to a domain of loss. In other words, a pregnancy or a 'baby' can be lost whereas an IVF treatment only fails. Again, the support network relies on the biological definitions of conception and implantation to assure her that her grief and her claim to motherhood are real experiences. The power to name also gives disciplines like medicine the power to construct and shape experience. Donna's narrative describes the need to collapse those biologically distinct moments defined as fertilisation, conception and pregnancy in order to point out the difficulty in defining exactly when motherhood – and consequently loss – begins. Donna finds satisfaction in this reinterpretation of her experience and is empowered by its endorsement by an official organisation. At the same time, this need to re-position her loss as a miscarriage reaffirms how fertility as the norm shapes everyday experiences for women who are trying to conceive.

(In)Conceivable: Contested Avenues for Grief

Infertility – the inability to have a child – has the potential to dominate your life. It can bring great personal despair and suffering. The feelings experienced by infertile couples include disbelief, pain, isolation, exclusion, bitterness, anger, confusion and depression. Unless addressed, the issues

> associated with infertility may encroach on your every waking moment,
> impinging on your self-esteem and sense of self – in short, infertility may
> cast a shadow over your creativity and leave you feeling utterly worthless as
> a human being. (NISIG website)[25]

There are a number of places where expressions and enactments of grief
and loss occur as Irish women and men search for ways to make sense of
their reproductive identities and infertility experiences from spiritual,
religious, medical and social perspectives. These include public and
familiar contexts associated with grieving and emotional support as personal memorials, religious services, cemeteries and support groups that
serve to materialise loss and make visible the identities of both parents
and children in an absence of conception. Grief and loss are constituted
as legitimate or illegitimate through professional and lay support
systems, and some tensions become evident as the nature and experience
of loss are defined and redefined. These stories also highlight the way
silence is sometimes sustained and sometimes bridged and broken when
people use grief as a means of communicating the depth of meaning
associated with a failure to conceive.

One of my first contacts in Ireland as I began my research was with a
small group of women who had formed a national support network –
the National Infertility Support and Information Group (NISIG). They
were exceptionally devoted to their cause and were very supportive of
my research as well. Their motto, which forms the basis for their
mandate, is 'Infertility can be an isolating experience. You are not alone'.
The network was organised by a group of women from Cork who have
had a variety of different experiences with infertility, treatment and
childlessness. The group organises meetings in a few cities and sponsors
a telephone support line, and this individual contact has been the main
focus and mandate of the group. This kind of support plays a role in
legitimating grief. In fact, the network has sponsored an interdenomina-
tional service in the past that has been framed as a memorial to
'unforgotten dreams', much like the mass Catherine describes at the
beginning of this chapter.

My initial intention, after meeting some of the executive prior to
beginning fieldwork, was to attend meetings of the support network.
However, shortly after I began the research, my participation at NISIG
group meetings was vetoed, after some sober second thought on the part
of the executive, on the basis of maintaining privacy for people who
might attend. Since it was not possible to predict who might attend any
specific meeting there was no formal way in which to ask permission
from participants. One facilitator told me that she had conducted meetings where people did not say a word, but simply cried for two hours – a

testament again to the need to create legitimate space for this kind of sorrow. People sometimes needed a safe place to express an embodied sensation that they found too powerful to articulate. I respected the executive for their desire to preserve this quality for people. Secrecy, confidentiality and isolation are locked in a complex embrace evident in both the motto and mandate of NISIG where they acknowledge isolation as a product of silence. I have written elsewhere about the powerful impact of silence as a product of social, political and familial relations in Ireland.[26]

The members of the executive were adamant that their purpose had never been political action and advocacy, but rather the provision of support for individuals. Kate, one of the founding members, points out that in providing a listening ear to others she was also reaching out as a result of needing emotional support for herself, perhaps the motivation for her forming a support community.

> KATE: *Now in hindsight looking back on NISIG, that three set it up and the three of us were embarking on infertility treatment. We used to facilitate the meetings all over Ireland and I'd have the helpline, mostly. So therefore I was there listening to everybody but there was nobody taking care of my needs. I didn't realise at the time, in hindsight when I look back. I realise I was still in the nursing role. You know, that I'd be listening to people crying. And I'd say yes, I know exactly how you are feeling because I had failed treatment a month ago. So because they were in such pain they couldn't give me comfort.*
> JILL: *No, no. Right, and they were calling you in the context of needing your support.*
> KATE: *And even if I say to them . . . I think that subconsciously I was reaching out. I didn't realise at the time. Looking back I think . . . I just don't know how I did it looking back. I really don't know how I did it. I suppose we all get an inner strength.*

Women who have been unable to conceive often draw on their experiences by organising support networks or counselling others. Franklin puts this kind of project in the context of 'women's work' as nurturers and care givers, suggesting that for many, this involvement provides a 'means of coming to terms with the end of treatment'.[27] In Ireland this might be defined as 'mothers' work' as well, deeply embedded in the social expectation that women provide stability and continuity in their role as mothers. Support networks provide a means for re-establishing a sense of order and continuity by giving meaning to shared experiences. Thus support networks provide a forum for both care giving and nurturing, and a mechanism for continuity as volunteers can sustain their own narratives of isolation, loss and pain. They also provide opportunities for women to participate in the affirmation of sensations of grief and loss without relinquishing an identity or 'coming to terms' with something – seen as a kind of resignation or acknowledgment of socially defined failure.

The support network also provides a context for dealing with relationships with family members and constituting a community of people who can be trusted to understand and legitimate one's feelings of loss, anger or resentment.

> KELLY: *And the amazing thing is when we went to NISIG first, it was such a nice thing to see everybody else's bitterness. [Laughing] We all laugh. We'd give out about people but you could still sense that it hadn't fazed the person. There was no deep hate within the person for whatever offhand comment somebody had made. They tried to deal with it with humour by giving out about it. There were two couples in particular that would be the same as us in that way. And the whole thing is you are laughing about it but you felt it was okay to laugh.*
> TARA: *We did actually. Even before people had children we did end up laughing. And it was good to laugh about it because you were laughing with people who understood, they were allowed to laugh.*

Being allowed to laugh indicates the feeling of legitimacy established by sharing the experiences of loss and absence. Such stories highlight people's need to find others who might validate the feelings and experiences that are often misunderstood by friends and family. Only someone who has experienced infertility can laugh at the situations that emerge from a lack of understanding by others.

Conclusion

I began this chapter with the suggestion that the presence of absence creates a conceptual space in which people who experience an inability to conceive can perform a kind of grieving that legitimates their sensation of loss while at once allowing them to sustain a sensation of being. As I described in the last chapter, many women redefined the parameters of the woman/mother paradigm, the meaning of motherhood and (in)fertility while becoming mothers in non-traditional circumstances. In a similar light, some women who remain childless are also redefining the paradigm by appropriating, embodying and redefining the terms within their life narratives, allowing them to claim conception and making them mothers in a very non-conventional sense. Thus, even in the absence of *becoming* a mother, some women still experience, subjectively, a sense of *being* that is motherhood.

The meanings of reproduction remain anchored to subjectivities powerfully inscribed on the gendered bodies of women and men. The reproductive body, particularly for infertile women, becomes a locus of experience for absence, disability and loss. Women experience the disorder of the reproductive body as a social failure in which there is an interruption to life narratives. The kind of conflicted subjectivity in which women feel as if they are 'always-already' mothers creates a need for social validation of their conformity with social ideals. This embodiment of maternal ideals challenges the margins of motherhood as an identity that begins with conception.

At the same time, avenues for the expression of the sensation of motherhood in the absence of children are limited in scope. Organisations and networks of support are products of the social environment and political context in which silence and secrecy dominate and there are few safe locations for either experiencing or expressing emotions around a presence of absence.

5. Eggs, Sperm and Conceptions of a Moral Nature

MAIREAD: I suppose the religious thing wouldn't have been as strong as . . . I mean my parents were very religious. They were Catholic to the core. But you know I wouldn't be as bothered by IVF. More in our family, if it gets the job done, get the job done. They wouldn't have cared as much as James' family would. And again, other friends have been through it and I know they've actually said that their family was just worried about, almost, the soul of the baby. But you know, then the baby is there and it's the best thing ever so it doesn't really matter. I suppose I can justify that to myself but maybe you can't justify . . . that the end justifies the means.

JAMES: I think my problems with IVF aren't so much religious. I think it's more just pumping your body with drugs and stimulating it and I just think it's unnatural.

JAMES: (reading from a report from their fertility specialist) 'The chances of a sperm meeting an oocyte in the fallopian tube are the same as a blind man finding a football in Cork railway station after the shops, obstacles and other buildings have all been removed.' This is the letter of medical recommendation from our doctor.

Infertility treatment has provoked a re-examination of the role of procreation in shaping the meanings of gender, sexuality, kinship and family. At the same time infertility confronts the role of nature in sexual, moral, biological and technological conception. This is not unique to the Irish social and cultural context but is part of the local moral world. What is significant is that this re-examination and confrontation mark out the heterosexual family, marriage and reproduction of family (biological and social) as sites in which morality, social responsibility and gender roles have been defined and contained in Ireland. This containment has also hinged on the way the heterosexual family has been naturalised and, in turn, shapes the contested meanings associated with nature and science in both procreation and assisted reproduction technologies. The moral and social dilemmas posed by ART are thus related to a number of issues including the way eggs and sperm are obtained, the relationship between sex and procreation, and a redefining of natural, biological, genetic and social bases for kinship identities and relationships. Nature is positioned and repositioned in institutional discourses as changing social conditions necessitate new attention to values. But as James and Mairead suggest in the epigraphs above, there is a kind of collision of discourses in which 'getting the job done' means dismissing nature as inefficient or inadequate and religious ethos as obstructive. Medicalisation is thus positioned in a new moral/normative light as a logical way to achieve a family. And since creating a family is framed as a moral objective in Ireland (and elsewhere), medicalisation of procreation gains a moral appeal for some people. At the same time there is an expectation that medical discourse *is* scientific discourse rather than mere metaphors about footballs and train stations and that what is deemed to be natural is the equivalent of health.

In the following chapters I will examine the ways that assisted repro-duction engenders moral, ethical, normative and social challenges and how people in Ireland talk about and work through those challenges. But at the same time, assisted reproduction operates within and sustains par-adigms of gender difference and associations between sexual reproduction and structures of moral meaning. The use of ART creates challenges for an imagined and idealised link between nature and sexual reproduction – the basis for claims to hetero-normative morality in family formation. Moreover, people who consider IVF as a means of dealing with infertility are not only confronted with new margins of acceptability for reproductive choices around conception but also new procreative outcomes such as 'leftover embryos' and genetic relations to strangers through donor gametes.

Feminist critiques highlight relations of power that have 'naturalised' gender difference and reproduction by incorporating them into the socially constituted rationale for patriarchal institutions and gendered political domains.[1] But beyond biology, nature and 'natural laws' have also been central to debates about the significance of gender difference in emotionally charged, ethical decision-making and the presumption of necessity rooted in logic for marriage and the family as political or legal arrangements.[2] Kelly Oliver argues, for example, that Hegel's theoretical use of the family depends on a binary construction in which women and the feminine are the keepers of irrational nature, thus allowing men to be associated with rational and ethical consciousness. In this light, then, the family can be seen as a site where ethical and conscious political actions are formulated while still being the locus for natural determinacy. In Hegel's construction, she argues, 'the family, then, is in the paradox-ical position of both challenging rational moral judgments and giving birth to rational moral judgements, challenging the nation and giving birth to the nation'.[3] The Irish Constitution's reliance on the family as

natural, moral and stabilising is similarly dependent on the political separation of roles wherein women are moral citizens by virtue of their
naturalised – and thus necessarily natural – domestic and maternal roles.

It is precisely the ambivalence around what is 'natural' about sex, sexuality, gender, kinship and family that makes nature a useful pivot
around which to redefine moral and social foundations as people accommodate new ways of being procreative. However, if the definition of
nature itself is fluid and culturally constituted, or the distinctions we
draw between nature and culture arbitrary and invented, it calls into
question any 'natural' basis for social arrangements such as family and
marriage. [4] Also contingent and contested, then, are presumptions about
nature and 'natural laws' as a basis for determining what is moral or for
establishing social norms. And yet, reproductive medicine and the scientific endeavours of ART have co-opted nature and employ the concept
in ways that make such technologies seem deeply embedded in the very
processes that are dismissed as inefficient.

Conceiving Miracles

In Ireland a reordering of frameworks for making moral decisions – not
the least of which are reproductive – has been precipitated, at least in
part, by the recent waning of the 'moral monopoly' held by the Catholic
Church and challenges to the dominant ethos on which procreative
meanings have been based. In Chapter 1, I described how the pronatalist
politics of the twentieth century that sustained a prohibition on contraception and abortion was also rooted in history and economics, and the
church, while arguably a dominant social institution, has always been
one institutional voice among many others. As I have argued, a kind of
residue of Catholic Church teaching lingers as an important, and occasionally influential, benchmark against which people reflect on social
change in reproductive and family mores, values and practices. As such
it is an important contextual reality, particularly where it continues to
shape motherhood as an enduring ideology. Changing views on the
church's role as an arbiter of reproductive decision-making is also
evident as a backdrop as people talk about assisted reproduction.

This tension between medical and religious discourses on procreation
was a theme in the artwork produced by Elsa, whom I introduced in the
Introduction. Much of this tension, as Elsa depicts it, revolves around the
way nature is defined, exploited and portrayed. Elsa's mixed media
artwork incorporates the use of different kinds of technology such as
photocopying and Photoshop. In a critical commentary on assisted
reproduction she used a metre-long board that held a single row of

dozens of test tubes lined up side by side. Inside each test tube, photocopied on paper of different colours, was a photograph of herself as an infant. The work plays on the popular description of *in vitro* fertilisation as producing 'test-tube babies'. Using a readily accessible technology that enabled her to easily reproduce a photo image of herself, Elsa challenges the idea that such technologies as IVF are increasingly considered accessible as a means of biologically reproducing oneself.

> ELSA: *I feel that everyone reads about it now in papers. Wonder child or children . . . wonder IVF treatments, mother in her sixties. And because of that, because it is available and it's something that's in the press, constantly being published, it comes across that if somebody wants a child they can just do it and it will work. I don't think anyone is aware of the fact that IVF has a success rate of 20%. And if you do tell people they are just . . . whoa . . .*

Beside the main board with the test tubes, Elsa placed surgical gloves and syringes, and a stack of small cards the size of a bookmark. The cards were copies of one of Raphael's famous paintings of the Madonna and Child with Elsa's added caption 'Thou shalt not conceive your own biological child'. Elsa said she made these cards as a kind of challenge to the influence of the Catholic Church and the valorisation of the Virgin Mary as an ideal for women. Contesting the meaning of an 'immaculate conception' as a natural occurrence, Elsa juxtaposes the scriptural explanations of Mary's supernatural conception with the idea of *in vitro* fertilisation as an intervention that can also be accomplished in the absence of sex and 'the stain of original sin'.[5] Critiquing portrayal of the miracle associated with conception and birth in Christian symbolism, Elsa also challenges the contradictory basis of the Catholic Church's opposition to IVF. Mary's miraculous conception required a supernatural intervention in the absence of biological sex; IVF offers women a similarly miraculous but scientific opportunity to fulfil the very iconic ideal of motherhood to which the church has elevated Mary as the mother of Jesus. What is debatable is IVF's relationship to what is defined as natural.

> ELSA: *I have taken on a lot you know, the Catholic Church, the Immaculate Conception, and in a way I'm asking, 'how did Mary get away with it?' [laughing] I have a serious problem with the Catholic Church, that they put so much emphasis on [the idea] that sex is dirty. On the one hand they are so pro-family and on the other hand they condemn IVF. This is something that I find hard. You know, I have a brain and I can see certain points about why they condemn IVF. That kind of ties to this [pointing to the cards]. But it's something like, 'Thou shalt not conceive naturally'. And she didn't – in a way she didn't conceive naturally. It was not natural.*

At the art show, to her surprise, people began taking the cards away with them. She recalled thinking it odd that people would take them and wondered what they were thinking as they picked them up. As Elsa describes above, her intention was to highlight that Mary's conception was not biological and, therefore, not natural either. And yet the Madonna's conception is celebrated as an achievement. Sarah Franklin's work on ART in the era of 'enterprise culture' in Thatcher's Britain reminds us that the kind of achievement conception is understood to be is rooted in the cultural, economic and historical relations of production. In the wake of diminishing Catholic influence in Ireland, conception continues to be seen as a moral achievement as people shift their allegiance from religion to science through a convenient slippage that allows nature to define what is both moral and healthy, and culture to determine what is natural.[6]

Contradictions and conflations that merge nature and biology with motherhood and the process of conceiving children are embedded in both the dilemmas and the resolutions for couples who must make choices among the technological options for aiding conception. These questions also relate to the way 'nature' becomes a basis for 'standards of the good, the beautiful, the just and the valuable' – in other words, how nature becomes the basis for moral authority.[7] But equally important is the challenge to the primacy of biology in the definition of one's 'own' child. For couples who consider adoption as a strategy for producing a family, the need to reconfigure the meaning of a child of 'one's own' requires that they be able to move beyond the discourse of biologically determined identity in constituting family. In a world where genetics and biological relationships increasingly determine our notions of potential for health and identity, the impact of biology on our social selves is often over-emphasised and the social significance of relatedness is lost.

Changing social meanings around reproduction and motherhood, greater access to choice and information and a more liberal social climate have contributed to shifting ethical boundaries and frameworks as the former monopoly of the church is now contested. It could be argued that such boundaries are necessarily always in a state of flux since they are products of social environments that are never static. However, Ireland's rapid economic growth coupled with the many revelations of abuse of power (and individuals) by the Catholic Church have coincided with the emergence of new technologies of procreation to which previous moral frameworks based on heterosexual marriage rules may not apply.

Jarrett Zigon differentiates between morality as an unconscious moment in decision-making based on a sense of right and wrong, and ethics as a moment when we are suddenly aware that our sense of right and wrong does not enable a smooth transition across difficult terrain. Ethics are in play when we must consciously think about choices and employ a set of principles based on values.[8] The changing social landscape, the shifting moral authority and tremendous advances in technology have created many such moments for people making decisions related to assisted reproduction in Ireland. In the past, people moved along what seemed to be a clear moral path in reproduction, defined by nature as the governing symbol for social norms around marriage, motherhood and reproduction. At the same time, what was natural was defined by the same social institutions of marriage, motherhood and reproduction. Thus, as the path between marriage, motherhood and reproduction is disrupted, so is the meaning of nature. Institutional discourses seeking to control the meaning of procreation must also be in control of the definition of what is natural. The key players in this game are the church, the state and medicine.

Changing Conceptual Frameworks for the Work of Ethics

The points of disjuncture between social ideals and the procreative choices available have also led to an apparent reanimation of a Catholic Church ethos in the current regulatory vacuum. This is not unique to Ireland, as new medical meanings must be articulated with existing religious and moral perspectives on procreation in a variety of cultural contexts. In India, a metaphysical cosmology is employed to enhance the seemingly inadequate biomedical model where failure is more prominent than succes, and stigmas associated with infertility remain deeply embedded in Hindu religious discourse.[9] In Egypt, entrenched gender roles, the importance of reproducing adherents, and orthodox Islamic views, have dictated and adapted the terms around the use of such practices as gamete donation.[10] Similarly, in Israel Kahn describes how orthodox Jews have faced the challenges of proscriptive religious rules on procreation by incorporating and adapting religious discourse, prayer and language to use in collaborative clinical settings.[11] In North America, Layne and Thompson both argue that religion and reproductive technologies do not reside in discrete domains, noting that important Christian ideals such as the power of conception as a gift and the meaning of the miracle are often absorbed by the discourse of science and technological innovation.[12] In Greece, recent changes to legislation have actually been shaped to fit the views of the Orthodox Church, and people work to smooth over contradictions between the meanings of procreation and motherhood and the availability of ART. The gendered meaning of ethical responsibility accommodates new ways of being a mother.[13]

This accommodation of religious perspective is less obvious in Ireland and there are elements of contradiction in many of the stories I collected. People often uncoupled their own reticence about assisted reproduction from the position of the Catholic Church, even as they acknowledged that the church had shaped much of their perspective in the past. Many of the people in my study could not totally distance themselves from the church teaching that has underwritten much of the meaning of reproduction and family building in Ireland, and yet were unwilling to follow the religious tenets of the Catholic Church, particularly with respect to IVF.[14] However, as the narrative excerpts in the epigraphs above suggest, people can sometimes accommodate their own ethical misgivings through recourse to nature and science, merging religious and secular values.

The social dimension of ART has been widely discussed in feminist social science literature that criticises the medicalisation of infertility and exploitation of women's reproductive bodies. The embrace of modern ideals around reproductive choice, as discussed above, with an increasing normalisation of reproductive technologies, further entrenches a reproductive imperative, discouraging rather than fostering expanded notions of reproductive choice as women feel compelled to try ART. At the same time, like others around the world, people in Ireland who rely on ART to procreate are challenging, redefining or reaffirming political, social and moral categories and meanings with respect to sex and sexuality, reproduction, family and gender. The Catholic Church in Ireland has been instrumental in developing much of the current moral/normative discourse and the most recent refrain from the church hierarchy seeks to sustain a hetero-normative definition of procreative morality. This definition emphasises a 'natural' unity between social and biological parenthood, one that has been perpetuated through gender and family politics in the past.

The Struggle for Renewed Moral Authority in the Regulatory Debate

The Catholic Church has been vocal about its position on assisted reproduction technologies in Ireland for some time. In a speech to the Life Society of St Patrick's College, Maynooth, on 2 March 1999, marking the thirtieth anniversary of the papal encyclical *Humanae Vitae*, the Archbishop of Dublin, Dr Desmond Connell, used assisted reproduction as a theme. His speech, quoted in part below, drew a firestorm of public protest that was, at the time, described as a sign that the Catholic Church hierarchy could no longer speak authoritatively on morality and repro-ductive choice in Ireland.[15]

> The wanted child is the child that is planned; the child produced by the decision of the parents begins to look more and more like a tech-nological product. This is clear in the case of *in vitro* fertilisation, surrogate motherhood, genetic engineering, cloning; but it may not be altogether absent in the practice of family planning. [. . .] A pro-found alteration in the relationship between parent and child may result when the child is no longer welcomed as a gift but produced as it were to order. Parental attitudes would thereby be affected, cre-ating a sense of consumer ownership as well as a new anxiety to win and retain the child's affection. The child no longer belongs to the family in a personal sense if it is radically a product rather than a person. (Extract from the full text of the Archbishop's speech pub-lished in *The Irish Times*, 8 March 1999.)

This excerpt draws on a wider doctrinal objection to ART but attempts to centre the arguments in the tight nexus that has contained and constrained sex, sexuality, procreation and marriage within the specifically defined heterosexual family – the very institution in which the church's moral monopoly was centred. Any separation, interference or reinterpretation of the basis for this tightly woven connection threatens the foundation for the church's authority over family relations. Nature is invoked as the obvious link between sex and marriage.

> Human sexuality is designed in such a way that the coming together of man and woman *as one flesh* is both an expression of intimacy *and* self-giving and the privileged context in which new life begins. This is not simply a statement of religious belief. It is evident from any realistic reflection on the facts of biology, physiology and human psychology.[16]

Much of the hierarchy's objection is thus rhetorically framed as common sense support for the naturalising of marriage as a procreative unit established for the purpose of receiving children from God. As Lydia points out below, the church also conflates nature and morality in unassisted conception in the same way that it promotes nature and morality in its prohibition of contraception.

> LYDIA: *But I mean the churches come on so much . . . and that's the other thing about the church, I remember going to work one morning and hearing the cardinal on the radio condemning people. I'm not sure what way he worded it but this is the way I interpreted it . . . People who did*

> *IVF were out to create a baby rather than . . . they were creating this baby*
> *rather than letting nature take its course. And I remember thinking . . .*
> *actually that was the point when I stopped going to mass. I got so angry.*
> *I remember thinking 'stop preaching; don't tell me what to do, don't tell*
> *me what to do'. I remember thinking 'you don't understand'. People who*
> *go through all of this really want a baby. And what about people who have*
> *ten children and who don't want them, or only wanted one? I can't accept*
> *the whole Catholic Church point you see, that whole thing. People who*
> *have as many babies as God . . . you know . . . I think they should be able*
> *to look after a baby. There has to be some thought. But I just feel, you*
> *know, having all these children and people can't look after them and*
> *encouraging children, I mean, where's the logic there?*

In spite of the popular protest and individual reactions like Lydia's, engendered by Dr Connell's speech, members of the hierarchy of the church have continued to seek opportunities to exert influence in the drafting of legislation that would govern the use of assisted reproduction technologies.[17] The church's concerns relating to the creation and use of embryos will be explored in detail in a subsequent chapter. However, the Irish Catholic Bishops' Conference on Bioethics has also produced position papers that reiterate the importance of the relationship between procreation and heterosexual marriage, particularly in reference to the doctrinal position on both IVF and gamete donation.[18] In framing the rationale for their arguments against assisted reproduction, they begin by stating that:

> The Catholic Church has a particular vision of human sexuality,
> which is rooted in the understanding of the human person found in
> the Scriptures, as well as in the natural law. [T]here will be many
> who, although they may not be religious, will share the belief (which
> traces its roots to the philosophy of ancient Greece) that our human
> reason enables us to discern a law written in nature itself, which leads
> us to recognise what is good.[19]

The idea of 'nature' and 'natural law' as a basis for both marriage and hetero-normative sexuality is a recurrent theme in Church documents.[20] This was problematic for Donna, who felt her marriage was subject to censure because it was not 'procreative'.

> DONNA: *And that goes back to the Catholic Church, right? When they say*
> *that how can a child be loved . . . that it's not created through love. We*
> *didn't ask for a Petri dish. And that's very insulting to us. To say that we*
> *cannot love our child. How many children are conceived through marital*
> *rape? Or an unloved relationship or rape in general or any unloved rela-*
> *tionship? They say that Harold and I shouldn't be making love now*
> *because we can't procreate. Good God, we're the greatest sinners, so . . .*
> *[laughing].*

The equation between natural and right works here when nature is defined in a particular way. The Catholic Church's focus on sex in a discourse of sin and morality is sustained by an emphasis on its procreative and, therefore, natural purpose. Conception becomes a more potent symbol in this context whereas in Greek Orthodoxy, for example, the greater moral association lies with birth and the quest for motherhood. Paxson argues that for women in Greece who adhere to an Orthodox Church ethos, the use of IVF is morally unproblematic; how conception takes place is seen as less significant than the birth itself.[21] Donna also challenges the naturalised link between sex and love that is presumed to be part of procreation, noting that it is often a fictional construct.

I spoke with a number of representatives of the Catholic Church before and after the release of the Commission on Assisted Human Reproduction report. It was explained to me on all these occasions that the Catholic Church's concerns with assisted reproduction and the CAHR report itself all stem from what the church sees as challenges to the primacy of heterosexual marriage, the marital family unit as natural and the importance of sexual procreation to sustaining the structure of both marriage and family. The document drafted in response to the CAHR report contains the following clause:

> The Church does not ask or expect the civil authority to legislate in accordance with her teaching, but hopes that legislators and all those who have an influence in the formation of public policy will recognise that the common good, which is their specific responsibility, can only be achieved when the rights of every human individual and the rights of the family are fully respected.[22]

The possibility that the rights of individuals and the rights of the family, as a unit, might contradict one another is sidestepped by the implied assumption that the family naturally has 'rights'. This is, of course, already naturalised in Article 41 of the Irish Constitution, as discussed in Chapter 1, where prescribed rights include protection from interference in education, social and marital relationships and privacy – rights to be protected for a common good rather than positive rights associated with individual aspirations.[23] Moreover, despite its conciliatory approach, the bishops' response above implies that in developing legislation, the state will be obligated by the ethical and moral interpretation of rights and the common good, as these have been defined by the Catholic Church.

Assisted reproduction thus poses a problem from the standpoint of Catholic Church ethos since physicians, while enabling people to meet a family ideal encouraged by church doctrine, offer a competing discourse on the nature and meaning of procreation.[24] One theologian told me that in an era of increasing access to medical technologies, people would have to be informed that IVF was not a moral choice. He noted that even students of theology 'had to be told, had to be taught that this was the case'. His concern rested on the fact that biomedical technology was now ubiquitous and that normalised medical practices in fertility medicine had created the opportunity for a kind of moral corruption.

The bishops' conference documents also convey a concern that offering such opportunities as IVF to couples in the guise of medical treatment will provide alternative ethical frameworks for couples, challenging and effectively weakening the influential reproductive morality shaped by Catholic social teaching in the past. These ethics might effect a political and social merger between nature and science, the kind of contradictory underside of what Bruno Latour describes as attempts to 'purify' or clarify these as separate domains in a categorically modern perspective. As Latour argues, modernity and its distinctions have always constituted 'hybrid' systems in which culture, politics, science, technology and nature mix.[25] Natural procreation has been appropriated and exploited as if it has a discrete and concrete meaning while doing so creates corrupted, hybrid concepts in the politics of gender, the science of religious discourse and the cultural realm of sexuality and family in Ireland. It is thus impossible to distil the meaning of nature from its cultural context.

Even among the people in my study who were practising Catholics, there were those who took issue with the position that medical practice was at odds with religious values and the position of the church. Attempts to 'purify' and categorise the technologies of reproductive medicine have only complicated its hybrid status as part of both science and nature.

> MARIE CLAIRE: *I decided to seek some spiritual help. So I went to a very nice priest and I explained very briefly the situation. I just wanted him to help me. But he was quite young and he did say, 'you know, you understand our position on IVF – the church's standing on IVF'. And I just thought you haven't got a clue. And I just thought if God had blessed these people, the fertility specialists, with special gifts to use so why would it be wrong, IVF? So this was a very tricky angle for me.*
> JILL: *Have you continued to go to church?*
> MARIE CLAIRE: *Oh, absolutely yes.*

Marie Claire finds a way to get around the priest's admonitions and still maintain her respect for the church. Pragmatic solutions such as this were not uncommon for people who were faced with dilemmas of faith. In Chapter 2 I discussed how some couples saw the use of IVF as a pivotal moment that distinguished their relationship with Catholicism from that of their parents' generation. But for some people like Marie Claire, the Catholic Church remained an important part of daily life and required a constant compromise that accommodated different perspectives on the morality and value of reproductive technologies as residing in both the realm of science and nature. Moral discordance can result when faith and values fail to produce the desired or expected outcomes; people question their faith and the moral frame it has established. People might question, for example, why God has not given them the child they desire.

The jarring clash of values for people who continue to adhere to Catholic teaching around producing children brings a practical accommodation in the face of moral discordance that necessitates and perhaps justifies picking and choosing what works. For others, the Catholic Church's position on IVF presented a clear obstacle.

> JILL: *So is religion important to you?*
> GAIL: *I converted. I was . . . we were both raised Catholic and after the first cycle of IVF, when it didn't work, on one hand I was very angry with God for doing that to me. And then on the other hand I needed Him. I needed to know that there was a reason for all of that. I decided to go to the Church of Ireland first and see how I got on and I was welcomed the first day with open arms and I thought I could stay.*
> MARTIN: *And the way they dealt with the IVF compared to the Catholic Church.*
> GAIL: *A big reason for me moving was that I could never have my child, if we ever did have a child, put in a situation where there was even a vague possibility that somebody in school would turn around to that child and say that the way you were conceived was a sin . . . Daniel has since been baptised in the Church of Ireland.*

Gail and Martin were one of two couples among my research participants who told me they left the Catholic Church and joined another Christian denomination.[26] Religious conviction is evident and it continues to play an important role in family life for many people, but for some couples the determination of particular kinds of reproduction as moral or amoral was simply untenable and infertility experiences sparked the abandonment of church ties altogether.

With the exception of two men and two women, all of my participants received their education under a school system that was influenced by the institutional hierarchy of the church. Given the reach of the moral monopoly, and the impact of church policies on reproductive education in the past, it is not surprising that the church's arguments against IVF and the use of donor gametes remain part of the ethical landscape that must be negotiated by people who are considering assisted reproduction in Ireland. The relationship between sex and procreation, the importance of clarity in the 'nature' of identities and kin relationships arise as problems in people's narratives about making decisions. Perhaps more importantly, however, the hierarchy of the Catholic Church has reanimated its ethos in ways that constitute particular kinds of social persons within families, both as parents and children and as women and men. In conjunction with these rigidly defined gender roles, the church also confines the moral conditions and obligations associated with procreation to the conjugal relationship in marriage and conflates identity with genealogy. This has implications for shaping both experience and subjectivity in relation to infertility treatment for people who practise the Catholic faith. At present the Catholic Church occupies a rather uncomfortable position as it promotes the ideal of motherhood and family but, at the same time, associates its position with a broader and perhaps more appealing bioethics rhetoric to promote its position for more restrictive regulation of assisted reproduction in the changing Irish state.

The contested morality of assisted reproduction is also apparent in the biological, medical and technological processes involved as these are both gendered and rendered as social in the Irish context. People draw upon the distinctions and overlaps between nature and science as they try to redefine moral obstacles within the technological frame of ART.

Gendering Morality: Medicalising Conception

Although it is more subtle and somewhat obscured by powerful scientific discourses, morality and ethics are also contested aspects of the medical profession's bid to define the *nature* of reproduction. Where gender, nature and morality intersect in assisted reproduction there are stories of alienated bodies and bodily elements, challenges to the meaning of sex and sexuality in procreation and the experience of having to absorb unknown 'others' into the procreative process, both physically and figuratively. The processes involved in assisted reproduction engender a number of moral and conceptual problems for people. Many of these challenges arise where medical and religious institutions compete for a moral high ground rooted in the ability to claim nature as the dominant foundation of their respective definitions of procreation.

Medical technologies of assisted reproduction seek to replicate or recreate a series of commonly occurring events in biological bodies that have come to be accepted as 'natural' reproduction. The events of reproduction must be appropriated or harnessed by medical interventions in ART but the process is nonetheless one of tinkering with or enhancing these events. The technologies blur the margins of natural and unnatural while sustaining the distinction that fertility is natural, infertility is unnatural. Technology tinkers and corrects.

During the process of *in vitro* fertilisation, acquiring the ova or 'eggs' from a woman requires a medical intervention that is not without risk, discomfort (many would argue pain) and an investment by practitioners in medical equipment and skills. Women are generally given a regimen of drugs which first suppress ovulation, usually the same drugs used as oral contraceptives, an irony not lost on many of the women who undertake this process to overcome a difficulty in conceiving. Once this process – known as 'down regulation' – is accomplished, the women are given a series of hormones by injection or by nasal spray to stimulate 'superovulation' in which their ovaries produce multiple ova rather than the normal one or two eggs regularly released each month. The process is closely monitored by ultrasound and when the follicles (the site where individual eggs develop) of the ovaries are maturing, women are given what people refer to as the hormonal 'trigger shot' of hCG (human chorionic gonadatropin) to promote the release of the eggs or ova.[27] The eggs are then collected, much like vacuuming, through a needle and suction tube inserted with the guidance of ultrasound into the woman's pelvic cavity. The eggs are collected into a dish and counted under the watchful eye (and microscope) of an embryologist and are mixed with the sperm that is intended to fertilise and create the embryos.

The experiences of infertility and the use of *in vitro* fertilisation sharpen the focus on the biological elements involved in conceiving a child. The body and its boundaries are challenged and reconfigured in new contexts whereby biomedical science creates extracorporeal body spaces in the lab that are merged back into the reproductive body once an embryo is returned. Donna Haraway describes the merging of technology and the body as a 'cyborg myth about transgressed boundaries, potent fusions and dangerous possibilities' in which the body becomes a contested site that no longer represents the distinction between nature and technology.[28] In a similar way the Petri dish in the lab becomes a technological extension of the womb. The boundaries between body and technology are both crossed and obscured by a relationship to the gametes that are at play in the process of IVF. In medical discourse the emphasis is placed on the way eggs and sperm facilitate a merger between the reproductive body and laboratory precisely because they themselves merge biologically or 'naturally' in the Petri dish; nature triumphs, with a little help from science. In reality, however, the use of IVF ties women and their partners to the Petri dish, making this bit of technology a permanent and predominant element in their effort to achieve a 'natural' outcome. Rather than a bit of technology in the processes of nature, there is a bit of nature in a highly technology-driven process.

> ANNE: *And when you're pregnant it's not 'woo-hoo, I can forget about my infertility'. You do meet a lot of people who are like that. 'Yeah, I can forget about infertility.' And then you want to meet somebody that's done donor egg. At the start of my pregnancy, something came about and I got so frightened I didn't know what I was doing. I rang the wrong people and they said to me 'well, you're not infertile, not any more'. There's nobody to ring then when you get pregnant from IVF. There's nowhere to go and that's a huge thing. I still consider myself infertile. To me, infertility is there and you need something outside to fix it.*

As Anne argues, infertility is part of one's reproductive identity because the technology is part of the reproductive body. For people who undergo infertility treatment, conception itself is perceived as a highly technical process experienced as quality control assessments that constitute their bodies as spaces in which success and failure are mapped and described. Eggs, sperm, embryos, fallopian tubes, ovaries, wombs, testes and hormones are all components that can be evaluated, graded and found wanting, both qualitatively and quantitatively. In addition, ovulation, spermatogenesis, ejaculation, fertilisation and implantation are all mechanical events to which success or failure can (although not always) be attributed.

The drug regimen, regular scans and an invasive process for collecting eggs place women into a medicalised realm that not only manages and 'enhances' their fertility but virtually takes control of their reproductive rhythm and sets their clocks on clinic time. While Sarah Franklin describes the sensation of IVF taking over in women's lives in terms of life management,[29] there is also a sense that bodies are taken over and functions appropriated by clinics. Several people spoke about losing their bodily rhythm to the clinic schedule and suggested it was all about maximising clinic efficiency and resources (making money) rather than about doing what was best for patients. Lara described this as 'batch cycling'. For women, this was particularly acute as their natural rhythms were appropriated and altered to suit a technological agenda, thus challenging the medical discourse that suggests ART is just helping nature along.

> NIAMH: *Yeah with the clinics you fall in with their thing and you do, you do. Because they totally control you. They slam you into menopause with*

the sniffer, first of all. And they tell you when to sniff. And then they keep you sniffing until . . . now this is my take on it and it might be totally nothing . . . they may do egg collections on Wednesday. So they organise it so your eggs are ripe on Wednesday. Now if I wanted to say I prefer if my eggs were ripe on the Monday they could organise that if they wanted to, probably, or the Thursday or . . . but basically they completely control you to get you to the Wednesday because that's the day when they do ten egg collections. But then you couldn't organise a clinic around emotional women on drugs saying when they want to do things. You are at their mercy in a way. But I don't see that it could be done any other way.

As Niamh points out, there would be few alternatives to the highly organised aspects of clinic regimes. With IVF offered in clinics in Cork city, Galway, Kilkenny and Dublin and its environs, people often have to travel several hours in each direction to get access to treatment. Coordinating treatment to maximise efficiency means that the body is both medicalised and mechanised to function as part of a larger process.

The treatment regimes for *in vitro* fertilisation are the same for women even if the problem in conceiving resides with a male partner (or perhaps with not having a male partner). The contributing male factor in infertility (usually identified in about 30% of cases) can result from the number, shape (morphology), or activity (motility) of sperm, and IVF can improve a man's chances of reproductive success by concentrating, washing and choosing the best actors or 'swimmers' in the process.[30] A more technological procedure known as Intracytoplasmic Sperm Injection (ICSI) is an advanced form of IVF often used for male factor infertility. Embryologists insert a single sperm (of their choosing) into the ovum, effecting a deliberate fertilisation under microscope. For a small number of people the issue of overriding nature was problematic with ICSI because the process interrupted the natural selection aspect of fertilisation.

> KRISTEN: *I have concerns about natural selection, that you're bypassing natural selection. Especially because with ICSI – we have to go through ICSI because of male factor – so it's not even that you're letting the best one through in the Petri dish. It's actually physically picking one out. We talked to the embryologist about it and they actually put them through what my husband would call a cryptofactor obstacle course. To get the best ones, you know. They wash them and then pick the ones off the top because they're faster and so I have a bit of a problem with that.*

One embryologist told me he originally had some questions about 'playing God' in this technique since he was choosing the sperm to inject in each ovum. His said his traditional Catholic upbringing had left him with some nagging questions about the ethics of IVF in general and certainly in his role working directly with embryos. In the end, however, in almost cliché fashion, he did what many Irish men (and men everywhere) do when faced with a problem – he asked his mother. She reassured him that what he was doing was of benefit to people and her response assuaged his religious and moral misgivings. The embryologist seemed able to rationalise his practice through an interchange of religious and scientific discourses, absorbing social good as a foundation for his professional ethics. Frith *et al.* describe a kind of 'boundary work' in which science and non-science are distinguished based on struggles for authority and legitimacy. Within the domain of ethics, 'scientists draw boundaries between what is ethically preferred such that ethics has become another line of demarcation, not so much from "non-science" as from "less ethical" positions'.[31] Some Irish clinicians were less able to bracket off their work in a clinical realm of expertise and claim a kind of 'settled morality' based on the routine nature of what they did; they readily acknowledged the high possibility of ethical dilemma in their work.[32]

Another form of moral discordance, or at least discomfort, is evident in the process of obtaining gametes or sperm from the male participant. The process is not complex or medically invasive as it is for women, and can be undertaken by the man himself with self-stimulation and ejaculation into a collection cup. This was referred to ubiquitously as obtaining 'the sperm sample' – a reference that suggests the medicalisation of the *product* even as it fails to medicalise fully an act that, for many men and some women, carries serious moral baggage.

> JILL: *So did you have infertility investigations?*
> CATHERINE: *They wanted a sperm sample and I had huge objections to that because I was the one that was in pain. I felt it had nothing to do with him. They kept saying, which is right I know, but the investigations of women are very invasive. So eventually we had to. Well the sperm sample, it was hilarious, we were trying to . . . it was just . . . [searching for words here] trying to be together. Well we ended up trying. I was so mad and we had a big huge fight and . . . well we had the whole bottle turned upside down. I didn't want that anger in our relationship. The only challenge that I had with IVF was producing the sperm sample. I would have done natural medication; if there was a machine that could produce the sperm sample I would have gone ahead with it. As much as I wanted a baby I wouldn't want his mother to know that he would have had to produce a sperm sample. [...]I'm not happy with that.*

> GRETCHEN: *Even if you wanted to have treatment it was not going to happen. And to have specific times to hand in semen and all that. My partner said, 'I'm not comfortable with that anyway'. In that way he is Catholic. Besides a lot of other things, he is still like that.*

In both these stories, the issue of masturbation comes up as a road-block to procreation with assisted technology. For Catherine in particular, the issue crosses into the relationship she and her husband have with other family members. If she gives in to her desire to be a mother by using IVF, she worries that she will be betraying a trust that her mother-in-law has given her to behave in a morally circumscribed manner within her marriage. She sees the moral transgressions associated with IVF as a potential threat to this tacit understanding that she is somehow the arbiter of values in her relationship. Such gendered moral responsibilities have been described in broader terms by Angela Martin who argues that women have borne an unequal burden of responsibility for the image of a moral Irish nation.[33] Gender is part of a system in which social, religious and biological meanings of motherhood shape what Paxson describes in Greece as 'a system of virtues'.[34] Women are thus held to account for the moral meanings of their procreative choices as part of national, local and familial expectations. Sex slips between the political, social and moral designations of nature and procreation when people are unable to see certain kinds of sex as natural or procreative. Science, in these stories, has been unable to rescue self-stimulation from a discourse of sin.

The moral/normative implications of procuring sperm through masturbation have been widely described in the literature on donor sperm in studies in the UK and US.[35] Evidence of social and institutional perceptions of deviance associated with donor sperm have been noted in the Warnock Report issued in the UK. Erica Haimes highlights how 'assumptions about gender and reproduction lead to egg donation being seen in a familial, clinical and asexual context whereas semen donation is seen in an individualistic, unregulated context of dubious sexual connotations'.[36] These differences relate to both the social perception of the means of acquiring sperm and the people who donate. With egg donations, the donor is 'doing the 'work' of a patient despite not being perceived as one.[37]

Gretchen and Catherine are not talking about gamete donation but rather about the process of procuring the gametes for treatment, even from within a marital relationship. Similarities arise in the gendered distinctions in the meanings associated with the process. For men the process is 'sexualised' and carries connotations of sexual deviance amplified by the presence of pornographic magazines as an aid to masturbation in most clinics. On the other hand, for women the process of egg collection is completely medicalised and devoid of sexual connotation, carrying, in addition, an attendant notion of risk and sacrifice.

Beyond the moral reticence to engage in masturbation necessary to produce the 'sample' there was a general sense of resentment about the seemingly callous, unprofessional and very un-medical perspective associated with the collection of sperm. However, my access to men's complaints in this regard was often filtered through women's stories that convey the sense of imbalance in the process even as women try to be sympathetic to what often seems like a trivial concern to them. Kristen talks about feeling completely exposed and invaded by the process which she contrasts with her husband's complaints.

> KRISTEN: *Sure I've no dignity left at all. Even the whole process itself is just intrusive on you as a woman. It's just so intrusive, you know. There's nothing left. Absolutely nothing left. And I do think . . . when Nick had to give his sperm sample, oh my God, it was just this dark little cubicle. I did say to him, 'just give it up. I'm here every month getting poked and prodded' and I suppose it wasn't very supportive of me but I just thought, 'oh get stuffed'.*

Maeve described how her husband Patrick felt threatened by the lack of privacy and potential disruption to his act of producing his own sperm. She is somewhat more sympathetic to the issues but nonetheless finds the worries trivial.

> MAEVE: *Well he did go on about the fact that it's the toilet, like. It's the only male toilet in the unit. And at the start he made it sound so traumatic, I thought it was one of those things with cubicles. But it's actually not and you can actually lock the door and nobody else can come in [laughing]. But I think he always has this panicky notion in his head that somebody might be dying to get into the toilet. It's just a most uncomfortable place to try and do it and then you have to try and make sure you don't spill anything or lose it or anything, there's all these added things anyways, you know. Ah, he jokes about it and stuff so he can't find it too bad but I know it can't be very nice and it's kind of pressurised.*

These gendered differences are aligned with normative roles in conception and even sexual activity in which women/eggs are constituted as passive and men/sperm are constituted as naturally active and aggressive.[38] Men are expected to concede to the demand to *perform* and *produce* while women are expected to *submit* to the rigours of treatment even as both processes seem degrading and humiliating. This construction can be contextualised with the stories of women as sexually näive, unsophisticated and passive in their sexuality in the past in Ireland.

Lisa's story begins with their more general feelings of apprehension and ambivalence about returning for another round of treatment after a miscarriage.

> LISA: *Actually, it was quite emotional going back and so my husband could see that I was happy that we had dealt with the issues. But, yeah, he was – he doesn't like going back. He never will, you know. And he hates the whole clinic thing itself, and the IUI (inter-uterine insemination) thing – I just know he's going to make a big fuss about it but . . .*
> JILL: *Which part of that – is it the medical aspect?*
> Lisa: *The donation of the sperm at the clinic – going into a room – you know, the porn. I think he thinks it's horrible – you know, it's hard and it's not natural and it's not right and . . . [trailing off] He finds it distasteful. It's not something that he would relate to. [. . .] Now, the last time he donated was . . . he actually had a fit and I just stood there and said I was upstairs having ice-cold stuff sprayed over my cervix, having saline inserted into my vagina. Like I mean, come on!*

Aside from the 'distasteful' aspects of producing sperm, Lisa also flags the issue of the 'nature' of sexual procreation as opposed to the clinical process of treatment and the disappointment that her husband might feel if they couldn't conceive through their sexual relationship. She suggests that self-stimulation is not 'natural' and 'not right'. Obviously the presence of pornography as an aid does little to undo this construction. Much of the distinction between natural/unnatural is based on a gold standard of sexual procreation as natural in opposition to medical interventions. The importance of the link between sex and procreation is not expressed in terms of religious values in this case but in terms of norms and relational values inherent in their performance.

> LISA: *He finds it all very distasteful and I think he'd be delighted if we conceived, yes, but he would be disappointed if, you know, that meant that it wasn't something like lovemaking as such. Part of a natural process.*
> JILL: *Right, and do you feel that way too? Or is this something that you deal with differently?*
> LISA: *I'm actually okay. [laughing] I just say that I don't care and it's something that I feel that I have to do to get the outcome, so I'll just deal with it. I think women are a little bit more kind of pragmatic about it. I mean the last time I was in the clinic having number twelve scan because I was ovulating, and I hopped up in the chair and I said – do you want me to do it myself?*

Lisa's narrative medicalises and de-sexualises the process of intrauterine insemination using her husband's sperm to the point where the loss of sexual intimacy reduces him to a 'sperm donor'. This becomes the basis for his own sense of social deviance. The equation of sex and nature is a common basis for a moralising discourse with respect to ART in general terms and most certainly from the point of view of the Catholic Church.[39] Lisa's pragmatism is a part of a willingness to sacrifice the natural for the necessary. This sentiment was expressed by several of my participants, including Mairead in the epigraph at the beginning of this chapter where 'getting the job done' is more important than privileging natural procreation as a means of sanitising sex. Discourses around ART have been shown to appropriate nature as a value when recipients and clinicians describe it as simply helping nature along.[40] In this case Lisa normalises the experience of the treatment itself as just part of her reproductive routine. However, she does not necessarily blur the boundaries between nature and technology, seeing natural or sexual reproduction as ideal and 'right' and ART as unnatural but necessary.

Some men, like John, felt clearly extraneous to the process and 'in the way' once they had handed over their sperm. Again, the gendered shift to the importance of the woman's body tends to medicalise women while leaving men feeling at least socially, if not organically, excluded from the procreative events that might result in their own child.

> JOHN: *Neither consultant was particularly embracing of us really as individuals or as a couple. They were very much typical consultants, standoffish and going through a process. Focusing on treatment and what was happening in Breda's body. So I was seen to be . . . and they kept saying, 'right, your sperm count is fine so just go over and sit over there' [laughing]. Now you've done your bit.*

While for some people reconciling the meaning of nature, procreative 'biology' and treatment seemed challenging, describing nature as the governing force in treatment outcomes was less problematic. This re-insertion of nature as an overarching force is evident in Carol Anne's story about how and why things happen and why science is not foolproof.

> CAROL ANNE: *There are trials and errors as in nature. A lot of it is just . . .*
> VINCE: *It's all down to nature.*
> CAROL ANNE: *It is. You could have all the medical intervention in the world and whatever, at the end of the day it's down to nature. And then once it goes into your womb it may not implant. And nobody can tell you anything. They can tell you blastocysts will increase, this will increase, that will increase but at the end of the day when it goes in it's down to nature whether it actually does.*

Nature is described as a guiding or even governing force at work, influencing the final outcome and whether technology will work. This sense that nature cannot be dominated exposes the kind of dualistic thinking that enables people to define nature as separate from science even as the processes of ART have merged them so completely. As a means of explaining the success or failure of ART, nature becomes a powerful trope. Nature can provide the moral high ground and become the scapegoat, both positions being rooted in the view that procreative events are essentially natural ones in the first place.

NaPro Technology: Conceiving a Moral ART

A number of attempts have been made to accommodate the Catholic Church's difficulty with IVF within a technological or scientific programme that assists reproduction. Various treatment approaches have bridged the fundamental challenge posed by separation of the sexual act from the procreative event of conception. Such processes as gamete intrafallopian transfer (GIFT) have been adjusted to incorporate 'unprotected' intercourse into the process. In GIFT, the eggs and sperm are retrieved in the same manner as in IVF and then transferred directly to the fallopian tube of the women by an invasive surgical procedure that uses laparoscopy.[41] This simulates what might happen following intercourse. While the Catholic Church has sanctioned the use of GIFT procedures, the expectation is that the sperm will be collected during sexual intercourse in a condom that has been perforated to ensure that the sexual act could result in a pregnancy.[42] Nobody in my study had used this procedure, but according to the CAHR report it has been offered in at least one clinic in Ireland.

Five couples who participated in my research had used a method of assisted reproduction that is endorsed by the Roman Catholic Church. Called NaPro or Natural Procreative Technology, it is an offshoot of the Billings method of rhythm contraception.[43] At the time of the research, there were two medical practitioners in Ireland who provided the treatment, along with a number of support counsellors in communities to assist people in the sometimes arduous charting and self-surveillance required.[44] The treatment uses fertility drugs to super-ovulate and then tracks using ultrasound and blood hormone levels in conjunction with rigorous temperature graphs and a requirement for women to monitor the consistency of mucous from their own cervix on a regular basis. In keeping with the link between sex and procreative morality, the process is designed to alert couples to the optimum moment for them to have sexual intercourse in order to conceive. As a treatment, it is viewed with scepticism in the medical community but for some people the emphasis on its, purportedly, more 'natural' attributes makes it more attractive even outside of its religious appeal. In fact all five of the couples I spoke with about NaPro appreciated that is was endorsed by the Catholic Church but most denied that this was their sole motivation for trying it. Mairead and James had a child after having tried both IUI in a standard fertility clinic and NaPro.

> MAIREAD: *And we put our name down for a programme called NaPro, a kind of natural reproduction . . . so we were on the waiting list for that. And then we also did the tests here with the gynaecologist. So the middle of*

> *March and we would have done a series of treatments right through the*
> *summer and then from there we went to the NaPro clinic and started doing*
> *the treatment there.*
> JAMES: *But the NaPro clinic, as well, is doing the injections and treatment.*
> *It's really following the Billings method and in Ireland in general and albeit*
> *drawn from the religion, yes. But here it was and it worked for us. One*
> *thing, it pays very close attention to the body and to the natural as opposed*
> *to the chemical.*

I visited the clinic of one well-known NaPro practitioner who was mentioned by many of the participants in my research. I was surprised to find his waiting room and office decorated almost entirely with religious icons such as statuettes of the Virgin Mary and crucifixes.[45] His waiting room also featured a large poster board covered with baby photos from his 'success stories'. James, who had considered the priesthood as a young man and spent two years in a seminary followed by two years of medical school, noted that he was somewhat put off by both these displays. As a practising Catholic himself, James appreciated the physician's obvious conviction to his religious beliefs but, as he explains below, felt this overt material display seemed overdone and out of place in the milieu of a medical practice.

> JAMES: *But also going there, you are confronted right away with statues of*
> *Our Lady and which, ordinarily, I would respect but not necessarily in the*
> *context of a medical practice. It was a little unusual.*
> MAIREAD: *Yes and again we found that interesting because I'd have been*
> *very Catholic at the time, if you look at the website it's not as . . . Was it*
> *Pope Pius?*
> JAMES: *Pope Paul VI.*
> MAIREAD: *Pope Paul VI. One of the interesting things about that is that at*
> *one stage you might have been requested to give a sample and in the Catholic*
> *religion that's not allowed . . . You tell that story . . .*
> JAMES: *It's a bit crazy really because . . . yeah masturbation is frowned upon*
> *so therefore they gave us a condom which was also marked as . . . not lubri-*
> *cant free but it doesn't have a spermicide.*
> JILL: *And they usually have a hole in it too, don't they?*
> JAMES: *[laughing]. Yes probably microscopic so nothing gets through but*
> *yeah [laughing]. And the instructions reading around that, it's just funny.*

In a letter to their GP, a portion of which is quoted in the epigraph for this chapter, the fertility specialist had suggested that their child could not have been a result of the NaPro treatment but rather a latent effect of his earlier ministrations. This statement made both James and Mairead laugh since they were inclined to think their daughter had been a result of neither technology and they had in fact, 'done it themselves'. Marie Claire did seek out the NaPro programme with an interest in its Catholic origins but was nonetheless disappointed when it did not produce the result she wanted.

> MARIE CLAIRE: *My religion would be extremely important so I'd say my faith is very strong. So I did pray for guidance. It's combined in the programme . . . The Pope developed the programme. I presume the doctor would understand how we felt.*

Niamh also described feeling that she must make a choice and move along a different path since NaPro had not resulted in the conception of the child she wants.

> NIAMH: *Yeah it's funny because I mean I know our NaPro doctor is completely anti-IVF but then it's a way of having a baby. I'd be very . . . It's easy to be that way if you're in the situation where there's no other choice. What do you do? Do you take the moral high ground or do you go with what might give you, you know, a new life? I think it's very difficult and I suppose it's age as well but you really get to a point in your life where until you can see things from other people's side of the road you can't make a judgement on it.*

As Niamh argues, there comes a point when you decide that you have little choice but to try everything available in order to achieve your objective. This becomes part of the construction of what Franklin describes as the choice of no choice, but often pivots on the idea of redefining the way nature and technology are categorically separated or hybridised in order to create the conditions in which choices are made. The importance of redefining the meaning of sexual intimacy, so crucial to the Catholic Church's distinction between nature and technology as the basis for moral reproductive decision, is another contested domain.

Conceiving of Sex as Irrelevant

At the first conference meeting of the newly-formed Irish Fertility Society, one of the speakers was a councillor from the HARI Unit at the Rotunda Hospital. Caroline Harrison, who also had a seat on the CAHR, told the crowd of clinicians, nurses, pharmaceutical representatives and veterinary medicine practitioners that one of the first questions she asks couples who come to her for counselling regarding infertility is, 'are you having sex?'[46] She pointed out that while it seemed rudimentary, in her experience many Irish couples who had been married for some time had lapsed into a kind of fraternal relationship in which they were disinclined to be intimate with one another. This was obviously a barrier to conceiving a child. It might also be contextualised against the historical repression of sex in Ireland, high rates of celibacy and patterns of family relations that meant marriage and romantic love, sexual intimacy and tenderness were discouraged in Irish social life until well into the twentieth century.[47] None of my participants described themselves as 'sexually repressed' or described moral reticence or a lack of sexual sophistication as contributing to their inability to conceive. However, many people spoke of emotional distress and conflicted feelings about trying to maintain some measure of sexual intimacy while attempting to conceive a child through assisted reproduction, whether IVF, NaPRo, or other forms of treatment.

> NIAMH: *Oh yeah, you'd be sitting around for the first couple of months because you think it's going to work. And then after years . . . you're going 'I don't want to go to bed tonight . . .' [laughing] 'Oh no, we have to do it . . . do we have to do it tonight?' [laughing] But you do it, but then you're kind of going, 'oh jeeze'.*
> Jill: *And then you get into the IVF and sex is completely out of the equation altogether.*
> Niamh: *Gone. Completely put aside.*

Niamh's comments point out how moral discord emerges in relation to the place of sexual intimacy within competing discourses on assisted reproduction. The importance of sustaining a sexual relationship in conjunction with treatment, as advocated by NaPro practitioners, is contrasted with IVF.

Infertility poses challenges to relationships on a number of levels. Most of the people I spoke with about infertility described their relationships as having endured challenges that were strengthening and had brought them closer together. One couple described infertility as having been a huge difficulty in their marriage and I spoke with two women who blamed the ultimate failure of their marriages on infertility and more specifically on IVF. Most of the people who told me about having used assisted reproduction also related the impact of treatment on their sexual relationships.

Sex had become routine or unpleasant, and for many, like Niamh above, and Gail and Martin below, an exercise that seemed to be without purpose in their endeavour to have a child. Gail is pragmatic about the fact that Martin has a very low sperm count. She says, 'certainly when you're trying to make a baby, sex is how you make a baby. But if you know nothing is going to work it just nukes sex out of the water.' When I asked Gail and Martin if their sexual intimacy might be something to reclaim, both laughed and said almost simultaneously, 'no, leave it on the shelf . . .' Gail went on to explain that until IVF was no longer in the picture, they would continue to leave sex out of the picture as well.

GAIL: *Leave it on the shelf until next year. And I suppose normal people with a five-month-old baby would be returning to normality or thinking about making another baby or all of that. For us there is no sex involved in making another baby so there isn't that rush to return to the normal husband–wife relationship. And I think also if having another IVF cycle . . . When the future state of IVF is removed . . . we just ideally would turn back into normal people.*

For other people the ongoing importance of intimacy in their relationship is disrupted by the regimental aspects of treatment and the need to abandon spontaneity. The medicalisation of their infertility also produces a medicalisation of their sexual relationship and sense of sexual failure which contributes to a stigmatisation and reticence to talk about infertility.[48] I found, in addition to this concern, an overwhelming sense of interference and pressure on couples who were striving to maintain a marital relationship in light of their difficulty in producing an idealised family.

LESLEY: *I think with all of this in the last four or five months . . . it's taking the spontaneity out of your love life. It's the worst part. For me anyways. It's the last thing you want to do, is have sex with somebody when you have to. The whole thing has brought us closer together but I definitely think that I've been cruel to my husband. It's difficult enough when you are helping but when you're not helping . . . I think for me that has been one of the worst aspects. Having to do it to a timer. I'd be ashamed if I had to go back to the consultant and chart our procreative matters alright because he'd be saying [laughing] go back to basics . . . I suppose what it does is just puts a spotlight on your sex life and it makes you feel inadequate and that you are not doing enough. It has been so medically oriented and so written down and 'what day is it today? . . . ' You kind of lose the 'woo me' and the romance and you know the caring and whatever. There have been times when we have had sex and I remember saying afterwards, 'I hope we didn't conceive a child there' because it was one of those times when we both didn't want to do it and it was just . . . having to have sex you start feeling, you start hating each other and going, 'this is horrible and it just can't be worth it'.*

In this narrative Lesley points out the stress that makes sex and intimacy a kind of chore in their relationship. Her story is evidence of the perception of sexual failure in the medicalisation of their sexual lives. The invasion of medical discourse, experienced as a kind of surveillance, is also apparent in Lesley's fear that a 'record' of their sex lives would lead physicians to see them as uncooperative, inadequate or failing to do what they need to do in order to conceive on their own or with minimal medical intervention. Lesley describes not only the frustration at the medicalisation of their sexual lives and the 'production' of their sexual inadequacy but also the inability to confirm what is 'normal' among peers since sexual discourse has largely been confined to the realm of reproductive health in their case. At the same time there is also an intense desire for intimacy and love in a procreative act that might result in the conception of a child. These stories present another facet of the tension around defining natural conception through spontaneous sex, confirming the moral and normative value associated with sex as natural. In this case, sex is equated with marital intimacy and love, which is lost in the clinical regulation of procreation in treatment.

This kind of loss of intimacy and imposition of a regimented sexual relationship was a frequent concern among my participants, young couples who were enjoying the new era of sexual freedom and sophistication described earlier. Such concerns are mentioned briefly in Becker's study of American couples but there is not a great deal of attention paid to this aspect of infertility treatment. The fact that my participants spoke about it frequently is perhaps a reflection of the lingering intensity with which moral/normative ideals have tended to link sex and procreation in Ireland.

> LISA: *And I'll tell you another one of the frustrating things is actually when you have to have sex a certain time of the month. I don't know if anyone else has mentioned that – that can be . . . that is frustrating because it's so by rote and it's so . . . it's difficult to get going, I suppose, for want of a better word. It makes your sex lives a lot more mechanical . . . a lot more emotional, actually, in a different way to what it would normally be, as in it's awkward and it's uncomfortable sometimes. And you feel like . . . You know, we have to do this! And particularly, with my husband again – back to the same issue about the donation and the clinic. He finds anything, where it's not just spontaneous, he doesn't like it, actually. So what I try to do is I warn him maybe a week in advance and say, 'in a about a week's time we're coming up to that time' – and I won't say anything else. I'll leave it up to him because he's so difficult.*
>
> MARIE CLAIRE: *Pressure starts coming in . . . you've got two days and maybe my husband and I might have an argument . . . that was tough because at home if you don't cooperate it means another month. So lo and behold, on the two days when we had to be . . . nice to each other we'd end up having an argument.*
> JILL: *So there was a lot of stress on your relationship?*
> MARIE CLAIRE: *Very stressful. Very, very stressful. The whole love side goes out the window. It's a function.*

The loss of spontaneity and the mechanical and 'functional' aspects of sex in the midst of both medical treatment and methods of tracking fertility at home add to the difficulty in sustaining the cooperative elements of the hetero-normative ideal. These stories show clearly how sex, intimacy and love can be disaggregated from the 'natural' procreation of children once they are slipped into the 'hybrid' domain of the science of reproduction.

Anne also notes the difficulty posed by the treatments themselves since hormones, the natural regulators of sexual desire and 'biological function', are the targets of ART and create conditions that are often not conducive to sexual relationships.

> JILL: *Can you tell me a little bit about what this does to your marital relationship? Does it alter your whole perception of intimacy at some point?*
> ANNE: *It did at the start because it meant we always made love and all of a sudden you're saying, 'but I can't ever get pregnant. I'm less of a woman'. And then having so many hormone drugs that you . . . The last two or three weeks if he even kissed me my skin crawled and I'd say 'go away'. Because that's what the hormone is after doing to me. I absolutely adore my husband and he's actually very much kissy and cuddly and so am I, but all of a sudden I'm like – no. It changes your whole hormones, your sex drive goes completely with it and I just, I feel nauseous the whole time. And I was reading something on TESA[49] the other day and one of the things is that every three days you have to make love. And my husband was like 'woo hoo'. And I was like, hmmmm, you could do it yourself. [laughing]*

Again, as part of treatment, sex seems like a chore for Anne while she maintains that her partner is still participating in the stereotypical role of an always-ready male. Unlike many of the stories above, the regimentation and lack of spontaneity is not an issue when sustaining a masculine ideal as part of the process. For Anne's partner it seems that reclaiming the meaning of an intimate relationship is more important in overcoming the medical construction of their sexual failure. Sexual inadequacy or failure, in this case, is construed as a result of the treatment rather than the reason for treatment.

Conclusion

As I note in previous chapters, motherhood and fertility are naturalised as foundations of social and political life but infertility disrupts the 'nature' and consistency of these foundations, challenging their hetero-normative basis. In this chapter I have pointed to the ways that some people in Ireland make sense of choices about infertility treatment in a maze of moral and medical discourses that rely on 'nature' as the foundation of their authority. In the process of making choices, however, people also challenge and/or reiterate the links between morality and social responsibility associated with procreation, sexuality and gender roles.

Assisted reproduction as part of a dialectic in which new ways of reproducing, that include technology, can be naturalised in the service of reshaping the moral discourse. However, this naturalisation is often at the expense of reinforcing gender difference in sexual mores and increasing the medicalisation of women's reproductive functions. Keeping the collection of sperm, for example, on the margins of the medical domain leaves men with no access to this new moral discourse as their contribution remains in the realm of sexual deviance. And for some people moral concerns are expressed not as religious ones but as an inability to dissociate the meaning of natural procreation from sexual intimacy. For some the clinical encounter cannot be easily articulated with definitions of what constitutes the natural. In this case, alternative 'technologies' such as NaPro might offer an opportunity to sustain a moral framework that tries to articulate nature and treatment. However, framing NaPro as 'treatment' draws it into a paradigm in which nature and sexual reproduction are still appropriated and clinically managed in opposition to, or outside of, what is perceived by many as natural reproduction.

Beyond the making of political persons in a legislative framework, the next chapter explores how new questions arise when people work through meanings of parenthood, kinship and family or offspring identities in relation to donor eggs and sperm (gametes). I will look at how people are working through new ideas about fertility, substance, donor gametes and morality in the constitution of family and kinship.

6. Conceptions of Contention:
Donor Challenge to the Dimensions of Relatedness

GAIL: And how I got over . . . well my own faith issues surrounding using donor sperm was when I was in the shower one day and I suddenly realised that Jesus was the ultimate 'donor baby'. And you know I thought if Mary and Joseph could raise a baby that not only wasn't his but was also the Messiah . . . Well you know I wasn't going to have to deal with the Messiah bit! So that really was the last hurdle for me to overcome.

Conventional definitions of parenthood often employ biology in order to naturalise ethical and moral assumptions implicit in social relationships. Eggs and sperm are important symbols in the construct of nature and parenthood as they are the biological building blocks of both offspring and relationships. In previous chapters, I have discussed the importance of motherhood not only as a social role in Ireland but a subjectivity produced in complex and contested relations of power. Stories about donor eggs allow us to tease out the ways in which biology is used in the service of relational, social and political definitions of motherhood. While nature and science could sometimes dance together in an ethical embrace with IVF, when egg and sperm donors enter, the rhythm changes, the steps falter and neither science nor nature provides the necessary discursive moral framework. Conceiving with another person's egg or sperm produces a fractured sense of parenthood and poses news possibilities for a child's identity.

David Schneider, in his work on Euro-American kinship, has suggested that the system is based on a logic that assumes 'kinship is defined as biogenetic. This definition says that kinship is whatever the biogenetic relationship is. If science discovers new facts about the biogenetic relationship, then that is what kinship is and was all along.'[1] Reproductive technologies at once facilitate parenthood, complicate it and make the biological processes highly visible and external to the embodied identities of the progenitors. New kinds of relationships are thus mediated in a scientific and disembodied context.[2] In this chapter I will examine how the use of donor eggs and sperm (gametes) relate to wider social and political discourses on motherhood, gender and sexual identity, morality, kinship and family responsibility that shape the local moral world in Ireland. The exchange of gametes creates not only complex gendered and sexual identities, but also a whole range of social identities and kinship relations for producers, recipients, and the children that are produced in the exchange, whether in assisted clinical reproduction or sexual reproduction. New concerns are created with respect to what Monica Konrad calls 'conjugal chaos' when procreation is no longer contained within marital relationships.[3]

As Schneider argues, science plays a role in shaping the social understanding of biogenetic facts. But science has reduced our notion of individual identities to the importance of the gene even as it creates ever more complex ways of defining and manipulating genetic material. In fact, donor conceptions represent a contradiction to the conventional biogenetic framework that emphasises genes and biological heritage as key to identity and future health and well-being. Blood is no longer the most powerful symbol of kin relations. The use of donor gametes also invites a re-examination of the role of genetics and birth in determining who is kin. McKinnon and Silverman challenge the growing modernist tendency to equate aspects of social personhood with genetics, locating the characteristics of individuals within a biological frame that reduces social relations and families to mere artifacts.[4] An emphasis on the role of nature as a basis for family relationships is both commonplace and contested, and we revisit again the malleability and constructedness of the concept of nature itself, particularly where it becomes the foundation for other constructed 'social facts'[5] and legal definitions of social relationships. In light of the importance of moral responsibilities attributed to motherhood and the family, Irish people who use donor eggs or sperm and ART must also navigate the meaning of biogenetic concepts in relation to the contested and changing social, legal and political ideas of family in Ireland.

Donor projects also constitute gametes more directly as body parts or objectified commodities, gifts or natural resources. As objects that are 'of the body', with embodied meanings, and yet necessarily disembodied, donor gametes are productive of complex identities and ethics as they transcend bodies in ways that contravene the norms of reproduction. Rhonda Shaw argues that ethics, in relation to an issue like egg donation, can only be understood in terms of embodiment if it is moved from the dimension of the theoretical to the practices grounded in everyday life.[6] These dimensions of the everyday are also gendered experiences, emphasising the intersection of social relationships and biology in reproduction – the space where gender difference is animated and defined as ethics that are enacted differently according to gendered expectations and responsibilities.[7] Gamete donation raises confusion and ethical dilemmas as people consider whether there is a moral and social responsibility associated with eggs and sperm that conveys a commitment to parenthood. The shifting location inside bodies and outside bodies, and the accompanying potential for embodied (recipients) or disembodied (donors) commitments to parenthood as a result of ART, creates dilemmas of relatedness embedded in the social value accorded to kin and family relations.[8] While many of these questions are not unique to Irish people, they are nonetheless shaped by the nuanced history of church and state relations as well as the stalled attempt to regulate the practices of assisted reproduction in Ireland. Given that family relationships are widely seen as sites for the formation of individual identity, social relations and stability, using donor gametes requires that people reimagine the importance of biological relationships in families.

The issue of donor gametes came up in about half of my forty interviews, three of which were with altruistic egg donors.[9] A willingness to consider donor eggs was mixed and always created a complex decision-making process that exposed the narrow scope of reproductive morality and normative practices that are based on sexual reproduction. About half of my participants had either considered or had undergone ART with donor eggs. But the only people who had used donor sperm were women without male partners. At the time of writing there were only two clinics in Ireland providing IVF with donor eggs. The waiting lists are long and many people wait several years for an opportunity or go abroad – Spain, Greece and, more recently, the Ukraine were available locations for accessing donor eggs. One clinic centred their clinical practice on a service in donor sperm and a couple of clinics offered the service but it was not used frequently. In spite of the challenges, however, in 2011 it was reported in *The Irish Times* that there are an estimated 500 babies born in Ireland each year through the use of donor gametes.[10] Clearly the use of donor gametes is going to continue to produce identities and kin relations in family-building projects in Ireland's pronatalist social context and has been absorbed, albeit with some discomfort, into the imperative to motherhood, maternity and morality defined through family.

Bodies of Truth: Social, Scientific and Regulatory Discourses

In an attempt to control the moral meanings associated with reproductive bodies, the Catholic Church in Ireland remains an insistent, if not influential, voice in the public debate and personal negotiation of the limits of acceptability in assisted reproduction, particularly in regard to donor gametes. Through the writings and press releases of the Irish Catholic Bishops' Conference on Bioethics in response to the CAHR, the church flags in particular a gap in 'parental responsibility' where the conception of a child through donor insemination or egg donation separates the contributors from any social relationship with that child.[11] Their position paper on the CAHR report states that 'the *nature* of human sexuality is such that it is the *norm* for a child to be born into a family where he/she has a mother and father who are in a stable relationship with another. This is why marriage is so fundamental to the well-being of children and society.'[12] As discussed in the last chapter, the church's documents rely on a rhetorical claim to a natural law and identify issues around the identity of the child as paramount. This suggests an irreconcilable gap between scientific possibility and moral logic dictated by what is defined as nature; our capacity to reason should, according to the tenets of natural law, provide us with the capacity to discern what is good by virtue of what is given in nature. It also emphasises an unproblematised link between nature as biology and identity. That the definition of 'nature' is of course culturally constituted in the first place is sidestepped again.

> LARA: *Well, the scriptures talk about the two shall become one. [. . .] I've always kind of understood that to mean the sexual act and possibly even the produce of the sexual act which would be a child – the fertilised egg – being the one. [. . .] And I know somebody did suggest to me that Jesus himself was a result of donor eggs. Well, I don't know whether he was or not, but a surrogate maybe [. . .] And it certainly does transcend my comfort zone – the use of donor eggs. I'm not comfortable with it. My husband isn't comfortable with it. I almost wish he were and that he would talk me into it because it makes so much scientific sense, and I wish I was prepared to. But it just doesn't sit well with me at all.*

The collision between faith-based morality and medical practices associated with donor conception is evident as people like Gail, in the epigraph of this chapter, and Lara juxtapose elements of infertility treatment and familiar religious meanings given to conception and reproduction. Like Elsa's artwork in an earlier chapter, the contested biogenetics in the conception of Jesus – a supernatural and thus unnatural event – is used to make sense of the shifting meaning of nature in science and reproduction. Lara struggles, for example, with the idea of a 'scientific sense' which is still at odds with her own moral understanding of the meaning of procreation and its components. Substituting a biomedical or scientific discourse for a religious one does not provide her with a basis for working out dilemmas of faith, challenges to parental identities or concepts of relatedness posed by the use of donated eggs. Egg donation adds new prospects to the biogenetic relationship without necessarily redefining it with clarity.

The moral reticence about donor gametes was not necessarily a product of religious sanctions, or difficulty making 'scientific sense', as Lara puts it. In some cases it related to the perceived social limits of acceptability. Niamh was in the midst of her fourth cycle of IVF as we sat at her kitchen table with a box of tissues between us; the pile of used ones mounted in her lap with the emotional intensity of her narrative. She spoke about the imaginary scenario that, for her, represents the moral boundaries of a biomedical solution to her infertility. Her story illustrates how conflict emerges in the very possibility of a dissociation, or transcendence, between gametes and wombs in determining maternal identity.

> JILL: *Has anyone ever suggested that you think about egg donation?*
> NIAMH: *[hesitating] . . . No. I wouldn't. And even my sister, you know. She said, 'Niamh, do you want me to carry a baby for you?' And I was thinking, now that's way too weird for me [laughing . . . and crying . . .]. She did offer and she was very genuine in her offer. But I couldn't do that. Like I would want it to be mine and Tommy's baby. And the only way it's going to be mine and Tommy's baby is if it is our bits that make it or if it's a child we go out and get together somewhere else in the world. Even if it's our bits that are in there I would still think it would be too weird. I mean how badly do I want it? I don't think my father would ever be able to come to terms with that [laughing]. I would have difficulty watching that baby growing in my sister. And then she's going to give birth and have to give me the child. I could just see way too much head-wrecking stuff there.*

The limitations and constraints that are inherent in both the meaning of motherhood and the presumed relationship between maternal bodies and the children they produce are tested and affirmed when women like Niamh consider how far they are willing to go in order to conceive a child and conceive of themselves as that child's mother. Even as she has allowed a kind of loosening of the boundary between her body and technology in the process of IVF, she relies on what seems like a clear border marked by the process of gestation in order to confirm the biological 'truth' of motherhood. Marilyn Strathern notes that '[i]t is a long-established supposition in the Euro-American cultural repertoire that the institutions of kinship and family 'regulate' biological processes for social ends'.[13] Niamh is concerned that even if the genetic 'bits' or gametes originate with her and her husband, having a child grow in her sister would

create too many intersections at the boundaries between social and biological parenthood and break too many regulations. A moral
ambivalence comes through as Niamh tries to imagine how she might
explain to her own father this porosity of bodily boundaries and sharing
of body parts. She struggles with this new image of the relationship
between a mother's body and motherhood, the relationship between the
gametes or 'bits' that constitute both the child and the kinship link, and
the possibility of watching her own pregnancy happening in someone
else's body. Niamh's reticence to employ her sister's body to become a
mother herself points out how current concepts of kinship and family
relations work normatively, making it difficult to accommodate new biological possibilities.

Such questions also revolve around the need to 'give cultural form to
the preservation of past biological truths', particularly as these truths are
now challenged by new possibilities in assisted reproduction.[14]
Preserving biological truths is important to a nation that has built its constitution around the importance of motherhood and family as the basis
for social stability and nationalist identity. While the CAHR recommends
in its report that birth be the deciding factor in determining the motherhood of a child in Ireland, in the case of donor gametes it is clear that for
people who contemplate these issues in their daily lives the lines are
much harder to draw. Conception and pregnancy remain important
markers even as hybrid forms involving technologies and disembodied
substance lurk beneath any notions of clarity around what constitutes
'natural' motherhood. The kind of surrogacy described above exposes
the need for new definitions of motherhood – definitions that can accommodate new kinds of biological truth in which pregnancy includes both
gestational and genetic maternal bodies but still privileges the social relationship implied by motherhood. But while recommendations can
promote regulatory processes that define motherhood a particular way,
the social comfort with the range of possibilities and implications for
identity lags behind.

The need for, and risks of, new regulatory and normative frameworks
in the practices of IVF and ART are perhaps understood most deeply by
those who are treading on new ground in the formation of biological
families through donor conceptions. I include a lengthy narrative from
Carol Anne and Vince here because it expresses some ambivalence on a
range of issues relating to the use of donor eggs from abroad. They also
point out that, in spite of longing for clarity, they recognise the complexity and range of issues that could become legal impediments in their
case, since Ireland has yet to clarify the legalities and regulate practices
such as donor conception. Carol Anne was diagnosed with unexplained

early menopause in her mid thirties and donor eggs offered the only realistic hope of conceiving.

> *JILL: So was the counselling more focused on your decision to do the egg donation and the issues around this?*
> *CAROL ANNE: Yeah, these are the issues. It was really to do with whether you have thought through the legality of it. I think in England because they have very strict guidelines, legally you would be the parent and there was no issue about that. But unfortunately in Ireland the CAHR still hasn't presented its findings and as far as I know if there is a problem . . . say I do get a donor and I do conceive . . . I don't know here if the legality of all that has been sorted. So I have the additional worry of will the child be legally mine here in Ireland? And I actually don't know. Under Spanish law and under English law when we went to the clinic in England they did spell that out.[. . .] I just had it in my mind that what if our marriage was to break up and I had given birth to a child? Could the court turn around and say that child is legally Vince's because he is the legal father but that child isn't legally yours and I could lose a custody battle on that basis? . . . It is a worry and it's something that I know even if I do conceive a child, all those issues won't go away. And nobody, no matter who I talk to, nobody can give you a solution. Because there's no law here in Ireland, so I come back here, give birth to a baby and just literally hope that the baby will be able to go through life without any issues because I wouldn't know how to deal with it.*
> *VINCE: If you've no law you can't do anything about it. I mean if you're registering a child there would be nothing on it saying, 'are you the genetic mother?'*
> *CAROL ANNE: It's a complete minefield really, isn't it? Normal IVF is difficult enough for couples but at least they know it's . . .*
> *VINCE: It's their own genetics.*

While answering my questions about the aims of counselling in the use of donor eggs, Carol Anne's most prominent recollection is about the legal issues. Her concern about the unequal claim to relatedness in a case such as theirs, in which she would have no genetic link to the child she might gestate, highlights a kind of disjuncture between birth and blood, or in this case genetics, as the basis for kinship codified in law. Monica Konrad describes the difficulty in analytical models of parenthood that seek to combine, in various ways, biological, social/emotional and legal definitions. Using Ward Goodenough's work as an example, she argues that 'jural rights are produced by a biological frame that naturalises these rights as causal relations for the ascription of an essentially sexed parenthood'.[15] This, she argues, conceals the extent to which legal definitions depend upon and are products of biological or emotional definitions of parenthood roles. The biological and emotional definitions of parenthood are thus posited as given in nature and unproblematised even as the terms are legally constructed. The 'Baby Anne' case in 2006 demonstrates the challenges when a young couple who had given up a child born to them outside marriage decided to contest the adoption two years later. In spite of the emotional trauma for adoptive parents and a child who had known no other family, Baby Anne was ordered by the court to be returned to the birth parents who had subsequently married.[16] Thus, biology and marriage became the basis for assuming the naturalised rights in this case.[17]

Carol Anne suggests that the complex issues regarding motherhood and identity that accompany a donor egg conception can also be reshaped as legal problems solved through regulatory discourses. Her case is an example in which the definition of 'biological mother' based on birth, while presumed to be natural, might not be adequate for the ascription of a legal definition of motherhood. As noted, Franklin challenges the attribution of social meaning to biological 'facts', arguing that such meanings as kin relationships are based on socially constituted meanings of nature and biology. Carol Anne further problematises the simplicity of this construction. She points out that while the social meaning of motherhood will be attributed to the biological fact of her gestating and giving birth, there is a need to attribute new legal meanings as well. Her concern speaks to the current uncertainty in Ireland that the social relationship – as the mother of a child to whom she gives birth – will also be legally recognised.[18] In fact the current laws in Ireland offer little protection since they are based on a biological family and have not incorporated the social family. Acknowledging that the law must be changed, the CAHR recommendations suggest that the gestational mother be recognised as the legal mother in the case of gamete donation.[19] However, at the time of writing such legislation has not yet been drafted in Ireland.

Another regulatory concern to people who use donor gametes is the question of anonymity and how this might protect recipient claims to parental identity. The implications of the removal of donor anonymity in regulations engenders ambivalence and uncertainty for recipients.[20] Anne is concerned that infertility is being constituted as different from other medical conditions, and gamete donation constructed as ethically and legally distinct from other organ donor programmes.

> ANNE: *But people have donated something huge like a kidney or a liver. It's still anonymous. Now because we're getting an egg – or a sperm [emphatically] – they're not dealing with us the same way and that is it. I've had many an argument with people who insist the children have the right to know. I said, 'no, we have the right to decide whether they ought to know'. [. . .] I think it should still be up to the parent. I think it should*

> *be anonymous if you want it anonymous and open if you want it open.*
> *What they wouldn't do to kidney or liver patients, why are they doing it*
> *to us because they are now making decisions in our lives and our families?*
> *Now, we're going to tell our child – sure. It's just . . . you know, we're*
> *allowed to do that because that's our decision. All of sudden it's 'oh this*
> *person is my real parent'. It's an emotional obligation. But for HFEA to*
> *turn around and be saying that this person is going to be so important in*
> *their life. That is just literally putting us right down on the totem pole*
> *again. And it feels absolutely terrible when in actual fact we are the*
> *parents – the biological parents – because I'll be the one giving birth to it.*

As her narrative suggests, Anne is concerned by recent changes in the UK to the Human Fertilisation and Embryology Act, mandating that information about donors be available to children conceived with donor gametes.[21] Although no such regulation currently exists in Ireland, the CAHR recommends a similar opportunity for children of donor gametes to have access to limited contact information, effectively eliminating anonymity for donors.[22] This focus on the rights of a child to gain access to information on the donors that contribute to their conception – the genetic parents – is a potential departure from the longstanding constitutional rights accorded to the family unit, as currently understood in Ireland, since contact with a donor threatens the integrity of the family based in marriage. The perceived threat comes from the insinuation of an outside other into the procreative relationship – a relationship that should ideally constitute two parents, not three. However, while donor practices have been seen as challenges to ideals of marriage and fidelity, many people in qualitative studies conducted in the UK were uncomfortable with the notion of total anonymity in receiving or providing donor gametes.[23]

In Ireland where the rights of the family are protected by constitutional law, the removal of anonymity inserts a privileged 'other' into the family unit, threatening the integrity of the parent–child relationship. The constitutionally ascribed rights of the family in Ireland are based on assumptions about birth and biology in tandem with marriage. Women who give birth are always accorded constitutionally protected rights in regard to the relationship with their children, whereas unmarried biological fathers have not been accorded any rights in the Constitution. While the Constitutional Review Group acknowledged the need for change in 1996, there continues to be an unequal recognition of the legal rights of parents who are not in a marital relationship.

A legislative framework that, on one hand, privileges the genetic connection by affirming the importance of a child's access to donor information might serve to diminish the importance of the commitment of social motherhood on the other. Marilyn Strathern notes that motherhood is a 'process of recognition and construction. In itself motherhood stands for the social construction of natural facts.'[24] For people like Anne and Carol Anne, the implications of possible legislative and regulatory constructions are threatening to their own legitimacy as mothers of a child to whom they are not genetically related. Any legal recognition of a donor's right to claim status as a parent, or their child's ability to seek out a donor as a parent, contests the validity of the social fact of motherhood and privileges the biogenetic. The natural facts could be socially and legally constructed in ways that work against Anne and Carol Anne.

Donated Relations: The New Substance of Kinship

In the previous section Anne was adamant that her own identity as a biological, gestational mother took precedence over any legal claims to motherhood by the egg donor as a genetic mother. For many women and their partners, these were conceptual problems in relation to the meaning and significance accorded to the notion of gametes as 'substance' in the making of kinship or family relations. For some it emerges as an imagined identity gap for the children produced through gamete donation. The use of donor sperm or eggs poses real and complex conceptual problems with respect to the issue of relatedness and potential for contact between children and gamete donors in the future. Most people who were considering using or had already used donor eggs were concerned with the perspective of the child, who might have an embodied sense of the unknown or a missing piece of their own identity. The child conceived with donor gametes comes with an unknown set of connections that must be accounted for in the process of determining who and what makes us 'related' and how this is meaningful for families.

The emphasis placed on genetics in relation to identity has served to emphasise continuity and individuality in ways that constitute challenges to previous assumptions about family relationships. Beyond a connection established by shared substance, for some of my participants the power and symbolism of genetics contained in a gamete constituted an identity for a child that seemed immutable, trumping their sense of kinship or relationship as parents.

Breda and John have had several courses of IVF without success and are now considering adoption. They have been told that donor eggs would be a worthwhile option since their difficulty with IVF has been attributed to 'egg quality'. The biggest hurdle for Breda is the risk of a conflicted identity for the child who might be produced through donor eggs. What are the implications for a child if genetic kin and biological kin are, in fact, not the same?

> BREDA: So I suppose there is still the other big open question which is donor eggs. I suppose John, he'd do it tomorrow. He's very into it and I suppose I would be as well if I didn't have to face the child . . . [laughing]. Just identity, you know. They'll be a person and they'll have to grow up with it. It's not me that will have to live with it. Well obviously I'll live with it in a different way but you'll be creating a whole new person who would have to . . . I suppose if it was the UK and if the donor didn't have the right to anonymity I might consider it. I would worry that there would be such a gap in the child's life. And if I was guaranteed that I could have twins maybe because then they could be each other's genetic link [laughing]. It's a big thing really because it means I'm denying John as well. I'd be denying him the chance to have his own genetic child and I'd love to have John's child. But for the child I have some problems. But then I sort of think well then the child becomes their own person like anybody and they'd be grateful to be alive and I wouldn't change that. I'd say probably the adoption is John's second choice. I shouldn't be speaking for him, but I think he'd probably prefer to go for the donor if I could get my head around it.
>
> JILL: Would John have been as accepting of the idea of a sperm donor, do you think?
>
> BREDA: Hmmm, I never asked him but I'd say so. He's a scientist you know so he'd be looking for the solution. I'd have the same questions . . . well obviously for me it's a loss because I wouldn't have my own genetic child but I mean it's a big thing to make up for it if I could carry a child and have a child. That would be fantastic but it's the child's identity and how they would grow up is my big question about it.
>
> JOHN: I know for Breda it's difficult when we think of the genetic identity of the child and it's a grey area in terms of contact with the genetic mother. Not an easy sort of thing whereas adoption has been there for so long that people are dealing with the circumstances around adoption.

Breda's narrative is full of contradictions. She is at once concerned that part of a child's identity might come from the egg donor but is also willing to concede that 'the child becomes their own person like anybody else'. She is concerned by the potential significance of a genetic identity for a child produced with a donor egg but is willing to consider adoption without seeming to question the same issues. But what is a 'genetic identity'? This duality ultimately becomes a source of ambivalence when women think about the identity embodied in the different genetics (nature) of a child that is nonetheless nurtured biologically by them. Breda is also, in contrast to some of the other people quoted above, comforted by the notion that a child produced with donor gametes would have access to information on their genetic parent. In this case, we see the locus of concern centred on the child's identity rather than on potential challenges to the parental identity of the recipient parent.

Not everyone sees the biogenetic continuum as natural. Gestating and giving birth to a child with no genetic relationship is not necessarily a critical part of parenthood. For Sarah, whom I spoke of in an earlier chapter, biogenetics held little meaning once she considered her options as a woman embarking on motherhood without a partner. After some careful consideration of the meaning of using donor gametes, she ultimately made the decision to abandon her original plan of using ART to conceive in favour of adoption.

> SARAH: *I began to think this isn't a good idea. This isn't going to work. What I'm really doing is adopting before birth. What's the difference? Adopting before birth or adopting after birth. Creating a child when there are so many children out there who are available. It didn't make sense to me. It was the ethical consideration that made me think 'go for a child that is already there'. Creating a child, it's an artificial thing. I suppose it felt like a kind of . . . like a selfishness there. It just made me think what's the point. And I thought, 'no, I'll look into adoption'. That was the turning point and I didn't go back to the fertility clinic.*

Sarah decided that using both donor egg and donor sperm meant she was effectively 'adopting' both the eggs and the sperm. Her sense of having a kin or blood relationship to a child conceived with both donor egg and sperm is the same as it would be if the child was born to another woman. She does not see her own gestational input as overriding the ultimate genetic heritage of a child created with donated gametes, not capable of infusing the child with a kind of blood relationship that would supersede the biological disconnection. But neither does she see this disconnection as impeding her ability to be a child's mother.

Sarah also suggests that the creation of a child with donor eggs and donor sperm would be 'artificial' in its separation from any natural, or 'genetic', link to her or a partner. The meaning of 'artificial' in this context is equally embedded in the social construction of a natural order in which the concept of nature itself is culturally determined and mediated. Sarah is ultimately influenced in her decision by pragmatism and logistics since, as a woman in her late forties, her age complicated the chance of success with donor IVF.

Anne, who had already conceived with donor eggs, finds another way to reshape the biogenetic relationship. In her narrative, she challenges the idea of genetics over gestation as the strongest link to a child and the greater claim on 'biological' motherhood. In the following I suggested that half of the genetic complement was her partner's, and she immediately incorporated her own body into the process as a genetic contributor.

> ANNE: *And that's it, at the best it's a third because, I mean how much of the DNA is actually made when it got into your body, when your blood is flowing through it?*
> JILL: *Yeah. So I suppose, yeah, there are all sorts of interactions with it because of the social and the environmental things.*
> ANNE: *But it's getting heart, lungs and a brain stem. That's all happening in your body. It's your blood flowing around. That's my way of thinking about it. So it's not just two people that made this baby. Do you know? There's three people's genetics in this – not two.*
> JILL: *That's such an interesting way to look at that, yeah.*
> ANNE: *That's the way I handle the people and they said, 'oh, you have a child with the genetics of the donor'. No. That's not the way it is. It shouldn't be that way.*

An important element in this story is the differentiation of the meaning of shared substance and kinship. Anne's idea of the 'formation' of an identity, even a genetic one, is based on maternity rather than conception. Her narrative disrupts the construct of genetics as fixed and encapsulated in a gamete by questioning the immutability of biology in identity formation. Claris Thompson describes a similar 'underdeterminacy of biogenetic ways of determining kinship' in her work in California fertility clinics.[25] In her study, one of her participants described her gestational activity as 'nourishing' with her blood, providing another conception of the sharing of blood as a substance that is more important than genetics. Both stories suggest that blood has a greater association with growth, nurturing and development in constituting at least a mother and child relationship, even if the tendency is to privilege genes as the hallmark of a wider kinship rooted in biogenetics.

These stories point out, on one hand, the reshaping of genetics as substance which might determine kinship connections. But on the other hand, they also illustrate people's willingness to re-order the meaning of substance as a determinant of kinship or relatedness, putting genetics in a less important position among substances in constituting relationships. There is evidence of pragmatism as women re-evaluate the power of their own maternity in shaping concepts of shared substance and kinship. They also re-evaluate the meaning of their maternity in the constitution of an identity for a child. Paxson, again, describes this significance in Greece where motherhood is valued and maternity accorded particular importance in influencing the makeup and identity of a child based on the flow of blood and sharing of substance in the womb.[26]

Gamete donors also provide interesting stories in which to explore the collision between what is socially constituted as kinship and what is seen as biologically meaningful. Laura, an egg donor who responded to my post on the Rollercoaster.ie website, explains her view of the meaning of the donation or 'gift'.

> LAURA: Yeah. Now I remember clearly when I first said it to my husband and he said, 'well what exactly does it involve? Would you not kind of feel that is was partly your baby?' And I said, 'No. I genuinely wouldn't'. So he said, 'well if you're okay with it I'm okay with it. Doesn't affect me at all'. To me I would liken it to giving blood. If I'm having children they are my children with my husband. So these were eggs. Now I know, yes it's part of me genetically and all that. But without my husband they were never going to be my children. And like I said, once a month there goes one and that's the way I see it.

Laura was an altruistic egg donor who undertook the process without the incentive of knowing someone who needed an egg donor. Based on research with egg donors and surrogate mothers in New Zealand, Rhonda Shaw describes such autonomous acts as body projects or 'projects of the self' undertaken to fulfil a need for the donor herself.[27]

> LAURA: And I would do it again. I mean they got twins so I don't know if they necessarily want to go again. And I don't know now ourselves, like, if we will go again. And I would like to know if they [recipient couple] did want to go I would like to offer them the chance. But if they just had twins I don't know if they want to go again right away. And in that respect if I did decide to donate again how would they feel about it?

As part of her project Laura takes the recipient couple's interests into consideration, recognising her own contribution to the potential genetic or 'blood' connection among other siblings in this family. She understands the kinship implications for the receiving couple if she provides another donation which might result in eggs going to a different couple. In this sense there are three families with children who share 'substance'. Laura highlights the issue of anonymity from the donor's perspective, suggesting that, on one hand, she is not kin to a child produced from her egg but, on the other hand, care will have to be taken to prevent her own children from getting into a relationship with a genetic half sibling, as remote as the possibility might be.

> LAURA: And the only thing that we did come across that we were sort of like thinking that could be a problem is in years to come if our children meet up with . . . and that's why I did ask when I went to talk to them about it. They had said they would let you know when the baby is born because that is all the information they were allowed. And the thing as

well with it being anonymous, it could be my next-door neighbours. But I don't mind and if I have a rough idea when they are born I can prepare both my children. I hate to think that when she starts dating in years to come that she's going to have this in the back of her mind, 'oh, could you be half related?', you know?

Laura suggests that the potential child of a donor egg is clearly related in some way to her own children. Konrad describes how anonymity in donor egg conceptions contributes to a kind of ambivalent 'relations of non-relations' through which a social relationship is formed by necessity of the gift but must then be obscured or 'effaced' from a network of kin relationships.[28] Anonymity, again, becomes a source of ambivalence in uncoupling the notion of kinship relations from donor conceptions as a way around the awkward issues of procreative and marital chaos described by Konrad, as well as the limits of procreative acceptance and the meanings of 'blood' relations and substance emphasised by Schneider.[29]

Kay, an egg donor who had considered the possibility of providing an altruistic donation after watching the *Making Babies* documentary programme on RTÉ television, ended up donating to an acquaintance who worked with her husband. The two women got into a conversation which resulted in their becoming aligned in a process of assisted reproduction.

KAY: *I had made a first appointment with the clinic but had to cancel last minute as I had no childcare that morning. The very next day I happened to be doing some professional work for a relation of my husband. I don't know how the conversation got around to infertility. I only knew this lady in a polite conversation way but we started chatting and I told her about my cancelled appointment and she said she had been on the waiting list for a donor for years and we took it from there. She had the option to use me as her donor or use me to get to the top of the waiting list by 'giving' me to the lady at the top of the list and swapping places with her. She decided that she would prefer me as her donor as I had proven fertility because I have two young children.[30]*

JILL: *I'm intrigued when you say that your egg is a 'building block' but I wonder if sometimes it might feel like more than that if you have some interaction with this child.*

KAY: *It was not much of an emotional challenge for me as our social circles are very different and I wouldn't see her regularly, weddings and funerals only, kind of thing. I would not have tried to see her more in case at some future point I might have developed an unhealthy interest or perceived an involvement with the child. Anyway, she hasn't had the child. She miscarried at seven weeks unfortunately so I can't say for 100% certain what it would feel like but I strongly feel that I would not have had a problem with it.*

Kay says she would tell her children later, 'when they are older perhaps with children of their own as I feel only then can you understand why a person would donate eggs'. Strathern argues that the more wide-reaching implications of kinship might reside with the families of donors as they also have unknown relations. She argues that complexities arise when a child 'that had the potential to create links (make relationships) could by the same token be seen as disrupting links (already based on relatedness)'.[31]

Konrad challenges the possibility that social relationships between gamete donors and recipients can be eclipsed or erased, even by legalised anonymity. She argues that part of the social self is constituted in the very act of the exchange and that body parts convey meanings to others in social interactions. From this perspective, donor and recipient 'each configure the other'[32] and these configurations are shaped within a legal and cultural context. The idea of non-relations becomes more complex when extended kin and family are considered in this procreative admixture of donors, recipients, genetic half siblings, and grandparents with genetic and social connections. In Ireland, it also pertains to what many people described as a past reticence on the part of family members to welcome an adopted child. It is beyond the scope of this volume to examine in detail but it is important to note that adoption also creates relations of non-relations as an unknown and unquantifiable entity.

Constituting Sexual and Gender Identities

An uncomplicated conception that occurs following sex eclipses not only the embodied social and moral value of gametes but the fact that they are objects or body parts with material value as well. Assisted reproduction creates the possibility of offering eggs, sperm and wombs for use by others in a new market designed for such an exchange. But more importantly, when disembodied, the components of sexual reproduction can be traded, sold, given away or lent/borrowed without the necessity of a sexual relationship. This shift has implications not only for the moral and normative complex of behaviours around sexual relationships and reproduction but for the meaning of biological substance in constituting relationships.

Eggs and sperm have particular kinds of value with the capacity to make social persons or parental identities. My interview with Lara took place in her living room over many cups of strong coffee. Lara described her very modern living space filled with glass tables and breakable objects as distinctly child *unfriendly* – a kind of aesthetic inversion to the role she longed to play but had yet to achieve. She noted that if she could not have kids she was not going to trouble herself with a child-friendly home. Her advanced maternal age was a point of contention in her marriage as her partner, who was younger, held Lara to account for their inability to conceive. In the following narrative she reflects on the options available to someone who is contemplating IVF at nearly forty years of age.

> LARA: *The difficulty I have with donor eggs is I'm unable to see eggs as a collection of cells, as merely an egg, as merely an ingredient. For me an egg . . . using another woman's egg . . . and it's not an ego thing. It's not that I think I'm so wonderful that my kids should have me in them. [. . .] With me it's probably religious scruples. I don't have the religious things all worked out. And how am I going to explain to my kid that I've used another woman for eggs but by the way, we don't want you to have adultery ever? It's morally wrong. It just kind of slips them into the grey zone. That it's going to blur the boundaries between right and wrong for the kids and that this somehow may be morally corrupting for them. It's a whole sort of moral and ethical thing and it sort of devalues the meaning of that contribution. It's a devaluing that takes place of that sort of union – marital union. To me there's something more to eggs than that. There's something more to sperm than just a cell or just something like a blood transfusion or if you need glasses you wear glasses. For me using somebody else's eggs and sperm has a whole load of social and moral connotations around it. If you're reproducing with someone who's not your spouse . . . I mean, okay, it's not a date; you're not meeting up directly. But you're essentially copulating.*

Lara frames her discomfort by talking about the cellular activities involved in fertilisation and conception as embodying the social meanings attached to sex in a relationship. Moral detachment is not an option in her story. Lara is concerned with the social and moral message implied by blurring the link between biological and genetic parenthood as it relates to issues of marital fidelity. Her story raises what Monica Konrad calls 'the perceived threat of conjugal chaos [. . .], the fear of being held to account' where there is a donor involved in the assisted conception as people fear they will be criticised for their introduction of a third party into a procreative partnership.[33] Lara and her husband Paul both made reference to the same biblical passage, suggesting that the 'two shall become one' might refer not only to the marital relationship but also to the biological moment of conception. This concern is not unique to Ireland, echoing findings in other studies in the UK in which people are uncomfortable with new kinds of marital infidelity or 'test tube adultery' arising from the use of gamete donors in ART.[34] The significance of fidelity links to concerns with containing the family in Ireland, like Katherine Conrad's description of the importance of the 'family cell' as a site for keeping foreign matter out. The emphasis on marriage and family as key to social stability in Ireland creates additional challenges for legislators who must decide how to regulate the use of donor gametes in Ireland.

Lara's story points to the depth of the meanings some people employ as they question whether their gametes (sperm and egg) are merely objects in a biological chain of events called sexual reproduction. In questioning the moral neutrality of mixing sperm and eggs, even in a Petri dish, Lara suggests that particular kinds of identities are produced for both donors and recipients in the generation and exchange of gametes.

The exchange in eggs and sperm objectifies them as they become disembodied elements, a concern raised by the Catholic Church and described in Dr Connell's speech discussed in the last chapter. The trade in gametes as products in and of themselves reduces the process to a transaction separate and apart from the 'procreative' commitment Lara feels should be part of having a child. While her perspective was an extreme example, it nonetheless represents part of a spectrum of issues related to the making of identities in procreative relationships. The issue for people is the potential for donor gametes to make or 'unmake' them as parents of the child that is conceived in the process.

An example of the use of donor gametes in making identities is evident in Gail and Martin's story. Faced with the implications of Martin's very low sperm count, they decided that a transactional relationship would ensure against any future dispute over the meaning of a biological investment to the personhood, identity and kinship connection of the child they might have with donor sperm.

> GAIL: *When the fresh IVF cycle didn't work we thought we'd fill in the adoption forms . . . Then we thought 'why do this when we can adopt sperm rather than adopting a baby . . .?'*
> JILL: *Interesting . . . you were more comfortable with donor sperm.*
> MARTIN: *It was the guilt factor . . . I would do anything to facilitate. The day I got the news [that he had almost no sperm] we sat down and I said, 'we'll do whatever it takes to make a baby'.*
> GAIL: *So my child is the child that I raise and that's what we decided with the donor sperm – that Martin would be the Daddy. We know any man can be a father. It takes a great man to be a Daddy. Martin had said right from the beginning that we would consider donor sperm and I said no way. Because I never wanted, in the heat of an argument, for him to say, 'take your child'. So what he said was that he would buy the sperm and then it would be his and he would do with it as he chose.*

The perspectives expressed by both of these couples might be seen as two ends of a spectrum of possibilities in which eggs and sperm are linked to the moral and social responsibility of parenthood. At one end of the spectrum, Paul and Lara eschew the material and transactional aspects of gamete exchange. They want to imagine the conception of their child as symbolic and performative, synonymous with the procreative ideal that links marriage with having children. Gail and Martin offer an alternative framework for making sense of this issue when they create a distinction between a biological relationship as a 'father' and the social relationship of a 'Daddy'. For Gail and Martin the taking of ethical and moral responsibility as a parent overrides any moral misgivings about perceived 'conjugal chaos'. In the absence of a genetic link, a social relationship is negotiated through what becomes a pragmatic monetary transaction. In this case, the 'Daddy' actually *owns* the sperm even if he has not produced it. The potential threat to family integrity posed by the presence of a third party in the procreative process may still exist in conceptual terms. However, owning sperm literally 'makes' Martin both a father and a Daddy and helps to detach and exclude the genetic father from the family picture.

'Making' a Mother: The Salvaged Egg

Gametes are constituted as items of exchange in other ways as well. The theme of a natural resource that is there to be recovered, exploited or utilised in some kind of transaction is apparent in stories about donor eggs. In many cases this theme of recovery is constituted as a means of overriding or at least compensating for what are construed as nature's inefficiencies. In Anne's story, typical of several on the use of donors, the donated egg is constituted as a 'salvaged' resource, destined to be otherwise wasted by normal bodily processes. In this case the egg is not necessarily a link between the woman who produced it and a child. The detachment is effected by this concept of gametes as discarded or wasted material as opposed to a commodity that is bought and paid for, as in Martin's story above.

> ANNE: *I mean like people said to me – 'would you consider the other woman to be the biological mother?' and I said, 'no'. I said, 'no, absolutely not'. Because to me she was ovulating and she didn't want to get pregnant and so those eggs would dissolve. And the baby would never have been born. But instead of taking the pill and letting them dissolve she's giving them to me; but that's not making a biological mother. Or any kind of mother.*

Anne takes this formulation somewhat further in challenging the discursive domain of genetics to determine who is the 'mother'. Like Gail and Martin, Anne argues that the gift of an egg *makes* her the mother. Anne does not see an egg donation as configuring a motherhood identity for the donor, and certainly not one that must be accounted for as part of the family construction in an imagined or real way.

Unlike the metaphorically constituted images of the 'active' production of sperm there is a powerful sense of passivity, lack of control, and waste in the inevitable loss of an egg during menstruation.[35] This contrasts significantly with the image of the active and purposeful production of sperm, as described in the last chapter, that contributes to associations between sperm donation and sexual deviance. Moreover, men can actively engage in the recovery of their gametes, and any 'waste' is, by and large, perceived as something they control. Women, on the other hand, must be assisted, by a technological investment, in the recovery of their resource. In this light, egg donation can also be constructed as compensating for nature, recouping a resource that is otherwise lost in natural processes.

This inevitability and wastefulness provided a framework through which there is a disconnection of the egg from its producer, decontextualising the maternal relationship and relocating maternal connections in the recipient's body. For Niamh, quoted earlier, the meaning of gestation and birth is complex and subject to moral and ethical re-evaluation in relation to the making of a motherhood identity. For most people who spoke to me about this issue, donor eggs were the basis for an imagined child once they are associated with a recipient maternal body, carefully delineated from the donor body. More importantly, in line with Konrad's findings in her UK study, this way of thinking about eggs as something that can be completely dissociated from the donor's body effectively eclipses any potential parental relationship to a resulting offspring.

A similar perspective was narrated in stories of people who have been egg donors. Alicia, an altruistic egg donor who describes herself as 'fascinated with fertility and infertility', heard about the need for donor eggs on a popular Irish radio talk show one afternoon. She called the clinic mentioned in the programme and set up an appointment. I asked her about her 'relationship' to the eggs she had donated.

> ALICIA: *What did I feel the egg was to me? For me, it's a piece of tissue that I don't need right now. I don't see it as an egg. I see it as a piece of tissue that I've absolutely no use for and somebody else could have a use for it. The counsellor asked me would I think that the baby is my child, biologically. And I said no, never, because for me the biological mother – I don't know from a legal point of view but from my point of view – the biological mother is the person who gives birth to this child and feeds the*

child while it's in the womb and looks after the health and well-being
while it's growing in the womb. So for me that's the mother. I don't feel,
ever, that I'm the mother of some baby out there somewhere. It's just . . .
people think differently but my thinking is it's not a baby I gave away. It
was a piece of tissue that made a baby for somebody else.

Alicia sees herself as having no part of the family life of a recipient couple. Nor was she being made a mother by virtue of the donation. In the exchange of a donor process, gametes are described as resources to be recovered or purchased, and ultimately owned as material property. Such transactions do not reduce the potential power of the gametes to make social persons. However, for many of the people I spoke with about donor egg reproduction any claim to a parental identity seemed more easily severed when the process was discussed using the metaphoric frame of economics or resource management.

While donated eggs can be dissociated from the bodies of their donors, the body of the recipient becomes very important through narratives of connection. Here the emphasis is on motherhood and nurturance as being part of the child's 'becoming'. The child that becomes a child only 'but for the mother' – because a woman provides a womb – is also part of the narratives that posit biological or gestational over genetic motherhood as the 'real' or significant identity. A tension emerges here as the use of donor eggs re-emphasises pregnancy and birth, shifting away from science and back to what is presumed to be both natural and highly gendered aspects of procreation. It is the performative aspects in which the woman who provides the nurturance and gives birth is affirmed as the real mother. Much like Niamh's concern for the making of a motherhood identity through surrogacy, the motherhood role and the kinship rules that determine it are constituted in the nature of birth. These stories also point to the importance of relationships as a determinant of ethical choice. Women shape their stories around the formation of a relational possibility between themselves and a child that might come from otherwise wasted eggs.

DONNA: *What I feel about donor eggs is that, like, if the pregnancy does*
occur, number one it would be a 50% genetic link whether it's donor egg
or donor sperm and also, number two, you're nurturing this baby. This
baby wouldn't be growing only for you. You know, like, you still could
deliver the child and then breastfeed the child. That was a hugely impor-
tant issue in my life.

As Donna suggests here, without the maternal body of the gestational mother life is not possible. This shifts procreative emphasis to the successful conception, the pregnancy and birth as a means of normalising egg donation as part of a continuum or process that is, in itself, a moral endeavour. Alicia, a practising Catholic, adds another layer of spiritual complexity suggesting that not only is the recipient gestational mother necessary for the conception, pregnancy and birth, but so is the intervention of God necessary to the process.

> ALICIA: *I wouldn't be over-religious, but the baby would never have been made or formed if God didn't want it to. I figured as well that if I was doing something incredibly wrong she wouldn't become pregnant. She wouldn't have the chance to have this baby if I was doing something really ethically and morally wrong. So I believe in fate. So I figured since I got that far it was meant to be.*

As in Gail's story in the opening of this chapter, religion is co-opted and shaped while sustaining the dominant assumption that conception, pregnancy and birth confirm a motherhood identity.

Gendered Donor Practices

Among my participants only Aoife and Cara, and Joan Marie, had used donor sperm. No one in a heterosexual relationship had used donor sperm. Gail and Martin had considered it but opted for technology instead, using ICSI. This apparent distinction along gender lines highlights the emphasis on biology and the unevenness of the meaning of donor gametes between men and women. Women can still participate in the sharing of substances by gestating and even feeding a child conceived with donor gametes. There is no similar opportunity for men. Like many other places in the world, the significance of gendered relations and the meaning of sexual performance and procreative actions influences the way these differences are experienced and addressed.[36]

The production and transmission of gametes sexually and the obtaining of gametes clinically often reiterates stereotypical images of masculinity and femininity. This gender differentiation is part of a social construction in which the need for a sperm donor poses challenges to notions of masculinity, sexual prowess and potency or performance. Many of the women I spoke to felt that even though women are often burdened with the assumption that they are biologically and/or socially responsible for a couple's childlessness, it was necessary to shield their male partner from the greater stigma associated with male infertility. Becker also suggests that such assumptions influence the secrecy involved in sperm donation in the USA, where patriarchy also underpins social norms that tend to emphasise the importance of genetic parentage.[37]

ANNE: *We wanted to keep some genetic link and men have such a hard time and people saying, 'oh you're shooting blanks' or 'oh, you couldn't even have kids' or 'you can't get it up' and smart comments like that. So that we'd never told anybody. His mother and my mother, that's it. Nobody else knows because I wanted to shield him from the pain of that. So there's the double standard. You can talk about donor eggs but the woman has still got the link because she's giving birth. Women, we internalise the questioning and you beat yourself up over it whereas with donor sperm, or male infertility, the outside world beats the men up as well as the men doing it themselves. So they've got it twice as bad. And it's not the same with donor eggs. It is still a stigma [for men].*

Anne's summation of the difficulty and stigma associated with public perceptions of male infertility is not unique to Ireland but is nuanced with the particular history around sexual repression, patriarchal marriage and family politics. Van Balen and Trimbos-Kemper discuss the challenges that such gendered assumptions can pose in an already strained marital relationship.[38]

Bridget and David were confronted with the issue of male infertility and despite feeling compelled to make an initial visit to a fertility clinic, they had been in agreement from the beginning that their approach would be adoption.

JILL: *And did you ever consider a sperm donor?*
BRIDGET: *I think we kind of felt that at the time if it wasn't going to belong to David we'd prefer that it didn't belong to either of us, you know? It's either related to both of us or we'd go for an adoption.*

For Bridget and David, an unequal material investment seemed threatening and unbalanced. This sense that gamete donation, particularly sperm donation, creates an unequal relationship is often expressed as the child being 'someone else's', a construct that again draws an outside 'other' into the family. Alexis and Ciaran were faced with numerous challenges to conceiving as she struggled with endometriosis. They discovered when beginning medical consultations for their infertility, much to their surprise, that he had virtually no sperm. Like Bridget and David, they were extremely reticent to use donor sperm.

ALEXIS: *No, definitely not. No, because even when we were talking about if the IVF doesn't work . . . like we were saying about . . . we'll go down the adoption route and we have no problem with that, and we both agreed and that's fine; but the doctor in the other clinic actually said to us would we not go with a donor. Ciaran's whole attitude was – oh no, you're not going to be carrying someone else's child. It has to be mine or adoption. So adoption was his route. When I was saying, 'But why? Because it'll be half mine or half yours, whichever half I don't mind.' I said, what if it's*

with his sperm and somebody else's egg? 'You'd still get to carry it,' he
said, so. Yeah. If it's not his sperm; it's not his child, you know, that's it.

Alexis' story points out that, in a case of donor eggs, women have
access to the experience of pregnancy and birth, which might augment
their sense of biological relatedness. The fact remains that, for Ciaran at
least, gametes convey a prior social and kinship relation as well as a
genetic relationship. As described above, the biological processes of conception and birth operate to favour the relational claims or 'blood ties' of
women over men when donor gametes are used.[39] The opportunity for
women to create biological relatedness through pregnancy even if they
used donor eggs was cited as an advantage by several couples.

> LEAH: *And yes, I know that I could go through a donor sperm if I wanted.*
> *And I did think about that obviously. It just did not appeal to me at all. I*
> *didn't like that fact that, even though I'm adopting a child and I do not*
> *know who their parents are, but the thought of carrying around somebody*
> *else's child that I did not know was too much to get my head around. My*
> *husband had no problem accepting it. I definitely had a problem. I just*
> *didn't like the idea at all. I don't believe in the clinic. Maybe I'm totally*
> *wrong but I always have this image, and they tell you like, about the*
> *father of the sperm or whatever and they're not that at all, you know.*

Studies have shown that the use of donor sperm in the US has
declined since the advent of intracytoplasmic sperm injection techniques.[40] This technique enables men with even minimal sperm counts
to father children. Of the twenty-three couples I spoke with who had
used IVF, eight had used ICSI and it had been recommended to at least
four of the couples who had not used IVF. Its use was deeply embedded
in the rhetoric of 'having a child of one's own'. For Gail and Martin, there
was an additional spin-off in revalidating Martin's masculinity.

> GAIL: *Especially because in that sort of two-week period between fertilisa-*
> *tion and when my period arrived, Martin was sort of re-given his . . .*
> MARTIN: *Manhood.*
> GAIL: *Manhood, yes, because we had 90% fertilisation. Of the ten [eggs]*
> *they could inject, nine fertilised and his sperm did their job and you know*
> *he was happy.*

As Gail says, that interim period of waiting after the embryos are
transferred back to her afforded her partner, who had a very low sperm
count, a chance to relish his own fertility. This confirmation of his
potency and fertility was demonstrated not by a positive pregnancy test
but the scene under a microscope enacted and witnessed by an embryologist and reported back to Gail and Martin by the clinic.[41] I will
explore this point again in the next chapter in relation to the visibility of

embryos, but the exposure of gametes and conception to the view of clinic staff and participants plays two key roles here. First, it is an important component in normalising the processes of IVF as scientific common sense. But more importantly, it reconfirms gender stereotypes associated with gametes in heterosexual performance through what Emily Martin has described as the imaginary 'romance' between eggs and sperm.[42] In this case both the romance and the gender roles are enacted under a microscope in a clinic. This confirmation of gender roles is important in order to offset potential social conceptions of sexual inadequacy that might emerge from the need for IVF. As Lara suggested in her narrative on donor eggs sex is, in fact, happening in a dish. And given Gail and Martin's admission that sex was temporarily 'on the shelf', this is the only place in which there is confirmation of Martin's sexual capability, an important element in a masculine identity.

Contesting the Body of Reproductive Ideals

While the use of donor gametes can participate in the process of redefining and building new social formations that constitute family on one hand, their use also demonstrates how access to 'assisted reproduction' as a reproductive strategy is legitimated in normative and regulatory terms. Debates about access to treatment by lesbian couples, for example, can disrupt the hetero-normative model of reproduction by redefining (in)fertility to include a wider set of sexual and procreative norms. What is apparent in the political and medical discourses on ART is a reaffirmation of the gendering associated with reproduction and definitions dependent upon sexed bodies.[43]

A brief public dialogue on access to assisted reproduction by lesbians was facilitated on RTÉ radio in autumn 2004 by an interview with a lesbian couple on Marian Finucane's daily morning programme.[44] Any attempt to normalise lesbian relationships as families with reproductive potential was undone, however, by another participant in the interview, the founder of an internet-based sperm donor service called ManNotIncluded.com (MNI).[45] The discussion on the use of this service by lesbians was framed not as one possible strategy for reproduction but rather as a titillating exposé on two women producing a child together. My field notes in subsequent days describe the response to RTÉ, in the form of phone-ins and emails, as primarily negative. People expressed religious objections to either the use of donor sperm or same-sex relationships (or both), often backed with biblical references.

While the discussion on the radio programme was intended to raise awareness of a new kind of reproduction, it quickly became a forum for many people to discuss the importance of the social nexus of hetero-normative marriage and family as the site for morally acceptable reproductive activity. What emerges again is concern with the moral and social fallout of separating sex and procreation and the challenge it would pose to hetero-normativity. Thus, in addition to the social and political difficulties equal access to treatment might pose, the idea of same-sex procreation disrupts the meaning of biology as a basis for confirming gendered identities and the social meanings attributed to biological 'facts'. Public debates that serve only to reaffirm the hetero-norms of reproduction do little to enable a dissociation between reproductive organs, reproduction as performance and embodied femininity for either infertile women or women in lesbian relationships. In other words, women will continue to be defined socially by the meanings attributed to their reproductive bodies.

It was some months after the radio programme, on 28 April 2005, that I attended the lecture at University College Hospital in Cork in which Dr Deirdre Madden spoke about the need for practitioners of assisted reproduction services to respect the laws established by the Equal Status Acts. However, in a climate of legal uncertainty it seems that most same-sex couples have quietly gone abroad to undertake assisted reproduction as Aoife and Cara, whose story I told in Chapter 3, had done.

In a debate of the Oireachtas Committee for Health and Children in 2006 Mr Fergal Goodman, a representative of the Department of Health and Children, presented a report to the committee. The members of the oireachtas committee were anticipating a presentation of draft legislation in response to the CAHR report. The report presented by the officer representing the Department for Health and Children failed to meet this expectation on the part of the committee. In addition, his statements on the Equal Status Acts were less than reassuring.

> With regard to other legislation that might be impacted, Mr McCormack referred to the issue of parentage and adoption, which would be a crucial issue in any discussion of donor programmes. [. . .] Similarly, the Equal Status Acts are discussed in the report. We talk colloquially about couples and so on but there are different understandings of what a 'couple' might be in present-day society. We must consider where we would go with this issue vis-à-vis equal status legislation and whether it is appropriate, depending on the policy direction the government would wish to take, to ask what legislative measures, if any, might be needed in this area.[46]

Here the representative suggests that, while the CAHR recommended that access to treatment must not discriminate based on sexual orientation, it might be up to the legislature or the state to determine who can legitimately be considered a 'couple' with access to assisted reproduction. This suggests that equal status might conflict with other constitutional protections, such as marriage and the heterosexual family, necessitating a kind of shoring up with additional legislation to contain assisted reproduction in closely defined social contexts. For couples dubiously distinguished as 'colloquial' in the rhetoric of the state, the prospect of any legislation forthcoming that will assure their equality and rights in reproduction appears uncertain.

Conclusion

Reconfigured social meanings attributed to gametes confront the moral meanings embodied in the eggs and sperm people produce, use, share, dispose of or even purchase. I began this chapter by suggesting that the most important issues related to the use of donor gametes in Ireland were those emergent in the moral and ethical questions people ask themselves. But gametes and embryos appear in regulatory discourses as objects over which control must be exercised for their use and availability to infertile couples seeking assisted conception. At the same time, they become subjects of institutional discourses that constitute them in relation to potential personhood by virtue of their relationship to the persons who produce or receive them. As a kind of substance, gametes embody potential relationships and convey potential identities between and among various people who are part of a reproductive exchange.

In a seemingly unlimited field of possibility presented by assisted reproduction technologies, people still seek some kind of boundaries or ethical framework for defining what constitutes family and the nature of their relationship to offspring. For a few people, a clear legal and/or regulatory code would provide a measure of comfort about their choices around using ART to conceive. But for others it is not about legal identities but rather the biogenetic and moral meaning associated with what is encapsulated in an egg or sperm. People do not put their faith in science to explain the relationship between the self and the genetic material that constitutes potential production of another. Science deals in concrete, material processes that embody reproductive properties in gametes but sidestep any metaphysical properties of personhood. Religious discourse fails to fulfil its promise of an embodied ethics through the logic constituted as natural law where ethics are products of human reason and the nature of reproductive bodies should furnish the basis. This relies on a socially constructed definition of nature and an untenable link between bodies, sex and social responsibility in a heterosexual matrix that excludes many from the moral framework.

There is no single discourse or framework that meets the needs of all the people who contemplate the use of ART, as recipients or donors. Religious ethos, attempts at legislation and a medicalised construction of infertility all sit in uneasy tension as people also work through new forms and formations of family. Their narratives are evidence of how people make pragmatic choices even as their understanding of the implications of donor gametes is ambivalent and contradictory. Such contestation reveals the multiple meanings of family/kin relationships in an ongoing process of social change in Ireland.

7. Embryos and the Ethics of Ambivalence

Up to 8,000 couples attend Irish fertility clinics every year, which results in 1,000 babies being born by assisted human reproduction techniques. But thousands of couples are being denied the chance of a baby because there is no legislation to regulate IVF treatments. The Oireachtas Health Committee heard yesterday that fertile parents who want to donate embryos to childless couples can't do so because of the lack of legal framework (Irish Examiner, 16 September 2005).[1]

As I spoke to people about their experiences with assisted reproduction, and IVF in particular, one of the most complicated issues that arose was how to decide the fate of embryos that are created in the process. Because IVF often results in more embryos than can safely be returned to a woman's body, there is now a possibility of 'supernumerary' or surplus embryos. But in Ireland, as elsewhere, the moral and legal status of such entities must now be determined in relation to social norms and expectations; this poses a challenge when medical, religious and social values and definitions appear at odds with one another.[2] Moreover, the legal status of embryos has been a site of contestation in light of the constitutional protection of a right to life afforded to the 'unborn' in Ireland.

In this chapter I move forward from the processes of *in vitro* fertilisation to look at the ethical difficulties engendered by the products of IVF. Both change and consistency are evident in social values associated with procreation, gender and family politics; both also contribute to the challenges posed by the indeterminate legal, political and social status of the embryo in Ireland. This indeterminacy results in embryos being given a variety of voices and meanings. Citing examples from the past century, Lynn Morgan describes how embryos are made to 'speak' for various interests as their 'meanings arise out of historically particular social anxieties and controversies' such as 'immigration policy, evolution, eugenics and "race betterment", and comparative anatomy'.[3] The dominant social and political values that contribute to symbols of national identity also contribute to the decision-making context around medical technologies such as embryo freezing in assisted reproduction.

149

For example, Rebecca Sullivan describes how attitudes towards embryo disposition in Canada reflect a greater emphasis on their value as part of the health economy, a value fostered in part by the social significance of the healthcare system as a whole in defining national identity in contrast to say the United States.[4] Similarly, Lisa Smyth's description of Ireland as a pro-life nation raises questions about a potential political expediency in promoting a disposition for embryos that is either pro-life or at least unlikely to be antagonistic to proponents of a pro-life politics.[5] As both individuals and institutional actors in Ireland incorporate embryos into various real and imagined scenarios, they become storied entities in and of themselves, representing or speaking for a number of important concepts and meanings associated with reproduction and family life. They become the object of what has been described as 'embryo custody disputes', and public debates, however unwilling and contentious, are provoked and sustained for periods of time without any regulatory resolution.[6]

The last chapter illustrates how the creation and use of embryos through assisted reproduction constitutes a variety of relationships, not only with the biological progenitors but with a host of potential kin. Such relationships are part of a broader social context in which embryos, as entities with characteristics and dimensions, can be understood to have a kind of cultural life of their own, shaped by institutional discourses, social values and their location in physical space. These relationships also require that actions and meanings associated with embryos in an Irish context be thought through in both moral and ethical terms that are also products of Irish history and social norms.

Flagging both the social and emotional elements in morality, Zigon suggests it is 'the negotiable, contextually manifested, embodied sensibilities that have been shaped over a lifetime of experience within a socio-historic-cultural range of possibilities'.[7] Ethics, on the other hand, refers to the moment in which this sense of right or wrong must be put into practice in the act of making a choice. Ethics is the process of realising that we must decide what course of action to take, but also that a clear sense of right and wrong is not intuitively felt or immediately evident in every situation. In many of my discussions with people about the use of embryos, a sense of this dissonance between morality and ethics was again part of a narrative of change in the wake of a shifting allegiance to (or declining fear of) the moral authority formerly held by the Catholic Church. Attempts at filling the gaps in moral authority with a legal framework have created challenges in constitutional, contractual and property law, all of which seem inadequate to address the emotional angst that people feel as they seek answers.[8]

What emerges is an ethics of ambivalence in which people can often articulate a moral standpoint with respect to the nature and use of embryos in abstract terms and yet are ambivalent about the application of various options in relation to the concrete reality of their own embryos. Ambivalence, in this case, creates a means of sustaining uncertainty; it enables people to come back from the brink of a difficult decision that did not, in the end, have to be made. The creation of embryos *in vitro* engenders ethical problems never before encountered, but as Margarit Schildrick notes, in spite of the 'intrinsically unfamiliar' moral and ethical grounds constituted by medical technology, 'there is a strong tendency to continue to rely on models of moral evaluation that derive from a belief in fixed and normative templates as adequate to all knowledge'.[9] Many of the people I spoke with were aware that such normative templates, while useful for creating consent forms and clinic documents, failed to provide them with the tools to address the practical, emotional implications of any of the options available for embryos. These options that comprise the imagined, the possible and the acceptable include embryo donation or 'embryo adoption', scientific research such as work with stem cells, indefinite storage in a clinic, or destruction.

Conceptions of Surplus: Leftover Embryos

While the epigraph at the start of this chapter suggests that it is the lack of legal framework that is preventing the free exchange of embryos in a donation/adoption network in Ireland, in reality it is more complex; the ethics of ambivalence emerges within a deep chasm between the conceptual idea of having embryos that can be defined as extras and actually donating embryos, to research or to others. People are similarly ambivalent when they consider the ethics of extended freezing and/or destruction. As people worked through the conceptual problem of how to deal with surplus or leftover embryos on the basis of a moral framework, they often recognised the contradictions of their own positions. An embodied sense of right and wrong about what should be the fate of embryos, in theoretical terms, sometimes contradicted what people thought they would actually do as they worked through the ethical challenge of dealing with their own embryos. Emotional uncertainty coincided with an acknowledged moral uncertainty about the humanness or relatedness of their own embryos and how to deal with it in practical terms.

The backdrop for this kind of angst includes the public efforts of the Catholic Church to sustain its pro-life agenda in spite of the loss of its former moral authority. As part of the social, historical and cultural context that constitutes the sensibilities called 'morality', the Catholic Church has, as discussed above, been an important factor. This coincides with the lack of an alternative basis for legitimating decision-making such as legislation or an independent regulatory body to address the practices of ART in Ireland. But more importantly, this ambivalence speaks to the complexity that emerges in Ireland as people try to reconcile contradictions embodied in an embryo that seems to be at once inside and outside the family, society and the procreative context of the body.

An important distinction must be made because embryos only become *extra* or *leftover* when there is a successful treatment and a decision must be made. They can only cease to be imagined as potential family members or children at the point when they become part of the cohort of 'new biologicals' as a result of IVF and now excess.[10] The Irish Catholic Bishops' Conference flags this point in a response to the CAHR report:

> [P]arenthood brings with it a responsibility of care. In the normal course of events, we would always recommend that the implications of this responsibility should be considered carefully *before* people become parents. In the case of assisted reproductive therapy, fertilisation takes place in a laboratory rather than in the mother's body. This distancing of the embryo from its parents does not, however, justify any abdication of the responsibility of care. The parents and, together with them, the 'quasi-parents' (those who assist them in the process) have no less an obligation to care for the embryo and to provide it with every possible opportunity of developing normally and coming to birth. To suggest that the embryos are 'surplus' is disingenuous if we have been responsible for the process which made them 'surplus' in the first place.[11]

The Bishops' Conference committee makes an interesting postmodern suggestion in calling the medical practitioners involved in an assisted conception 'quasi-parents'. They are emphasising their point that 'procreation' and everything about it, including the production and exchange of gametes, is about parental responsibility. While the statement above is obviously an extreme example of the church's stance on the meaning of procreation, the question about how embryos are constituted as surplus identities exposes the slippery distinctions and artifice of nature, culture and science as discrete categories when embryos refuse to stay in one line or another. Instead they move between adoptable family members, products of nature, and scientific objects. How does an embryo become a leftover and what is its moral status?

In the following story, Lara describes the complex social position of embryos and her own thoughts on the ethics of embryo donation. This is a possibility she *imagines* for excess embryos as she continues her narrative about the options she and her partner have considered in their quest to conceive. She tells her story from the point of view of a potential beneficiary but also as a potential saviour who might rescue embryos as an alternative to the forever-frozen scenario that is now a possibility as a result of *in vitro* fertilisation technologies.

> LARA: *Now this moves me on to donor embryos. This is something I'm very interested in because it seems to me that it solves the problem for a lot of people concerned. First of all there are a lot of leftover embryos from IVF in freezers all over the world, and they're going to be there until kingdom come if somebody doesn't rescue them. I know before our first IVF we thought about what happens if there are leftover embryos – and we thought we'd keep going back and we'd use them all up. Well, as it happens, we only had three maximum, ever, but there was never any question of us abandoning them in a freezer forever. [. . .] I wouldn't be comfortable getting donor embryos from parents who are not married to each other. So in other words if people who use say, donor egg or donor sperm to create their embryos, I wouldn't be comfortable. For the very reason that I feel that I need to explain to my kids . . . you know, where they come from – I feel they have the right to know that for medical reasons and all that. I feel we'll probably end up using donor embryos. The problem is you can't do it in this country and we'd have to go abroad and more money, more hassles, and probably more failures. But anyway donor embryo seems to be the way to go ethically, and also you're looking after them previously. You know that the parents who begat them because they did IVF they were expecting to get pregnant, so they ate well. They were probably more than likely in good shape.*

Lara's discussion of the moral grey zone in which embryos might be donated and received is rooted firmly in the association between marriage and kinship relations and yet alludes to the 'leftover' embryo as a potential child. But how does an entity constituted as a 'leftover' fit into a moral framework embedded in state discourses in which sexual morality, reproduction, motherhood and family have been marshalled into the politics of nationalist identity? It is here that the ethics of ambivalence is produced in the zone between objectified embryos as leftovers and subjectified embryos as potential offspring, sometimes left in limbo. While the Irish state seems unable to provide any objective framework for how to define the former, individuals struggle to make sense of an entity that can be a subject in its relationship to the progenitors and an object in its potential for exchange.

As discussed in the last chapter, assisted reproduction technologies participate in the redefining of kinship, relatedness, parenthood and family. The complexity continues, and perhaps deepens, with the fusing of gametes as the search for meanings moves beyond biological or genetic relatedness to incorporate notions of potential personhood and actual social relationships beyond kinship.[12] The stories in this chapter will highlight how people locate embryos in previously unimagined contexts in terms of space and kinship relations. These stories also show how a number of ethical perspectives are challenged, upheld or proven inadequate to the task of understanding the embryo in subjective, spatial and familial terms in the Irish social and political context. What becomes apparent is that context, as well as the decontextualisation and recontextualisation[13] of embryos as 'new biologicals', plays an important role in the contested and reluctant public discourse on new reproductive technologies in Ireland.

Competing Discourses

The legislative and regulatory void with respect to ART is perhaps most profound when it comes to the treatment of embryos *in vitro*. A number of events widely discussed in the media, including the release of the CAHR report in 2005 and a court case involving the fate of frozen embryos in 2006, have also framed opportunities for public debate on regulation and have provided a space in which embryos are made to 'speak' on behalf of a number of interests. Marilyn Strathern suggests that regulatory debates and legislative change provide an obvious place for social scientists to examine social tension.[14] However, as many of the stories below will illustrate, it is also important to explore how people, for whom such regulation matters, might employ institutional discourses in their own stories.

The designation 'unborn' in Article 40.3.3 of the Irish Constitution has hinged on the idea of moral personhood and human dignity that is central to the pro-life position on abortion.[15] I revisit this here because the question of personhood in embryos underpins much of the ethical reticence that is a feature of both public debate and private deliberation about embryos created through IVF in Ireland. Historically, even in the ethos of the Roman Catholic Church, the moral status for the foetus has been contested and has changed over time. The embryo's current status of moral personhood from the moment of conception can be traced to Pope Pius IX who, in 1869 dropped a prior distinction between the *foetus animatus* and *foetus inanimatus* originating in the teachings of Aristotle and incorporated by Thomas Aquinas.[16] Nonetheless, the pro-life arguments put forward by the church have exerted a dampening effect on public debate around ART.

Looking at it from the perspective of Foucault's 'repressive hypothesis', a proliferation of discourses that speak of the unspeakable aspects of something that deviates from norms simultaneously reinforces the established norms through both discipline and pleasure. The perpetual discussion about the need for regulation has tended to reinforce the moral and ethical edginess of the whole ART process.[17] Orla McDonnell has also argued that the reticence of the Irish state to open the debate too widely is the legacy of the painful and divisive politics during the abortion referenda in the 1980s.[18] Moreover, the apparent refusal of the government to address the issue directly operates to consolidate further the norm of heterosexual fertility and a perception of abnormality associated with an inability to conceive without biomedical assistance.

In spite of the rather solidly entrenched moral and ethical value base in the Eighth Amendment of the Irish Constitution, the Catholic Church and conservative pro-life advocates find themselves in need of a secular platform from which to argue their perspective in the debate around ART. The hierarchy of the Catholic Church has employed bioethics as a kind of 'metaframe' to add weight to their arguments even as they assert the ethical primacy of their position over all others.[19] In its discursive turn to a bioethics platform, the church is reanimating its own ethical position that privileges the 'right to life' over reproductive choice using the rational and authoritative terms of science and medicine as an exercise in semantics. The Bishops' Conference draws on an embryology textbook, emphasising 'organic unity' and arguing that the fertilised ovum is 'biologically human'.[20] The CAHR report, on the other hand, established at the outset that it would not engage in an exercise of semantics around such terms as 'pre-embryo' in describing various stages of development of the fertilised ovum, suggesting this only adds confusion.[21] Biological terminology is used as if it refers to both natural and social fact in an effort to assert authority in bioethical discourses. This is evident not only in legislative or regulatory debates, as a means of redefining the object of regulation, but also in discourses of medical practice as a means of sidestepping the contested term 'embryo' by focusing on a subdivision of its stages of development.[22]

This bioethics platform has been the site where power relations and collisions between church and medicine play out, sometimes publicly and sometimes behind closed doors. For example, in October 2005 it came to light that the ethics committees at both the Mater Hospital and St Vincent's in Dublin had 'deferred' participation, effectively denying patients in their institutions the opportunity to participate in an international study for a treatment protocol for lung cancer. Their refusal was based on the fact that, as criteria for participation, women were required to use contraception to prevent pregnancy while they were on the study drug. One oncologist reported his intention to bypass the ethics committee since new rules governing European drug trials allow physicians to avoid hospitals with a religious affiliation.[23]

The long-awaited release of the CAHR's final report in May 2005[24] revealed that the issue of the status of the 'unborn' as it applied to embryos *in vitro* was, predictably, the major obstruction to development of regulation or public policy on ART.[25] In spite of its clear recommendation that 'implantation' of the embryo in the womb should be the basis for defining 'unborn', the commission did not successfully reconcile assisted reproduction and the production of supernumerary embryos with Article 40.3.3 of the Irish Constitution. While the recommendations were drafted and a report made public, there were two letters of dissent from members of the Commission attached to the final report that garnered some media attention at the time.[26] The fallout from competing ethical discourses resonates beyond the Commission itself as the institutions of church, state and medicine have all acknowledged a need for some kind of regulatory framework for the practice of ART in Ireland.

Parliamentary debates that led to the Human Embryology and Fertilisation Act in the UK in 1990 focused on defining embryogenesis and establishing precise biological timeframes that could be employed as a basis for the social determination of individual personhood.[27] Language matters and the concern for precision in the terminology and the appropriation of particular discourses by various actors indicate the intense desire to convey the image of clarity, authority and objectivity around the issue. Franklin points to this as an example of 'natural' facts woven into social logics that create meanings and come to underwrite regulation in reproduction and kinship.[28] Attempts to define, authoritatively, the 'nature' of the embryo also feature in Irish regulatory discourses.

A Precarious Existence: Decontextualised Embryos

> *The child has the right to be conceived, carried in the womb, brought into the world and brought up within marriage: it is through the secure and recognised relationship to his own parents that the child can discover his own identity and achieve his own proper human development. (Donum Vitae – Instruction on Respect for Human Life in its Origin and on the Dignity of Procreation).[29]*

In addition to the issue of stages, time and process of cellular development, another aspect is significant in the burgeoning, albeit limited, political discussions around developing regulation. The release of the CAHR report and recommendations in 2005 was one of a number of contested but important attempts at defining the scope and meaning of the term 'unborn' in relation to embryos produced *in vitro* in Ireland through discourse and authority. This event, along with another, brought the regulatory debate on ART into public focus in ways that drew attention to the importance of embryo context. The second, which I will discuss later in this section, is a recent High Court ruling, later upheld by the Supreme Court on appeal, in a case involving three frozen embryos.[30] Both propose it is only through implantation – a spatial association with women's reproductive bodies – that the embryo gains the status of being unborn and, by implication, the legal protection of the Constitution. In both cases, the indeterminate meaning of 'unborn' in the Irish Constitution has been a point of contention and the issue that confounds, most directly, attempts to establish conceptual clarity in moving forward with regulation.[31] Such debates also animate discussion among people who contemplate IVF. As Niamh suggests below, there are points of biological necessity that can be used to define when the embryo moves from something to a living being or someone.

> NIAMH: *While I was doing philosophy I was going out with a scientist. And he'd always put a spanner in the whole works [laughter]. But I don't know. I don't allow myself to think about it, probably. I probably don't allow myself to think about it but I really can't see anything happening until implantation occurs. I think once you have implantation . . . but until you have implantation, yeah something is there but I don't see it as being a living being in the end, right? It's not a person, right? It needs to be fed by another living being and it needs to be in the little box it's kept in . . .*

Strathern notes that assisted reproduction represents 'the paradox of a context whose rationale of boundless opportunity is substantively "about" decontextualisation'.[32] In Ireland, this paradox means that efforts to regulate the production of embryos are stalled by questions of a conceptual context in which the embryos produced may or may not retain the same political, social and moral status outside the womb as inside the womb; context is everything, and embryos outside a procreative context are potential free radicals without an embodied identity.

In the record of the debate that took place in the Oireachtas Committee for Health and Children in July 2005 regarding the recently presented CAHR report, Deputy Liam Twomey challenges Mr Brian Mullen, the principal officer of the CAHR, on the issue of clarity.

> DEPUTY TWOMEY: Before we start on the issues, can we have Mr Mullen's views on how far this committee can go in this regard? One issue that continually crops up in the report concerns Article 40.3.3° of the Constitution and when the unborn child gets the

protection of the State. Until such time as that decision is made – this committee cannot make that decision – we are in territory about which we can do nothing. [. . .] It seems, therefore, that the most contentious aspects of the report [. . .] cannot go any further until either the Supreme Court decides whether the unborn child is protected *in vitro* or *in utero* or until we have a referendum on the matter. Has this been discussed by the Department? It is important to do that so that this committee can know how far it can go on the issue. [. . .]

MR MULLEN: The issue of the unborn and when it is afforded the protection of Article 40.3.3° is discussed in detail in Appendix III of the commission's report. The deputy is right that this issue runs through the report. Until there is clarification on the issue, the question of when the embryo is afforded protection and when human life begins is an issue crucial to the whole area of embryo research, destruction of surplus embryos and similar issues. [. . .]

DEPUTY TWOMEY: The Supreme Court could decide one way or another. Currently, if people allow embryos to 'perish', they will be considered by some to have committed murder. The same goes with regard to embryonic stem cell research. It cannot be carried out until the issue is clarified. The medical opinions on the issue do not matter. This is both a legal and constitutional issue and we must deal with it.[33]

Two issues emerge from this exchange between these political actors, as they try to define the terms of a debate that has not yet happened. The first is that the question of an embryo's entitlement to protection under Article 40.3.3 is never challenged. Instead both parties in this exchange are in apparent agreement that the embryo is, as Deputy Twomey clearly states, an 'unborn child'. They suggest that the only issue to be clarified is when and under what conditions the embryos will be included under the protection of the 'right to life' constitutional clause. The second is Deputy Twomey's exclusion of the medical profession from a regulatory decision-making process.[34] It is perhaps most significant that, in spite of a recognised need, there has not been, to date, any full-scale legislative debate on the issue of ART in Ireland. The subject appears instead as an occasional topic on the agenda of committee and subcommittee meetings such as the one cited above, and most often in discussions around subsidising the cost of fertility drugs or providing tax relief for such expenditures.[35]

In addition to debates about the constitutional definition, there is another important point in relation to the definition of the embryo as 'unborn' that employs the context of implantation in the womb. In 2006, a case was brought before the Irish courts which set assisted reproduction technologies on a collision course with the legal and bioethical conundrum created by Ireland's Eighth Amendment. The case involved a couple who had divorced some time after successfully conceiving their second child with a course of IVF at a fertility clinic in Dublin in 2004.[36] They were left with three frozen embryos, preserved in a kind of cryo-limbo. The moral, ethical and legal conundrum was forced into the public domain of the courts when the woman involved asked the clinic to transfer the embryos to her body in 2006. While she argued that the embryos have a 'right to life' as her unborn children and as siblings for her existing children,[37] her former husband argued that he agreed only to the treatment as a means of conceiving a second child and did not want to use the remaining embryos to have any more children with his former wife.[38] The case was argued on the basis of the contractual elements, since the courts rely on case law and require some basis from which to draw a decision.

While the arguments are obviously nuanced in terms of the particulars of this marital dispute and arguments over custody, support and ongoing family relations, this case highlighted, for Irish legislators and policy makers as well as the public, the need to build a consensus in order to make a decision rather than passing the problem from one committee to another. A spokesperson for the National Infertility Support and Information Group and a spokesperson for the Pro-Life Campaign both agreed that the situation was a result of a lack of legislation. However, despite their consensus on the need for regulation, they represented opposing sides of the debate about whether embryo freezing should occur at all.[39] Similar sentiments were widely expressed in the media by physicians who argued that this case was an example of the difficulties that emerge for clinical practice in the absence of clear legislation or regulation.

This case shows how the creation of embryos *in vitro* forces a re-evaluation of the term 'unborn' since the embryo in cryo-preservation is not yet part of the dependent and connected relationship of pregnancy through which it might achieve the *capacity* to be born – a feature that would, as has been argued, seem a necessity if one is to be called 'unborn'. In June 2006, the High Court brought down a ruling that seemed to concur with the CAHR recommendation that the embryo did not merit status as 'unborn', which would require that the state intervene to protect it until it was 'implanted' in the womb.[40] Justice Brian McGovern ruled against the woman in the R vs R case based only on the contractual elements related to the intention in creating the embryos. The decision was appealed and the Supreme Court upheld the ruling in its decision in December 2009. Nonetheless, the court rulings and the recommendation of the CAHR have implications for re-imagining the meaning of women's reproductive bodies as political spaces since it is the location of the embryo that now determines its status as an 'unborn citizen' protected by the state.[41]

The ruling has resulted in no legal clarity and the *in vitro* embryo remains a biological entity with an indeterminate and as yet undefined political and social status in Ireland. Any measure of clarity pertains only to 'when' the constitutional protection applies to embryos as 'unborn', sidestepping the issue of whether embryos are in fact 'unborn' in any case. Indeed, High Court Justice Brian McGovern compelled fertility clinics to maintain embryos indefinitely until legislation could be passed, saying that rather than the courts, the people of Ireland should decide by a referendum whether the word 'unborn' should include embryos resulting from IVF treatment. He noted that 'in the absence of any rules or regulations in this jurisdiction, embryos outside the womb have a very precarious existence'.[42] This indeterminacy was sustained in the ruling on appeal by five Supreme Court judges in 2009.[43] Such clashes between different perspectives on when life begins and the meaning of events in the process of fertilisation and/or conception are not new; nor are they unique to Ireland. They are, however, uniquely nuanced in terms of the political significance of the current impasse.[44] The lack of legislation becomes both the reason for and the result of the sustained lack of clarity. The legislators have argued that the Irish court must decide, and the High Court and Supreme Court have clearly passed the ball back to the legislators. Meanwhile, clinics already have practices in place, discussed in more detail below. Medical protocols have been established around the pragmatism of logistics and cost for maintaining embryos indefinitely, based on the construction of a scientific sense that embryos cannot remain viable in cryo-preservation indefinitely. Because people are paying for the service, it seems that clinics are only obligated to store embryos as long as the fees are paid, and would seem to be released from culpability even in light of Justice McGovern's warning.

The case before the Irish courts regarding the fate of the frozen embryos was much discussed on the IVF support boards such as *IVFConnections* and *Rollercoaster* which I continued to follow after I left the field. I asked one of my participants with whom I keep in touch for her thoughts on the dispute between the couple.

> GAIL: *As far as I am concerned any embryo that is suitable for transfer is one of my children. Therefore any embryo that is frozen is already our child and we are already its parents. A lot of what is said . . . usually by the father in these cases, is about the fact that they don't want to have any more children with the woman involved or that they don't want to be a*

father at this time. Well you know what? TOUGH SHIT!! You are
already a father. You became one the day you handed over the sample on
the day the eggs were retrieved. What you don't want now is to be a Dad.

When she asked her husband what he would want to do if they had frozen embryos and their marriage ended he replied, 'sell them on eBay'. Humour aside, Gail clearly draws on a discourse of parental responsibility that constitutes the embryos in a particular linear perspective that begins with the sperm and egg in the process of reproduction. When it comes to the challenges of regulating IVF in Ireland, embryos have been made to speak in the interests of both medical and religious perspectives. What is interesting is that embryos are made to speak as moral subjects about themselves as moral objects; as individual family members apart from and external to an embodied procreative relationship.

Frozen in Cryo-Limbo

The freezing of embryos in Ireland has had political and moral implications as its meaning shifted from cutting-edge technology to saviour science. The ethics of technology is the purview of the medical profession and in spite of Deputy Twomey's argument in the section above, the Irish Medical Council has been an active institutional player in the bioethics/regulatory debate. The Council has been a 'self-regulating' overseer and has progressively, albeit quietly, made amendments to its Ethical Guidelines to accommodate changes in the practice of ART over a twenty-year period. The revisions in 1998 to *A Guide to Ethical Conduct and Behaviour and Fitness to Practice* (4th edition) addressed the issue of embryo freezing.[45] Prior to the technological capacity to freeze in the late 1990s, all embryos created *in vitro* had to be transferred to the body of the mother and physicians had sometimes used creative ways of dealing with the presence of multiple embryos. It came to light during a television debate in 1999 that 'supernumerary' embryos were often placed in the cervix rather than the womb during the embryo transfer phase of IVF, virtually guaranteeing that they would have no hope of successfully implanting and going on to a pregnancy. This practice enabled physicians to follow the letter of the law, since all the embryos created were being transferred to the body of the mother, but still prevented the possibility of a triplet, quadruplet or higher multiple pregnancy.[46] At least one of my participants made her decision to seek treatment in the UK at this time, based on an ethical adversity to this practice.

DONNA: *I'd gone to England because here there was no freezing of embryos at that time. And I couldn't cope with the fact of extra embryos being left at the neck of your womb which happened here in Ireland at the time.*

The advent of cryo-preservation or embryo freezing was spun by Irish medical practitioners as a positive advance in the effort to preserve the life of embryos created by IVF. The difficulty in arriving at a consensus within the medical community is highlighted by the report of a subcommittee of the Executive Council of the Institute of Obstetricians and Gynecologists. The subcommittee executed a questionnaire to physicians around the country asking, rather ambiguously, whether freezing should be available. The question, as it was posed to physicians at the time, required further clarification in order to elicit answers from the medical community and a breakdown of the terms under which this might be allowed.[47]

However, while placing embryos in the cervix attempted to solve, quietly, the dilemma posed by a treatment process that regularly created a surplus, embryo freezing has quietly continued without any regulatory provision for the ongoing maintenance of these entities, or their disposal in any circumstances. During an interview, one embryologist noted there is also a quiet practice of allowing embryos to perish on the bench of labs when people no longer wish to support them in storage or when they are deemed past their 'best before date' (five years in most clinics).[48] While no statistics are readily available, at least one media story in 2006 reported speculative estimates of between one hundred and two hundred frozen embryos in each of four clinics offering the service.[49] The cost of storing embryos varies between €150 and €1,000 per year in Irish clinics with differing initial freezing costs included or added to the cost of treatment.[50] The cost and the logistics often provoke the realisation that, as strategy, ambivalence and avoidance have limits, and people who have supernumerary embryos must ultimately make a decision about the fate of their own embryos.

For Siobhan embryo freezing represented no salvation or solution to a dilemma about what to do with 'extra embryos'. Her narrative begins with what she describes as the 'disappointment before it is a disappointment'. She felt that because so many embryos perished during the thawing procedure, leaving fewer to work with in the subsequent treatment cycle, the preparation for the IVF cycle seemed like a futile and painful exercise. This constituted a failure of a different sort since the embryos already existed and she and her partner had eagerly anticipated their return in the embryo transfer process. The embryos seemed to them to be potential children and their loss only compounded the disappointment.

SIOBHAN: No, I think there was only one put back. They had three, and then the first day it went to two, and then the second day it went to one. I think that was partly what put us off as well, because you start off with three which seems to be reasonable and the frozen cycle was supposed to be less trouble. But as far as I was concerned it wasn't really less trouble because you still ended up taking the same amount of drugs and yes, you know, you had the embryos. But then after you've gone through all of this, they ended up just putting back in one. And it went nowhere. So it was kind of like, the odds are against you. [. . .] It was actually kind of a disappointment even before it was a disappointment, so. I guess that was just our particular situation but if you don't do that [freeze] then what do you do with them? [. . .] Really that wasn't our dilemma but that would be a dilemma. It wouldn't be because of what the Catholic Church says but it would be just a moral dilemma in its own right. [. . .] I think I would have had a problem with that alright. The situation didn't arrive for us. It gets really crazy thinking about whether you leave them or whether you would go back for them. But anyhow I guess our sort of chapter closed neatly so it's not really a problem for us.

It is clear that for Siobhan and her partner, embryo freezing was not a panacea for either the moral or ethical dilemma of having made more embryos than could be used. If anything, the option made the process more fraught with difficult choices and painful surprises when so many of the embryos seemed to be lost in the freezing and thawing process itself. While the medical discourse is built on minimising the 'loss' of embryos and reducing the ethical difficulties and physiological hardships for couples, clearly this is not the case in reality for many couples in treatment who are trading in a kind of economy of hope.[51]

There is currently no mechanism for donating embryos to research or to other infertile couples in Ireland. Medical Council guidelines were changed in 2004 to accommodate the prospect that embryos created through IVF could be donated to couples other than the genetic contributors. In an article in *The Irish Times*, an unidentified Medical Council representative stated that couples receiving a donated embryo should be screened in a similar way to couples seeking adoption.[52] There is a suggestion in this and related articles at the time that screening may be done through the Adoption Board associated with regional health boards.[53] This portrayal of the embryo as an 'adoptee' participates in the discourse of embryo 'citizenship' being debated in relation to the constitutional meaning of the 'unborn' for which the right to life obtains.[54] This nebulous suggestion of personhood might thus accommodate pro-life concerns but risks creating not only a moral but legal dilemma for people who have undergone IVF and must consider what they will do with their 'spare' embryos.

Since that fleeting and unrealised potential for embryo adoption was codified in the Medical Council Guidelines, the guidelines have changed again. The most recent edition of the *Guide to Professional Conduct and Ethics* was published in 2009 and among the changes pertaining to the practice of assisted reproduction is an absence with respect to the treatment of embryos. While in 2004 the Medical Council guidelines suggested that embryos could be adopted, there is in fact a 'repeal' or deletion of this reference. Walsh *et al.* suggest that this leaves embryos in an even more precarious position since there seems to be no professional ethical imperative to consider their fate. They argue that this is partly a result of the changes in governance in the Medical Council with a shift towards non-medical majority, and distinctly less pro-life, membership as directed by the Medical Practitioners Act of 2007.[55] Here embryos speak for changing dynamics in the politics of medicine as the loss of power on the Medical Council is seen by some to put embryos in greater peril in clinics across the country, even as it is clearly a move to shift the balance of values within the committee itself.

The suggestion that embryos might be *adopted* raises the difficult position vis-à-vis the constitutional protection of the 'inalienable and imprescriptible rights' accorded to the family unit. Clearly the Medical Council was unable to find any tenable way to enable the process. However, the absence of guidelines creates an even wider regulatory gap and even fewer roadmaps for people.

Conceived in Paradox

Lara's story, discussed above, highlights an ethical dilemma people face when trying to imagine who or what embryos are and to whom they are related in a new complex that incorporates both kinship and biological categories of meaning. Embryos, as 'new biologicals', are part of what Franklin describes as 'new biologies [. . .] the material-semiotic practices of the contemporary sciences' effected by a 'conflation of a system of knowledge and its object'.[56] Like gamete donation, the discursive exploitation of 'nature' in defining aspects of procreation is powerful in establishing normative and moral limits. The capacity of science to claim and define both biology and 'biologicals' as part of a domain of expertise similarly constitutes the power to legitimate certain practices in assisted reproduction.

The idea of nature as a model of, or for, culture has been widely challenged. The focus of this critique as discussed in previous chapters includes exposing the ways in which cultural meanings define what is 'nature' and 'the natural'[57] and exploring the extent to which nature, as a concept, is re-invented to fit cultural definitions.[58] As Franklin notes, this creates an interesting frame for postmodernist arguments that have dissociated kinship and gender from essentialised biological or natural definitions; this is all the more significant since the meaning of what is biological is now under scrutiny from within the discipline of science itself.[59] In her work in Greece, Paxson found that the use of IVF could be aligned with the social construct of 'realising nature', harnessing technology to accomplish what is naturally determined by gender.[60] The shifting meaning of nature and biology thus adds to the complexities and dilemmas that arise when people make decisions about embryos since it is both the biological and social nature of embryos that makes their place in families and laboratories so difficult to define.

One obstacle, as I have argued, is the constitutional primacy of maintaining the integrity of the family and guarding against divisive or disruptive interventions – principles that have animated much of the legislation on family policy in Ireland. State policies that favour the legal integrity of the procreative family unit and the constitutional protection of the 'unborn' shape the political background against which people imagine opportunities for exchanging 'leftover' embryos. In her work in Ecuador, also a predominantly Roman Catholic country, Elizabeth Roberts explores how people draw on two seemingly incompatible ethical frameworks when making decisions about embryos created through IVF. She describes a distinction between 'life ethics', which holds to the fundamental personhood of embryos, and 'kin ethics' which is based on a desire to 'regulate the legitimate boundaries of kin relations'.[61] This distinction operates at the level of decision making for couples who have 'spare' embryos after IVF and must decide whether to freeze them or destroy them. Social and biological meanings of kin relations form seemingly opposing logics in decisions to preserve or destroy embryos.

Roberts describes how kin ethics underpin a concern that frozen embryos might be used by others, breaching the boundaries of the family and kin relations. An ethics based on this framework favours the destruction of unused embryos as a means of containing them within the family. The opposing pro-life view which provides for the donation of embryos to preserve them as life in fact objectifies the embryos as commodities which can be exchanged – a concept that seems at odds with a perspective that would personify embryos as subjects. I would argue, however, that the divide is not so neatly effected in Ireland in spite of a strongly developed notion of the importance of family and kinship relations as described in earlier chapters. In this case, embryo-speak is part of discourse which sustains the ideal procreative family household as a site of social and political stability, as reassuringly hetero-normative. For most people, the idea of destroying their own embryos in order to preserve the integrity and biological cohesion of the family unit was unthinkable, and discarding embryos was only spoken of in hypothetical terms as a kind of worst-case scenario that might be experienced by someone else.

The difficulty in Ireland, as Lara points out, is that the possibility for donation of embryos exists only in the political and social imagination. Lara's story suggests that, even as she values embryos as offspring, they are still potential objects of exchange. And yet, a different kind of kin ethics is also at play here, since Lara wants embryos to be both produced and contained within a household family unit circumscribed by a marriage.

Cryo-Limbo: Embryos in Suspension

I met Gail and Martin at their home in a small urban centre and we conducted the interview in their sitting room amid blankets and plush toys and baby gear of every description. It was a Mothercare[62] mother lode and their son was clearly the centre of their lives (and sometimes our interview). I asked Gail and Martin about an upcoming cycle of IVF and the possibility of having frozen embryos as a result. Their first child had come to them through IVF and was the result not of the original cycle but a cycle using frozen embryos after the first attempt had not succeeded. Their perspective is of course deeply influenced by the fact that a frozen cycle was successful for them and that one of the embryos they had waiting in cryo-preservation before that cycle would ultimately become their son. They spoke about the promise that a frozen cycle can hold in the face of a failed IVF treatment. And yet their response was somewhat surprising.

> JILL: *What will you do if this cycle works but you have frozen embryos? Will you go back again?*
> GAIL: *We've talked about that and Martin's response was that, well by that stage we'll be able to donate the embryos. I'd love to be able to do that if there was embryo donation. I'd have absolutely no problem at all with that. And I would hope ultimately to do a donor egg cycle after we've had our second baby because two was our number anyway. Because we were bordering on doing a donor sperm, having a child that wasn't genetically both of ours. And if I can give couples this opportunity then it would be the greatest honour, to me, to offer that to somebody.*
> JILL: *And the prospect of there being a genetic sibling if you donated embryos, out there somewhere, does that bother you?*
> GAIL: *I would need it to be . . . I would need the legislation surrounding it to be the same as with an adoption situation where at eighteen there was a possibility of contact situation [. . .] I would like to be in a situation*

where somebody might be able to look me up. There is a risk of him [their own son] meeting his half-sister.
JILL: But if there is no possibility for donating embryos will you cycle again with frozen embryos?
GAIL: I personally would feel that I have to have IVF because otherwise the embryos are not given a reasonable chance. Now if they're just put in the right environment, the idea of just leaving them sit on the counter and letting them slowly die . . .
[she lets her voice trail here]

Gail's narrative reflects a certain faith in state legislation or regulation to legitimise the kind of conflation of kin and life ethics that embryo donation (or 'embryo adoption') might provide. But more importantly, like most people, when asked about the potential for losing embryos in the process of treatment, freezing or thawing, Gail makes the comparison with 'nature' in which embryos might not implant or are miscarried and lost on a regular basis.[63] In Gail's narrative, there even appears to be little or no margin between eggs that are 'lost' or not used in menstrual cycles and the embryos that are lost in the processes of IVF.

The blurring of natural and medical events involving the loss or wastage (as described in Chapter 8) of both gametes and embryos shapes an ethical explanation that draws on biology and nature to justify what is 'naturally' inevitable. Paxson describes how the merging of nature and ART in Greece is part of an ethics in which nature is being realised or attained, in which the end – the achievement of one's nature – justifies the means. However, for people like Gail in Ireland, this merger acknowledges that the ethical problem with IVF lies in the moral emphasis that values the meaning of conception. People must 'fold' the events of an IVF conception into nature in the same way that Paxson describes how Greek women are able to absorb IVF as part of nature in their emphasis on gestation and birth.[64] When conception is the site of moral debates, loss of embryos becomes more important and thus the dominant focus of attempts to reconcile nature and IVF.

When asked about the issue of donated embryos being genetic siblings (like fraternal twins) for a child they might have using IVF, Gail relates it to an adoption. In fact, she suggests that legislation would be required for her to make the necessary move to effectively 'give up' an embryo to another family. The desire to protect and ensure that embryos become members of a family, if not the family who generated them, can again be linked to that complex ethics that moves between seeing embryos as objects that can be given away and as subjects who are members of one's family.[65] It is this ambiguous and indeterminate aspect of embryo 'nature' or identity that is so hard to locate in concrete terms in stories like Gail's.

Among the forty women/couples I interviewed, twenty-one had undertaken IVF, and only one had not yet used all the embryos that were created from their gametes. This couple had frozen embryos that were produced from donor gametes on both sides. The people who spoke favourably of the idea of donating embryos to other couples were generally in the midst of a treatment cycle that had not yet produced any embryos. This was a hopeful stage in which they imagined themselves successfully conceiving in the first round of IVF, thus leaving them with the luxury of a 'choice' about spare embryos. As I noted above, the Medical Council had, in its earlier guidelines, incorporated the possibility of a kind of embryo 'adoption' into its regulatory framework but since this option is not available in Ireland it was an imaginary scenario in the interviews in which it came up.

It is revealing that in these imaginary scenarios the embryo is described as if it is a child for someone else, another couple who will become its parents. Having constituted scientifically and medically the personhood of embryos in their visibility and existence outside the body, as a kind of patient-hood, it is all but impossible *not* to envision embryos as having a social position, relationships and attributes as well.[66] It is this construction of personhood that animates the desire for embryo donation among the people I spoke with in Ireland and yet, as Gail's story suggests, this also makes embryos objects of exchange. While she thinks of any frozen embryo as her child, she can also see the potential to relinquish it to another family. Roberts notes in her work that the perception of embryos as being part of kin networks tends to limit the 'circulation' of embryos as objects of exchange that might have a market value. In contrast, in Ireland the imaginary opportunity to 'gift' or offer embryos to others suggests an exchange mechanism in which the givers are benevolent and helpful and the embryos are children for someone else. This has the effect of rendering, in hypothetical terms at least, the problem of spare embryos as moot.

Not everyone thought that this was a solution, however. Tara and Kelly have two children conceived with assisted reproduction.

> JILL: *Would you think about donating embryos to somebody else?*
> KELLY: *I don't think I could.*
> TARA: *I don't think so. Because if I was going to go through that again I'd be doing that for myself.*
> KELLY: *And I couldn't bear the thought of my own child being out there. And I know that's very greedy. I know that's denying somebody something that I have. That we have.*

TARA: [*speaking to her husband*] *But embryos, I think with embryos it would be you. It would be the two of us. But with eggs it's different.*
KELLY: *I think I could reconcile myself to eggs or sperm. But the fact that it's ours. I suppose maybe that means that I do think about it as a life and you know that with . . . It's a difficult one, I have to say, having gone through IVF and all that and I try not to think about it too much. It is a weird one because we talked about adoption a lot when we were on the adoption list . . . You know certainly I think we'd make the decision in our mind about the adoption that the child would be ours. Genetically it just doesn't matter. It is the bond that you form with the child that is the most important thing. And yet I couldn't bear to think of . . . our own child out there. That's why it is such a problem because your views are contradictory. It brings up many emotions. It's very much, you know, scientifically this is where it's at, medically it's worth that but there's absolutely no account of people's feelings in it. You meet up with that in NISIG, people just feel emotionally separated from it. As if this all happens here in the middle and it is nothing to do with you. It's doctors and obstetricians and all those people and they really just screw around with you. Very clinical detachment, I suppose the detachment needs to be there so most people can do their jobs, but there are times when they shouldn't be so detached from it.*

The incorporation of science and medicine into a procreative and family-building process is not comfortable for many people. Ambivalence provides the means of accommodating an inability to reconcile or make a decision – it becomes an ethical stance in and of itself. Tara and Kelly acknowledge contradiction when they think about their own embryos, as products of their gametes, as both life and kin. They can envision donating gametes and can rationalise the benefits of donation with respect to embryos that are not their own, but their embryos are family members and siblings for their children. This kind of challenge has also been described in American research as couples think much differently about an embryo as a product of both people in a relationship; the focus is less on genetics in this case and more on the shared project of conception.[67] Kelly also raises an important issue about the alienation of the reproductive body. This dislocation, 'detachment'[68] or 'decontextualisation' of the embryo from its procreative parents contributes to the ethical struggle people face as they have to work at recontextualising and relocating their own emotional relationship to the products of conception – embryos in a freezer – in a clinic.

The personhood of an embryo becomes all the more real when people confront the potential for its future social relations in the wider community. Gail described the risks of a kind of inadvertent incest occurring with donating embryos, much like the concerns discussed in the preceding chapter with respect to gamete donation. Again, she feels that regulation might mitigate the possibility of her son having a relationship with someone who was a genetic sibling as a result of embryo donation. Sonya is less certain about this possibility from the outset and bases her concern on her knowledge of the problems that already exist in her family as a result of 'similar genes' circulating within the small population of her community.

> JILL: *Some people are hoping that down the line there will be an opportunity to donate the embryos to someone else.*
> SONYA: *The gene pool is quite narrow here in Ireland. You know, I think . . . we came across it slightly . . . Evan's brother S. has one little boy, born last April. And he has arterial calcification where calcium builds in his veins. It's very rare. It usually happens if parents are related. So one of the first things they were asked is 'are you related?' and they said 'no'. And like Evan's mother could go back five generations . . . They went back, you're probably talking five generations because they can trace it at that. Genetically. They have to go for counselling and see but it could be that their genes are similar and that is the cause of it. So that's another thing. If you had donation I wouldn't be sure . . . Yeah.*

> SIOBHAN: *But I don't think I'd be too keen to give them to somebody else. It would be a little bit weird, especially because Dublin is a small place. And I don't know whether you'd ever find out whether it was successful or not but it would be . . . it would be a little weird if you had a kid when you didn't want to.*

Siobhan also raises the issue of the 'smallness' of Ireland and the risk of having children out there that you do not plan to have if embryos are donated to others. These concerns align with ethnographic studies undertaken in the UK. These studies showed that the potential for incest, however remote in reality, formed a kind of boundary for social acceptance of certain practices in ART rooted in the prior understanding of kinship relations.[69] Not unlike the concern for avoiding 'conjugal chaos' described in the last chapter, moral and normative boundaries are often established with reference to prior notions of the meaning of biological connections.

Anne, who was expecting a child as a result of donor egg IVF at the time of our second meeting together, was the only person in my study group who did have frozen embryos. She and her husband were considering the option of donating frozen embryos but their situation was different from any of the other people I spoke with as their remaining embryos were not genetically related to either her or her husband. Because they had suffered multiple setbacks that were related to low sperm counts, antibodies and poor egg quality they had opted, on their last treatment cycle, to fertilise half the donor eggs with her husband's sperm and half with donor sperm to try to ensure a positive outcome. In this narrative the benevolence associated with the gift of embryos addresses both the difficulty of infertility and the additional burden posed by financial hardship.

> JILL: *Do you have frozen embryos then?*
> ANNE: *There are; there are six frozen embryos and they're donor sperm and donor egg, which doesn't make a difference to us. We'd still use them both and we actually said . . . because it would be a while before I would want to do that again, that even if I do that we actually told them to give them to a couple that needed them so we're going to donate our embryos to somebody else that may be financially . . . hasn't got the money to do what needs to be done.*

In Anne's case, if the pregnancy does not succeed they will retrieve the embryos they have frozen. This is almost universal as a strategy among couples in the midst of treatment. All these stories about frozen embryos are predicated on the possibility that they might become 'left over' embryos.

There are circumstances in which embryos are neither imagined children nor excess embryos, but rather objects that engender the kind of ambivalence necessary to abandon them altogether. Following the traffic of postings on the websites and through stories told about third parties, it is apparent that occasionally people who have had repeated failures of IVF decide to leave embryos in cryo-storage or destroy them. This is almost always done because emotionally people are not prepared to undertake another round of treatment. No one I spoke with was in this position but several couples knew of other people who made this choice.

> SIOBHAN: *What we had is gone. I actually know some people who have adopted and actually still have some embryos frozen somewhere. But we don't have that problem.*
>
> TARA: *I was talking to a couple at the weekend and, you know, they have frozen embryos now and they have no intention of going again. Because their situation is just, they are older now and he just said to me I don't know what to do. And what do you do? You know what I mean? I don't know whether I could leave them sitting there.*
> KELLY: *I don't think I'd have the answer.*
> TARA: *You can't know until you are in that situation.*

Much is said about this on the bulletin boards where women are quick to offer reassurance to others who are faced with this difficult dilemma. It is interesting to note, however, that in the Irish cyber-world of infertility support websites the imaginary possibility of donating embryos was never mentioned.

The Numbers Game: Competing Embryo Discourses

The process of constituting a 'story' for embryos as social and moral entities involves the significance of numbers in relation to quantity, quality and time. Implantation, the natural proactive process, is ultimately something the embryo 'does'. It was Breda who pointed out to me that calling the medical process of returning the embryos to the body 'implantation' was giving medical practitioners more credit than they are due since only the embryo could 'implant'. In the following story Leah shifts the proactive motion of 'implantation' to the medical practitioners as she describes how they make decisions about her embryos. Like the stories above, the maternal body is merely the passive recipient. Medical discourses posit a quantitative framework that grades and qualifies, on a numerical scale, which embryos will be chosen and why numbers matter.

> LEAH: *It was a frozen one after the first time. I think I had the frozen cycle after that. Then I did it a second time and they weren't good enough to freeze. And then I guess it was the same on the third time and the fourth. I was getting older and there was less each time. I can't even remember, I have it all written down somewhere but it was different numbers, different eggs and different grades and stuff like that but when they went through they kept telling me the grades were very good, very good quality and the ones they were implanting were really high quality.*

Embryos created by embryologists are dissociated from the influence of the maternal body and located as biological entities with medical histories. Such histories and diagnoses are constituted as 'grades' and embryologists themselves as the embryos' very own medical specialist.[70]

> NIAMH: *No it's always been just two or three and they put the two back and they would be always really positive. 'These are really good.' You're better off with two really good ones than seven really dodgy ones.*

In some cases, the application of quantitative bases for decisions can be difficult for people. Grading the quality and choosing which embryos will be used is only part of the numerical game in IVF. Carol Anne describes the moral challenge posed by the realisation that only the best embryos would be used for IVF or frozen in the clinic she attended in England.

> CAROL ANNE: *I think actually some of the clinics in Ireland they would put the embryos in and they may disintegrate naturally in the womb but you see in England they don't put them in. They just destroy them. So that for me was just a little bit traumatic. Because I wouldn't necessarily agree with the destruction of embryos. But I felt it was out of my control and it was something that the clinic . . . that was the way they operated.*

And I just had to abide by that. When you're going down this road you have to accept every clinic operates differently and if you're putting yourself in their hands you have to kind of go with whatever their ethics are and whether you agree with them or not is beside the point.

Carol Anne accepts that clinics operate under a set of ethics that may differ from her own Catholic-based values. Moreover, these clinic regulations took decisions out of her hands and relieved her of the burden of responsibility. She is willing to concede that her desire to reproduce is in the 'hands' of the clinic and a sensation of ambivalence seems to neutralise her moral concerns and 'life ethics'. Carol Anne is willing to let the ethics determined by the clinic override her own as a way of sidestepping the challenges. The role of ambivalence as an ethical stance is evident here as she notes that her own moral misgivings are 'beside the point'. The shift to a medical discourse from a religious-based ethics can alleviate some of the anxiety around supernumerary embryos.

Medical decision-making processes are contentious for some people when the issue revolves around embryo quality and personhood. In a conversation with Breda around the Catholic Church's determination that from the moment of fertilisation there is a genetically distinct human being, she replied, 'they obviously haven't seen my embryos then'. Breda and John have been told that in the four IVF treatments they have undertaken their embryos have a high degree of 'fragmentation', reducing the likelihood that they will implant and progress. The discursive constitution of embryos as a collection of fragmenting cells makes it difficult for Breda to imagine them as distinctly human.

Clinical decision-making can sometimes be redefined as a kind of ethical discourse that takes precedence when it comes to the number of embryos returned to a mother during treatment cycles. Donna describes the challenge in balancing her desire to conceive with scientific sense that became an ethical logic.

DONNA: *And then the frozen cycles depend on how many . . . how many embryos you have. For me, it wasn't really the number of cycles as the number of embryos put back. I just wanted to make sure. In actual fact when I had twelve embryos and for one fresh cycle – at least for the fresh cycle – I asked them to put back six. And they asked me why. I just said I felt I couldn't have four times [for IVF treatments] hanging over me. It just felt too long to me and they were appalled.*
JILL: *So did they agree in the end?*
DONNA: *No. The embryologist came to me and said, 'what if they're all good?' and explained why they are frozen. They have their criteria and only the best ones are frozen. So anyway, I agreed. And so I eventually came to an agreement for five. So then I went back to the apartment I was renting and I rang my husband. And he was appalled! He thought it was*

such a waste of embryos. He thought that there could be at the very most
four. So then each time I went – I went three times – and each time one
didn't survive the thawing so three were put back.

Donna's husband provided a kind of intermediary between her own desire to get as many embryos as possible put back and the clinician's concern for what might occur. Donna was concerned with how many times she would have to prepare emotionally and physically for the process of IVF while her partner was concerned for the embryos themselves. The physicians were concerned, one assumes, with the possibility of high-risk multiple pregnancy. Donna spoke about her struggles with her Catholic values as she feels the church often does not understand or make room for the kinds of challenges people face as individuals dealing with a difficulty conceiving a child. But this narrative reveals how Donna's desire to increase her chances of success contradicted not only the teachings of the Catholic Church but the bioethical framework employed as a value base by medical practitioners. Most clinics have established protocols for returning embryos to the womb that limit the number returned to two or three at a maximum to reduce the risks associated with multiple pregnancies – twins, triplets or greater. But as Donna describes it, the issue of value and getting a better deal for one's monetary outlay is significant in many situations.

> DONNA: *I definitely wanted the option of triplets. I definitely wanted that*
> *because I was paying a lot of money . . . and I'd prepared myself . . . And*
> *I'd be happy with twins. There are lots of young couples especially if they*
> *don't see, it's difficult initially. I think that it needs to be discussed more.*
> *And I think also that society has to understand that it's very tough on*
> *people when you only have one child as well. Because society can be quite*
> *nasty to them as well . . . 'oh she'll be an only child' and on and on . . .*
> *'All alone . . .' Why don't you have another child?' You know that can be*
> *quite oppressive for the couple and they don't have the option of a sibling*
> *so easily because they have an IVF child. And if they haven't been able to*
> *conceive naturally it's very tough on them. So jeezus, you can't please*
> *anybody.*

There is a definite shift in Donna's story from the difficulty and emotional stress of travelling to the clinic for treatment as reflected in the earlier part of her story to the logical and monetary reality of having two or more babies for the cost of a single treatment. This shift signals the paradox of assisted reproduction as simultaneously a subjective and arduous medical experience and a commoditised process shaped by getting more for your money and having an 'instant family' with siblings already in place. Such discourses play into the construct of the ideal family in which siblings are assumed to be not only important but vital.

Decisions about the number of embryos is an important example of how women are often pragmatic advocates for themselves in questioning dominant discourse and reshaping the meaning of medicalisation.[71]

Anne had told me about her insistence on returning four or five embryos with each cycle. She was aware of the risks of multiple pregnancies such a practice involved but maintains that this was the only solution for her. She was also prepared to make some difficult choices in order to have a successful pregnancy.

> ANNE: *Some people are just lucky and they can put in one and eventually it'll work. But for me – I put in four or five each time. This is the first achieved pregnancy. Before we make that decision, you have to talk about selective reduction and everything else. And even though we are totally against going for it you have to look at it as saving the life of one child rather than killing – or whatever you want to call it – another if . . . because that's what it comes to. So I think that's a good thing when the doctor explained to me and they make you face the fact, make you face your religion and . . . Because they were Catholic too. It's a thing that they knew would be hard for us, but you have to make that decision before you put them in.*

This is probably the most direct intersection of ART and abortion among all the conversations I had with people who had used or contemplated IVF. Anne faced the prospect of 'reduction' with the same logic that many people used when faced with the idea that IVF necessarily involves the loss of some embryos. In the context of creating and sustaining life, such choices are again framed in pragmatism, offering the best opportunity (or any opportunity). The womb is constituted as an ethical grey zone where the politics of choice is contextualised by both the knowledge of nature and the phenomenon of loss that infertile couples experience as a constant. For many people in Ireland, however, the relationship between their spiritual backgrounds and the roots of ethical decision-making around IVF is very evident, even if contested.

Moving Morality: Hybrid Ethical Frameworks

Religious values and, more specifically, Catholic Church values did appear directly in several places in some people's narratives, often when people discussed their conceptualisation of morality and reproduction. In fact, a number of people began their stories by describing their upbringing in Catholic families. I wondered what that meant to the competing discourses with which they had to negotiate in considering assisted reproduction. I asked Jane if she had any moral or ethical concerns around IVF itself and if these were related to her own religious upbringing in a strongly Catholic family.

JANE: No. Not as a Catholic. I would be a recovering Catholic or a lapsed Catholic depending which way you look at it [laughing]. It's funny. There's obviously the church as a thing in the background. I can't ever really remember explicitly hearing anything about IVF from the Catholic religion. But obviously when you get into thinking about some of the spiritual questions then those sort of filter in. But I do know the church has a loose position on it. My reading of it, they approach it as sort of a grey area and they don't want to get too involved. They realise the difficulty for childless couples and they probably haven't had a strong . . . now that is my perception but I could be quite wrong about that. But just that would be my idea as I haven't seen anything quite forceful about some of the grey areas that would actually be around IVF. You know the selection, the embryo selection and the sort of selective process where maybe more embryos are created than go on to become . . . So I would have spiritual questions about that. Not concerning religion but I myself would have questions about creating embryos and what happens to them. And I don't know about that whole sort of soul question but I would spend a bit of time thinking about stuff like that.

Jane's perception of a kind of neutrality on the part of the church is situated against her own ethical questions about the creation of embryos. This perhaps speaks more clearly to the extent of Jane's 'lapse' in Catholic practice since she doesn't appear to have a clear picture of the position of the Catholic Church hierarchy or how extensively they have lobbied on these issues. She does suggest that her own point of view would be in consensus with the views of the church on embryo selection, even if she believes her position is independent of church influence. For other people, the process of IVF forces them to confront ethical concepts and religious discourses directly.

JILL: And in terms of your personal perspective, it hasn't come up as an issue in making decisions about IVF?
LESLIE: No. It hasn't. We wouldn't be I suppose overly religious ourselves. We're the kind of going to mass on Christmas kind of Catholics. But until we went to the information meeting, I never ever thought about it in relation to the IVF, about the embryos. It never entered my head about whether to discard or destruct or if people don't choose to freeze embryos. It never entered my head and I thought 'my God! That's something of interest'. Potentially, so people could maybe turn around and say that's a form of abortion; that you're aborting an embryo life or destroying the soul. And that is the sort of thing that I hadn't really thought about.

TARA: I mean before we did IVF we wouldn't have thought of it, the whole religious kind of thing.
KELLY: It made me think about the ones that are implanted that have no chance of surviving.
TARA: And we certainly had given it some thought because we had agreed to freeze embryos but we didn't have any.

KELLY: *We did think about the fact that it was there and is it life or is it not. I mean it was something we talked about but it wasn't something we could really say this is what we'd do. And if somebody confronted me with it [the issue of right to life] I think I'd just be very angry. Probably because I don't have an answer right now for it. I can't rationalise it. You couldn't say well you know, if that was the choice I wouldn't have them. I think we'd have said . . . whatever it takes.*

It is not surprising that people realise only when confronted with the processes of IVF that there are potential moral and religious conflicts. The challenge in Ireland is that regulatory decisions and legislation, particularly around any constitutional changes, will have to involve some measure of public debate. The absence of public debate leaves most of the population in the same state of unawares that people like Tara, Kelly and Leslie describe. But without having gone through the process of IVF, the meaning of embryo freezing had not been important to them. The meaning of the embryo in moral and perhaps religious terms was presented to Leslie in the form of what could be construed as a competing medical discourse. But as Kelly notes, doing whatever it takes mobilises the complex ethical processes I have been talking about, in which people have ambivalent feelings about whether some aspects of IVF are right or wrong. They shift this ambivalence into the ethics of making decisions based on the 'rightness' of the outcome of IVF, rather than the process itself, as the moral guidepost.

Kristen, who had finished several courses of IUI and was now contemplating IVF had a very succinct idea of the Catholic Church's position and her own willingness to set aside doctrinal objections in spite of her own adherence to religious practice.

KRISTEN: *I'll go in and light candles and everything and at the same time I know IVF is going against the Catholic Church. That doesn't cross my mind. Whatever belief I have, I have a belief in a God that says we can do whatever we need to get or to have our baby. I suppose, I actually go to the Poor Clares myself sometimes, for different reasons. But I do think the way I see it is in relation to God, I have my own relationship with Him. I don't think my belief is strong enough for Knock or for Lourdes at the moment.*

Kristen argues, as did several other people in the study, that the technology for ART was enabled by God and therefore fits her own moral agenda even as a practising Catholic. The naturalisation of the technological means to an essentially moral procreative objective moves beyond 'helping nature do what it would have done anyway'[72] or what Greek women describe as repairing or overriding nature's damage or failings.[73] In this case the technology itself is seen as God-given and absorbed into the means of achieving a procreative ideal. Kristen is able to merge her visits to a fertility clinic with her visit to petition the Poor Clares for spiritual intercession with health issues including infertility. I moved her into a discussion on IVF as an offshoot of this discussion on religion.

> JILL: *Does IVF worry you in any way?*
> KRISTEN: *Not religiously, no. I don't think religiously. And then they were talking about freezing. I'd have to think about that. I'm not 100% where I am on that, really. RTÉ talked about this yesterday, about the stem cell research and you know with some of the medical conditions in my family – I'd have always been so against it and you know I don't know now. This could save some of their lives. I don't know where my head is really on that. But I don't think it's from a religious place. Mind you, that's probably where it stems from.*

As Kristen's narrative moves from faith in a religious context to faith in science she questions the wisdom of interfering with the 'natural selection' of sperm. Her willingness to rethink her own perspective on stem cell research aligns with her need to accept medical intervention for infertility. As she admits, it was not something she was in favour of, from an ethical perspective, until some members of her own family faced health crises in which biomedical research into the potential of stems cells offered some promise of benefit. She moves between questioning what should happen to embryos as subjects and the idea that as biological objects, science can use them for positive ends. This points to what Sarah Franklin describes as the interface between reproductive technologies and stem cell research in shifting forms of 'reproductive hope', moving from hope for a baby to hope for a cure.[74] Kristen felt compelled to rethink her ethical stance on many issues along a trajectory that places IVF in a continuum with medical technologies that previously seemed morally unthinkable.

Kelly and Tara also introduce the idea of stem cell research as an extension of reproductive technology.

> KELLY: *Certainly we've come to think about stem cell research. You tend to think of it more and should we be doing it or not. Certainly this whole thing with cloning, that's where I would definitely draw a line but stem cell research you tend to think well . . .*
> TARA: *No. I know if I had them frozen I would want to try and have a baby with them.*
> KELLY: *For us I don't think it would have happened because if we had one [an embryo] it would definitely be going into Tara. I think in kind of general terms like 'should they do it or not . . .?' I definitely think in stem cell research there is a huge benefit to it. It's not just tinkering with nature for the sheer hell of it. Let's just do this because we can. I think with cloning it's just that extra little bit. It's just too . . . something not quite right in it.*

Again, the narrative of potential and benefit is dominant here. While Kelly is willing to accept the idea of stem cell research as socially beneficial and morally acceptable, the idea of cloning extended too far beyond the 'natural' boundaries established by notions of relatedness. As Edwards' study in the UK suggests, there are moral limits to what people conceptualise as acceptable in reproduction, and these limits are often based on how closely practices seem to replicate what is understood to be natural or follow the normative model of kinship and family-building.[75] Thus while cloning may be part of a continuum that begins with IVF, it is not seen through the same ethical lens in the decision-making process.

Stem cells have created challenges in Ireland in recent years as two universities, University College Cork and Trinity College Dublin, have agreed to allow their research centres to use human embryonic stem cells (hES) in spite of the lack of clarity and regulation in the nation itself. Both institutions have stipulated that cell lines have to have been produced outside the country and research supported by external funding but there has been no actual reported research at either university. Arguments revolve around the need to support innovative potential that people like Kelly and Kristen have identified as morally sound rationale. Political parties have diverged on their positions on embryonic stem cells and while Fianna Fáil made regulation of ART an election promise in 2009, it also disbanded the Irish Council for Bioethics, an independent oversight organisation that had called for Ireland to regulate hES in line with other EU countries.[76]

One way that the ethical stickiness of using embryos for research is negotiated is through the notion of gratitude. While Donna went through every opportunity to use her embryos in spite of the emotional hardship she describes above, she is nonetheless supportive of the idea of 'giving' to research.

> DONNA: *For some couples they are comfortable with the idea of giving back to science what science gave to them. They are grateful for the child they have and want to give something back.*

Franklin notes that in the UK where embryo donation for stem cell research is occurring, more than 80% of couples who donated embryos did so out of 'a desire to "give something back"'.[77] The fact that the possibility does not currently exist in Ireland does not diminish the sentiment for people like Donna who see the potential medical science offers as part of the economy of hope.

Conclusion

The complex meanings people attribute to embryos are part of an emerging tug of war between institutional interests in Ireland over the regulation, terms of use and moral meanings of assisted reproduction. In a nation that has historically shaped issues of reproductive choice into legislative and constitutional statutes, an emphasis on procreative morality associated with national identity has come at a high price for women. In the current climate of social change there is no longer a single voice purporting to be the basis for any moral consensus on reproduction. In fact, embryos are now part of an increasingly complex ethical dialogue in which they seem to speak on behalf of opposing positions held by the biomedical and religious institutions with a stake in defining the embryo's status. But current challenges to reconciling the relationship of embryos created *in vitro* with the constitutional protection of the 'right to life of the unborn' in Article 40.3.3 indicate the depth and complexity of any attempt to legislate or regulate on the basis of presumed ethical consensus, and legislators have been slow to move forward on regulation of ART.

The recent rulings on 'implantation' shape the womb as a naturalised political space in which embryos enact their *becoming* as humans and perhaps as citizens. Rather than empower women with choice, the rulings embody the responsibility for providing a space in which all embryos might realise their potential. In Ireland the ethical questions around ART are thus also part of the reshaping of an embodied ideal of motherhood. These new meanings shape, in turn, the ambivalence many people feel towards particular definitions of morality as the uncontested basis for arguments against ART. For couples who just want to realise their desire for a child, the decisions they make include compromise and discomfort as often as they include clarity.

The perception of rapid social change in Ireland, particularly with respect to the constitution of families, commitment to the ideals of marriage and the meaning of reproductive choice, has left people struggling to make decisions around the products of ART in a climate of shifting moral certainty and social norms. They are often left with a sense of fatalism or gratitude that they did not have to make difficult choices, particularly with respect to freezing embryos. The current situation provides no clear policy and thus no regulatory or bioethical point of reference for people who continue to adhere to the values of the Catholic Church but want to participate fully in the social experience of having and raising children.

8. Conclusion:
Confirmation and Contestation in a Changing Ireland

'Oh but Ireland has changed . . .' I heard this refrain about change from virtually everyone I spoke with in the course of eighteen months of field-work. People were referring generally to the way the rapid economic development known as the 'Celtic Tiger' had facilitated new employ-ment opportunities and an improved lifestyle for many Irish families. Talk of change also refers to what people perceive as the end of an era in which the Catholic Church held a monopoly on dictating the normative values of sex, marriage, procreation and family. Change thus animated many discussions on issues like sex and sexuality, reproductive decision-making and reproductive health.

While the dominant basis for reproductive morality, as both a sense of right and wrong and driver of social norms, has long been established and perpetuated by the church in Ireland, other institutions have also made use of reproduction as a means of establishing the terms for gender difference and naturalised inequality. Following from this point, church, political and medical institutions also employ the concept of nature, from a number of perspectives, as a means of legitimising claims to moral authority. My research has focused on both institutional discourses and individual narratives about an inability to conceive in Ireland. Through the lens of infertility the research portrays the very real dilemmas that emerge from inconsistencies and contradictions in attempts to define, cat-egorically, the place of nature in reproductive decision-making and in the local moral world in which these decisions are made. We also see how the changing concept of nature creates space for talk of social change.

These questions also relate to the way 'nature' becomes a basis for 'standards of the good, the beautiful, the just, and the valuable' – in other words how nature becomes the basis for moral authority.[1] But equally important is the challenge to the primacy of biology in the defi-nition of one's 'own' child. For couples who consider adoption as a strategy for producing a family, the subject for another book perhaps, and beyond the scope of this work, the need to reconfigure the meaning of a child of 'one's own' requires that they be enabled to move beyond the discourse of biologically determined identity in constituting family. In a world where genetics and biological relationships increasingly determine our notions of potential for health and identity, the impact of biology on our social selves is often over-emphasised and the social significance of relatedness is lost.

The more I spoke to people about infertility the more I began to understand it as an experience that ran against the grain of many meanings associated with reproduction. Through their stories about experiences with infertility people often contested the foundational meanings and naturalised differences that informed reproductive politics in Ireland's past. At the same time, it is apparent that there is no consensus on the meaning of the concept of change in Ireland's present. Infertility is, however, an experience through which change can be marked, precisely because it is steeped in the meanings associated with past idealisms and the desire for some sense of continuity in the present.

I have endeavoured to provide, through an emphasis on ethnographic empathy, an understanding of what people face when they are unable to conceive a child. I focus on the way an absence of conception exposes embodied and gendered identities as contingent rather than 'natural' or immutable; how infertility alters the meaning of personal, family, social and institutional relationships; how it forces people to confront, often for the first time, the very roots of their ethical decision-making with respect to reproduction; the complicated politics of adoption and the imaginary gap it creates between the biology of reproduction and the social commitment of parenthood; and how people's experiences can sometimes simultaneously contest, contradict and reaffirm the dominant meanings of procreation from biological, medical, social and religious viewpoints. I have also tried to locate this array of issues in this particular moment in Irish history – a moment that everyone describes as only just beyond a point marked by something called change.

The most important discovery for me, as a researcher, and the most complex analytical issue, has been the consistent presence of conflicted feelings, contested ideals, and ambivalence that is evident in narratives as people describe the difficult decisions they make in relation to reproduction and infertility. In her examination of the debate surrounding the divorce referendum in November 1995, and the high number of 'No' votes Carol Coulter suggests a similar ambivalence and contradictory approach to changing social values. Coulter sees this seeming reticence to sanction even popular change as indicative of a concern for growing materialism and 'the deep unease with this vision of the future and the widespread desire to stem its advance'.[2] There is no clean break that signals change; no moment when 'tradition' defines something absolute; no point where the values of the past no longer have meaning in the present. As a narrative trope, the theme of change allows people to locate these sensations of uncertainty in a wider social context for the meaning of reproduction and family, acknowledging in some way the need to forge a new path and still look behind to see where they have been.

Reproducing Borders

Some overarching questions remain, however. Experiences of infertility increasingly provoke questions about the status quo of family politics in Ireland, particularly as this pertains to changing family composition, reproductive politics, medical breakthroughs and ethical dilemmas. What is unclear is whether the boundaries and borders of women's bodies will be rethought and whether women's reproductive autonomy is likely to increase in light of greater access to technological control. Even more oblique is the way reproductive bodies, as contested political spaces, will be harnessed to the symbolic value they have for national identity-building. The salience of such questions is evident as the right to travel continues to be tested and political negotiations with the EU continue to produce questions around alignment of social values.

In 2007 a young woman, called Miss D in the media, applied for a passport in order to leave the country to terminate a pregnancy when she discovered her child had many anomalies and would not survive birth. Much like the well-known 'X' case in 1992, the state tried to intervene and contain the woman in order to prevent her seeking an abortion. The case was complicated by the fact that the young woman was a ward of the state and her interests as a minor were pitted against the right to travel and the right to life of the unborn in a structural morass that made it difficult to determine whose interests were in fact being protected. She won her case in court and was granted a passport to travel. As Lisa Smyth argues, the case presented an opportunity to examine the relevance of Article 40.3.3 in relation to circumstances where the foetus will not survive but this did not occur. Instead, she points out, the case merely reaffirmed a number of entrenched assumptions and social norms as well as the importance of the right to travel.[3] The right to travel for the purpose of assisted reproduction, at this point, remains unchallenged but given that women's reproductive capacities have been site and source of much biopolitical power in the last century, people are right to approach their reproductive projects abroad with some caution. Relations with other EU nations that have regulations and differing perspectives on the use and availability of ART will be important for Irish women seeking fertility treatment abroad. The frequent travel to Spain, Greece and Eastern European nations where waiting lists are shorter and opportunities greater for donor gametes demonstrates that borders are porous when it suits the state's pronatalist agenda.

Reproductive politics continue to animate many debates about Ireland's citizenship and relationship to the EU. Sarah Bottini suggests that although Ireland's provision for protecting the unborn is unique, the political alliance with the EU is creating new avenues for contesting Article 40.3.3 through the European Court of Human Rights. She suggests that this might well force a change. In a 2005 case not unlike the case of Miss D, where a foetal anomaly was the issue, the Irish government responded to a challenge by saying that the courts were 'unlikely to interpret the provision with remorseless logic, particularly when the facts were exceptional'.[4] However, there is little reassurance since clearly each case will be argued on a fragment of the story that pertains to a particular element of the law, foreclosing opportunities to argue fully the merits, meanings and challenges posed by the constitutional protection of the 'unborn'.

Borders have been even more distinctly significant with respect to the kind of persons who should be produced and reproduced in Ireland. A citizenship referendum in 2004 asked people to decide whether birth on Irish soil should continue to confer citizenship. The majority decision by a wide margin (79% agreed to the change) was that citizenship would now be determined on the basis of blood or familial links rather than by birth as it had been in the past. The referendum was propelled in part by a growing concern for illegal immigration by pregnant women seeking a way into Ireland and the EU. The media described it as pregnancy tourism and found doctors willing to describe the maternity wards overrun with foreign women giving birth. There were wider concerns regarding access to EU citizenship since Ireland was the only EU nation that continued to grant citizenship on the basis of birthright. As Lisa Smyth notes, the issues of borders and women's bodies have been a frequent concern for Ireland as women have historically been prevented from leaving in order to seek abortions and were now, ironically, being prevented from entering to give birth.[5] John Harrington argues that 'women's reproductive work has been the subject of popular anxiety about porous borders promoted by moral entrepreneurs within and at the edges of the official political system'.[6] He describes the referendum as an example of biopolitics operating in the name of a 'post-nationalist' modern and developing nation that sought to distance itself from its colonial past.

Ireland's constitutional structure requires that changes in EU governance structure be ratified by national referendum. This was evident when the people of Ireland were asked, in 2008 and again in 2009, to vote in a referendum to amend the Irish Constitution allowing the state to ratify the Lisbon Treaty. The treaty altered the previous constitutional format and voting structure for EU member states, making it closer to a federation of states with a single overarching constitutional framework that supersedes the constitutions of member states, should there be a disagreement. As had happened with the Maastricht Treaty in 1992, Ireland once again sought and was granted a Protocol (No. 35) to protect against any attempt to override Article 40.3.3 of the Irish Constitution.[7] While the main issues revolved around the agricultural economy and military neutrality, the issue of abortion surfaced in the campaign. On 13 June 2008 Ireland voted against the necessary constitutional changes to ratify the Lisbon Treaty, much to the chagrin of many other member states.[8] An exit poll conducted by the European Commission noted that a significant factor among those who did not vote at all and those who voted 'No' was a lack of information about the treaty. John O'Brennan argues that the foremost reason for a 'No' vote was 'an enduring Irish attachment to an overwhelmingly exclusivist national identity' which was easily exploited by opponents of wider integration to portray the EU 'as an existential threat to Ireland's values and interests'.[9] In reality, however, only 60% of those voting 'No' thought that this would ensure that Ireland would retain its political identity and its current legislation on abortion, gay marriage and euthanasia.[10] In October 2009, the electorate voted in favour of the Lisbon Treaty but it was widely reported that it was economic uncertainty that provided the necessary momentum for Irish voters to cast in with the EU.

Locating Change

Ethnographic studies illustrate that the experiences of and the responses to infertility are often marked by key moments of political and social innovation. Sarah Franklin's account of assisted conception in the 'enterprise culture' emergent in the UK under Margaret Thatcher's conservatism and Heather Paxson's discussion of infertility and the 'modernisation' of motherhood in late-twentieth-century Greece are two examples.[11] I have thus sought ways to explore the experiences of infertility that provoke and resist changing ideals and values and at the same time reflect the tension that some changes create, particularly at the blurred and contested boundaries of social, moral, political and medical domains of reproduction. But the stories in this book also show how the concept of change is, itself, unclear and contested; the meanings are thus inconsistent among the many people who view their infertility experiences through this lens.

My research suggests that the values associated with fertility, family and motherhood demonstrate aspects of continuity as often as they indicate shifts in perspective. And while infertility is often a 'disruption' to a life narrative, plan or self-identity, it can also be an experience through which people reaffirm their life goals and seek ways of re-engaging with the values that underpin a sense of continuity in their lives.[12] In other words, in the face of fertility challenges, people who strive to overcome difficulties can often promote most vigorously the values and ideals from which they feel they have been excluded as a result of infertility.

From a wider social perspective, while people speak of a groundswell of social change in terms of reproductive values in Ireland, the actual depth and reality of that change, as well as its inconsistencies, are evident in the structures that support or fail to support people struggling to conceive. For example, the Catholic Church remains a site of obstructive moral politics on the issue of reproductive choice and ART. People who are both Catholic and infertile must either negotiate a pragmatic anti-clericalism, by working around advice from priests and advisers in the Catholic Church, or reject the prospect of using *in vitro* fertilisation to resolve their infertility.

Women's narratives about their infertility experiences often drew comparisons between their identities as mothers (or potential mothers) and what they believed to be the reproductive and social experiences of their own mothers. Such insights are embedded in both contestation and affirmation as women often identify themselves and their reproductive experiences as representative of change. This was particularly evident where they saw themselves as better informed than their mothers and better able to act with a measure of agency in planning families. These stories were narrated against a backdrop of what is widely described as 'tradition'.

Tradition, in this light, has become a cultural idiom, following Michael Herzfeld's usage, conveying culturally embedded meanings, especially in reference to hetero-normative family forms and Catholic identity, in the context of its use.[13] The definition and constitution of families is largely measured against a hetero-normative anchor glossed as 'traditional'. These stories also convey an affirmation of the ideal of women as mothers; indeed, most of the women I spoke with were committed to embracing motherhood and forming a family with all the hallmarks of the hetero-normative ideal. Even as the shape of the family they envisioned for themselves differed very little from what they described as tradition, the idiom nonetheless conveyed an essence and an identity that they associated with a different era marked by generational difference. Infertility narratives show how, in Ireland, the values endure even as the meaning of tradition implies, somewhat paradoxically, a change.

There is little doubt that there has been a shift in predominant social values that has seen the shape of relationships and families change in Ireland, even if the mainstream or official political discourse reflects a persistent refusal to acknowledge changing patterns. This refusal is evident in the reticence of various Irish parliamentary committees and commissions to broaden a definition of family or to recognise alternatives to hetero-normative families such as those formed by same-sex couples. Cohabiting couples, children born outside marriage, divorce and same-sex couples do, in fact, represent the diversity of family form in Ireland, as elsewhere. But in spite of an increasing visibility of families that do not adhere to a hetero-normative standard, what endures is the sustained importance of children and, indeed, birth to Irish family life. Therefore, couples who struggle to conceive continue to be subject to a pro-family social climate that promotes, as the norm, fertility and motherhood. The contradiction is that this pro-family politics occurs where the margins of sexual and moral politics continue to overlap in the provision of reproductive health services.

While birth outside of marriage and single motherhood are both accepted in the climate of changing social values, there is no recognition of a sense of loss for infertile women who have remained unmarried, even if they have long-term partners. This failure suggests that motherhood outside marriage is still perceived largely as a failure of 'reproductive choice' (contraception) rather than a proactive 'opting in' on the part of women. Cormac Ó Gráda argues that the rising age of single mothers in Ireland, from 23.6 in 1990 to 27.1 in 2006, might correlate with some measure of planning on the part of unmarried women and their partners, as they find new ways to conform to expected norms of social stability in family and marital relationships.[14] I suggest, however, that a shift in norms to accommodate this trend, in terms of public perception of single women as mothers, has lagged behind reality. There is a lingering assumption that maternal desire itself is only a feature of a marital relationship. This is also structurally confirmed by the lack of access to clinical services for infertility for same-sex couples and the refusal of some clinics to treat unmarried people even as couples in Ireland.

While much has changed in the way families are constituted in Ireland, infertility experiences remain a site where hetero-norms are exploited and perpetuated in medical, church and state discourses. There have, of course, been challenges to the heterosexual ideal that remains enshrined in the Irish Constitution. Same-sex couples are seeking ways to gain recognition as families and some are using reproductive strategies such as ART and adoption even if the opportunities to do so are convoluted and complex. At the same time, lesbian women in particular are challenging the hetero-normative structures in which 'infertility' itself is defined since unprotected intercourse will not yield a conception for people with the same gametes.

Another challenge posed by the issue of sexuality is aimed at the conflation of conception and nature in the politics of the family. While my study only touched the edges of this subject, with two women in a lesbian relationship who were in the process of trying to conceive a child, the issue relates to my observations about infertility as a point of challenge to the hetero-normative definition of family. The medicalisation of infertility and the defining of an inability to conceive as a medical issue draw directly on the social understanding of what is natural about reproduction. Even with the use of ART human reproduction remains, biologically speaking, a process involving gametes from two chromosomally different sexes. This has continued to animate the refusal of alternative models of family as a basis for reproduction. The same hetero-normative framework also constitutes gender as a direct product of a sexualised body. And yet the uncoupling of sex and procreation should create the space for same-sex couples to seek opportunities to become parents in spite of the gamete challenges they face within their sexual relationship. In other words, ART should help us to re-envision the importance of social relations in defining family, parenthood and procreation itself. The fusion of gametes is not sexual – it is merely an event on a cellular level. Everything that preceeds and follows is socially mediated.

The Silence Continues

Despite what I had been told about changing social values in Ireland, the most significant issue that I faced in reality was widespread political silence on the subject of infertility. The difficulty with the silence around infertility is that it leaves unquestioned the idea of the universality, accessibility and imperative of fertility and conception as natural. By concealing, even denying, the challenge posed by infertility to the normative ideals that follow these naturalised assumptions, silence sustains an image of infertility as deviating from a presumed biological and social norm. Silence also obscures the extent to which hetero-normative structures and the ideologies of motherhood continue to shape the gendered distribution of power based on the possibilities and venues in which a voice can be heard.[15] Silence on the wider implications of infertility tends to contain women's voices on reproductive politics within the institutions of family and marriage.

On a broader level, silence is part of discourse and an element of dialogue that operates to sustain gender, motherhood and family ideologies that are embedded in Irish political and social life.[16] The persistent, even chronic, lack of public debate on regulation noted in the literature is echoed by the absence of conversations within some families about the use of ART.[17] But silence also enables some aspects of change and challenge to occur unseen and obscured from institutional critique or public debate. For example, public and political silences have contributed to the growth of clinics that provide ART in Ireland, enabling it to become a somewhat normalised medical service existing quietly but nonetheless known to many medical practitioners and recipients of the technology. In spite of this space afforded by silence, infertility treatment is political in much the same way that abortion, contraception and reproduction itself are political. Infertility treatments now require political attention in order that they be regulated and legislated. In this light, infertility and ART are destined to be the focal point for an ongoing debate in Ireland about access to reproductive choice and the meaning of planning families in a pronatalist political climate.

The slow pace at which the Irish government has moved towards regulation only serves to highlight the difficulty in finding common ground between assisted reproduction, a pronatalist politics and the bioethical debate on the human-ness of embryos. The reticence to restrict technologies is driven, in part, by the interests of medical practitioners who want to provide optimum, state-of-the-art care and the interests of the population who would receive it. At the same time discussion about regulation is most often framed as an ethical necessity rather than a medical one.

There is no question that the regulatory challenges and inconsistencies in the move towards legislation of ART in Ireland are immersed in institutional, national and international politics. This has been described as a legacy of the abortion debate[18] and the complexities of family law.[19] The 2008 decision by the Board of Regents at University College Cork to allow research on embryonic stem cells points to the contradictions between the policies put forward by the state in its negotiations with the EU and the practices related to ART and its spin-off technologies.[20] These contradictions are part of the increasingly untenable position wherein the Irish state uses its constitutional protection of the 'right to life of the unborn' in Article 40.3.3 to identify its position on a number of issues related to medical and bioethical politics without clarifying the meaning of the terms of this article beyond its original intention in the context of the abortion debate.

The increasing normalisation of IVF in everyday medical practice can be contrasted with the discursive portrayal of stem cell research as the real bioethical challenge in current political statements. In Ireland, discussions on stem cell research have recently been marshalled into the ongoing discourse on reproductive, gender and family politics, sometimes to the exclusion of a bioethical debate on the value of medical technology in addressing reproductive needs. Moreover, as has happened in the past with the issue of abortion, discussion on policy has been used to define Ireland as unique in relation to political others in the EU.[21] Whereas elsewhere stem cell research is shaped by the scientific community as part of the healing and regenerative medicine paradigm, in Ireland stem cell research is discussed largely from the point of view of its relationship to embryos as potential life.[22]

And there can be no doubt that anger, fear and a willingness to defend beliefs aggressively attends the very idea of reproductive technology in some facets of Irish society. The concern for safety and attracting the attention of an activist pro-life backlash is not unfounded. In late February 2008, bullets and a fake bomb were mailed to several fertility clinics as well as the Minister for Health in Ireland. A group calling itself the Irish Citizens Defence Force claimed it was a protest against the freezing of embryos. No one was injured but the same potential for militancy as is often associated with anti-abortion campaigns is evident.[23]

My purpose in this research has not been to determine the impact or extent of social, political or economic change in Ireland. Rather, in my analysis, I seek to locate the meaning of reproduction and fertility in relation to people's perceptions of a changing social climate in which the politics of reproduction is negotiated. I do not propose to come to any direct conclusions on the extent to which Ireland has changed but rather to explore how people think about their experiences and articulate meanings in their reproductive lives at a point in time when the idea of social change appears to dominate many people's perception of Irish life. Moreover, I have tried to show that social change becomes not only a backdrop but an active motif that facilitates many aspects of their stories. But where do we go from here? Clearly if change is a theme in Irish social and political life it must also resonate with the politics of reproduction. In this light a number of contradictions and questions remain with regard to the meaning of both fertility and infertility in Ireland. The answers may depend on the shape that regulatory debates and legislative statutes take and the willingness to provide flexibility in the meanings associated with reproduction and family.

It has been my contention throughout this project that a study of the meaning of reproduction, from the point of view of people who have faced challenges in conceiving children, is a critical source of information about Irish social, cultural and political life. The inability to conceive a child is a historically specific and culturally contextualised experience and is nuanced with the politics of reproduction, the meaning of procreation and the significance of family. It is precisely these issues that have been at the heart of many changes in social life in Ireland in recent decades. What is clear, however, is that the meanings of fertility and infertility from the past are continually drawn into the stories, idioms and rhetorical constructions of reproductive politics of the present in Ireland. As an ethnographic project, a study of the experience of infertility is also a study of discontinuity and misaligned experiences. Infertility stories are also reproductive stories that illustrate the cracks and fissures where presumed norms of embodied potential do not necessarily align with the many definitions of reproductive success. The fact that reproduction continues to be measured in terms of success and failure is what makes fertility matter, in Ireland and elsewhere.

Afterword

In a story about change and continuity in Ireland's approach to motherhood, choice and procreation, there have been many events that both serve as and hearken to touchstones marking time and history. Two such events took place as this book was going to press. The purported social and political magnitude of one event rippled beyond Ireland, garnering worldwide media attention. In fact I was in a coffee shop in Kathmandu, Nepal, when the story of the passing of the Protection of Life During Pregnancy Bill 2013 in Ireland was broadcast as a breaking news flash. The other story was scarcely covered by the local press and yet, I would argue, will have much deeper philosophical and social consequences in the years to come. It is the High Court decision in March of 2013 that the genetic mother of twins born through the use of a surrogate mother would be named on the birth certificate rather than the woman (her sister) who actually gave birth to the babies.

On 12 July 2013, Ireland's parliament passed a bill that states with certainty that abortion can be performed in the country to save the life of the mother. Of course, the genesis of this story is very old indeed and while it has been linked to the recent ruling by the European Court of Human Rights, the Protection of Life During Pregnancy Bill 2013 that was passed in both houses of the Irish Parliament by a wide majority is only the latest in a long series of mergers between policy and ideology that have sought to control women's reproduction in the name of Irish identity. The bill was signed into law on 30 July 2013 by President Michael Higgins after he called a meeting of the Council of State to seek advice about referring the bill to the Supreme Court for an assessment of its constitutionality. This call is an indication of the politically challenging and potentially divisive nature of the bill, but it was in fact passed into law without the necessity of further legal examination. This bill is meant to accomplish what the court ruling in the infamous 'X' case in 1992 had not – to ensure with clarity that the life of a woman will not be put at medical risk because she is pregnant. In fact, often referred to as the 'X' case Legislation, the bill spells out the regulatory framework under which physicians are allowed to perform an abortion where the life of the mother is endangered should the pregnancy continue, including by risk of suicide. Since the 1992 case and in two subsequent referenda the Irish populace have, in fact, upheld the right of women to access an abortion to save their lives. However, there has never been, nor will there be with the passing of this new legislation, any political or legal recognition of a woman's right to refuse the biological and social role of motherhood once a pregnancy has begun. The decision to terminate a pregnancy is not a matter of choice but rather, remains a matter of medical necessity as determined by not one but two or three physicians, depending on the circumstance.

There continues to be little political room to manoeuvre on the issue of a woman's right to make this decision and many women have argued compellingly for some measure of compassion for the hardship they face in cases of physical and mental illness, fetuses with disabilities and anomalies that are incompatible with life. In 2010, the European Court of Human Rights gave its ruling on the A, B, & C v. Ireland case brought before the Court by three women who had sought abortions outside Ireland because of the prohibitive laws. Highlighting the complexity of reproductive rights as human rights, the court did not deem Ireland's restrictive laws on access to abortion in violation of the European Convention on Human Rights (ECHR). However, the European Court of Human Rights (ECtHR) did point out that the Irish government's lack of legislative clarity and process with respect to access to abortion to save the life of woman was a violation of Article 8 of the ECHR.[1] An Expert Group was subsequently established in order to explore the implications of the ruling and make recommendations how best to comply with the European Convention on Human Rights and implement the decision of the ECtHR.[2]

This lack of clarity would haunt the government and health officials in a very real way in October 2012 when a 31-year-old dentist in Galway was denied an abortion even though she was suffering a miscarriage at seventeen weeks pregnant and subsequently died of complications. A health services investigation revealed that that the physicians who were caring for Savita Halapannavar, reportedly thought they were obligated to preserve the life of the foetus and, as a result, did not perform a termination that would have prevented the septicaemia – blood poisoning – that led to her death.[3] At the time, it was widely reported that family members were told no abortion could be performed while there was still evidence of a foetal heartbeat because 'Ireland was a Catholic country'.[4] Savita Halapannavar's health care providers have since contested the importance of this statement in the overall approach to the care provided. However, it suggests that while a pro-life ethos defined by its treatment of women and attitude toward reproductive choice is discussed openly in the pulpit and the Oireachtas, it is also a subtext for practice in the labour and delivery room of hospitals. Women continue to pay a heavy price in Ireland for their role as icons of an Irishness deeply marked by those traces of motherhood as morality.

As I have argued throughout this book, the presence or absence of legislation on reproductive health and access to services has animated debate around the meaning of reproductive choice in Ireland, sometimes at the expense of meaningful discussion on gender equality and the social norms that shape women's identity. Reproductive decision-making remains an institutional domain and while medicine may have gained the upper hand, the Church ethos of maternal responsibility looms large. Even the name of the bill speaks to a paternalism and protection of the vulnerable that implies women are to be cared for rather than respected as decision-makers. In the case of Savita Halapannavar physicians claimed a lack of clarity around their capacity to make a decision to terminate a pregnancy since the 'X' case resulted in a High Court decision but no actual regulation. With the passing of the new Protection of Life During Pregnancy Bill, the decision-making is framed around the medical judgment call, albeit in very restricted and specific circumstances. The bill is really as much about reiterating Article 40.3.3 and the protection of the life of the unborn as it is about protecting the lives of women. This is apparent through its constant enjoinder that medical practitioners' opinions as to the risk to the life of a woman be 'formed in good faith which has regard to the need to preserve unborn human life as far as possible'.[5]

O'Sullivan et al. highlight that the Report on Public Hearings held by the Expert Group in 2013 was an 'acknowledgement of the silent majority in Irish society who occupy 'middle ground . . . giving voice to the members of the public who are not mobilised on either side of the debate but represent the majority of citizens'.[6] This awareness that the populace of Ireland is perhaps weary of polemics has not translated into a lessening of the power of the State to govern reproduction; if anything, the bill more succinctly outlines the prohibitions on reproductive choice by stating ever more clearly the responsibilities of women as mothers and defining more soundly the citizenship of the unborn. It short, it entrenches the gender inequality inherent in a system that refuses women the right to make decisions over their own bodies. It seems that Ireland's national identity and political distinction remains tied to a religious ethos enforced through a pro-life politics, embodied in a reproductive responsibility for women and enacted through medical decision-making in reproductive health.

The other event I have flagged as significant, and which received much less local attention and no international fanfare, has greater potential to challenge the values and meaning associated with the ideology of motherhood since it speaks to the way motherhood is defined and determined. Justice Henry Abbott ruled against the State and its refusal to name the genetic mother on the birth certificate of the twins conceived through assisted reproduction.[7] In this case the woman who gestated and gave birth to her sister's genetic offspring did not contest the request.[8] However, her biological work on the part of her sister will be negated from the children's official origin stories. I have discussed throughout this book the complexity and fluidity associated with motherhood as a social commitment and identity as much as a biological relationship. The shift in the legal definition suggested by this ruling may have interesting consequences as assisted reproduction becomes more accessible and more commonplace in Irish society. The need to name and thus create a 'presence' of one kind of motherhood – biological, social, genetic – as the 'real', the recognised and the legal mother facilitates an absence of the other relationships. In its separation of birth from motherhood the ruling suggests that even birth is not a 'fact' of kin relations, forcing a re-examination of the concept of a birth mother and the contested, but nonetheless significant, role played in the kinship imaginaries of many who are adopted or conceived through assisted reproduction. More worrisome perhaps for women who use donor eggs is the potential to allow genetics to trump birth as the defining feature of maternal relationships. In the past, as the CAHR had recommended in cases of egg or embryo donation, birth would ensure a donor could not lay claim to a child produced through assisted reproduction.[9] In short, the ruling creates potential for an even greater lack of clarity in the defining of kin relations in Ireland's future. While the Protection of Life During Pregnancy Bill re-emphasises the social and moral responsibility inherent in the biological process of pregnancy, the High Court ruling in the surrogacy case would seem to challenge the ideology of motherhood on which this responsibility is based.

While legislation and legal rulings offer some firm grounds for decision-making in some areas of life, they cannot be relied upon to address the nuanced and often fraught process of reproductive decision-making. In this domain of social life regulation and legislation cannot account for complexity in the decision to have a child, the diversity of values that shape such decisions, the unique circumstances and hardships that can be created and the suffering and joy that are associated with motherhood. Even the seemingly bold and progressive move to recognise the genetic mother on a birth certificate suggests an inability to accommodate alternative and multiple ways of being a mother. These recent events in Ireland point to the fact that social change cannot truly occur while sustaining existing normative values. Nowhere is this more evident than in Ireland's ongoing definition of the role of women as mothers.

Bibliography

Achino-Loeb, M.L. *Silence: The Currency of Power* (New York: Berghahn Books, 2006)

All-Party Oireachtas Committee on the Constitution, *Tenth Progress Report: The Family* (Dublin: Stationery Office, 2006) (http://www.constitution.ie/reports/10th-Report-Family.pdf [accessed 1 November 2012])

Allison, Jill, 'Conceiving Silence: Infertility as Discursive Contradiction in Ireland', *Medical Anthropology Quarterly*, vol. 25, no. 1, 2011

Alonso, Ana Maria, 'The Use and Abuse of Feminist Theory: Fear, Dust and Commensality', in Alejandro Lugo and Bill Maurer (eds), *Gender Matters: Rereading Michelle Rosaldo* (Ann Arbor, MI: University of Michigan Press, 2000)

Althusser, Louis, *Essays on Ideology* (London: Verso, 1970)

Arensberg, Conrad, and Solon Toothaker Kimball, *Family and Community in Ireland*, 2nd edn (Cambridge, MA: Harvard University Press, 1968)

Asma, S.T. 'Abortion and the Embarrassing Saint [Thomas Aquinas]', *The Humanist*, vol. 54 (May/June 1994), pp. 30–3

Backus, Margot Gayle, *The Gothic Family Romance: Heterosexuality, Child Sacrifice and the Anglo–Irish Colonial Order* (Durham, NC: Duke University Press, 1999)

Badone, Ellen, *Religious Orthodoxy and Popular Faith in European Society* (Princeton, NJ: Princeton University Press, 1990)

Banfield, Edward C., *The Moral Basis for a Backward Society* (Glencoe, IL: Free Press, 1958)

Barry, Ursula, 'Movement, Change and Reaction: The Struggle Over Reproductive Rights in Ireland', in Ailbhe Smyth (ed.), *The Abortion Papers Ireland* (Dublin: Attic Press, 1993)

Battersby, Christine, *The Phenomenal Woman: Feminist Metaphysics and the Patterns of Identity* (New York: Routledge, 1998)

Becker, Gay, *The Elusive Embryo: How Women and Men Approach New Reproductive Technologies* (Berkeley: University of California Press, 2000)

Becker, Gay, *Disrupted Lives: How People Create Meaning in a Chaotic World* (Berkeley: University of California Press, 1997)

Becker, Gay, and Robert E. Nachtigall, 'Eager for Medicalization: The Social Production of Infertility as a Disease', *Sociology of Health and Illness*, vol. 14, 1992, pp. 456–71

Behar, Ruth, *The Vulnerable Observer: Anthropology that Breaks Your Heart* (Boston: Beacon Press, 1996)

Benhabib, Seyla, *Feminist Contentions: A Philosophical Exchange* (New York: Routledge, 1995)

Bharadwaj, Aditya, 'Sacred Conceptions: Clinical Theodicies, Uncertain Science and Technologies of Procreation in India', *Culture, Medicine and Psychiatry*, vol. 30, no. 4, 2006, pp. 451–65

Bharadwaj, Aditya, 'Sacred Modernity: Religion, Infertility and Technoscientific Conception Around the Globe', *Culture, Medicine and Psychiatry*, vol. 30, no. 4, 2006, pp. 423–45

Biehl, João Guilherme, Byron Good and Arthur Kleinman, *Subjectivity: Ethnographic Investigations* (Berkeley: University of California Press, 2007)

Boland, Eavan, *The War Horse: Poems by Eavan Boland* (London: Gollancz, 1975)

Bottini, Sarah Pentz, 'Europe's Rebellious Daughter: Will Ireland Be Forced to Conform Its Abortion Law to That of Its Neighbors?', *Journal of Church and State*, vol. 49, no. 2, 2007, pp. 211–49

Bouquet, Mary, 'Making Kinship, with an Old Reproductive Technology', in Sarah Franklin and Susan McKinnon (eds), *Relative Values: Reconfiguring Kinship Studies* (Durham, NC: Duke University Press, 2001), pp. 85–116

Bourdieu, Pierre, *Outline of a Theory of Practice* (Cambridge: Cambridge University Press, 1977)

Bourke, Angela, 'Irish Stories of Weather, Time and Gender: St Brigid', in Marilyn Cohen and Nancy J. Curtin (eds), *Reclaiming Gender: Transgressive Identities in Modern Ireland* (New York: St Martin's Press, 1999), pp. 13–32

Bourke, Angela, *The Burning of Bridget Cleary: A True Story* (London: Pimlico, 1999)

Bradley, Anthony, and Maryann Gialanella Valiulis, *Gender and Sexuality in Modern Ireland* (Amherst, MA: University of Massachusetts Press, 1997)

Brettell, Caroline B. 'Breton Folklore of Anticlericalism', in Ellen Badone (ed.), *Religious Orthodoxy and Popular Faith in European Society* (Princeton, NJ: Princeton University Press, 1990)

Brettell, Caroline B., and Carolyn Fishel Sargent, *Gender in Cross-Cultural Perspective* (Upper Saddle River, NJ: Prentice Hall, 2001)

Brody, Hugh, *Inishkillane: Change and Decline in the West of Ireland* (London: Allen Lane, 1973)

Brogan, Patricia Burke, 'The Magdalen Experience', in Patricia Kennedy (ed.), *Motherhood in Ireland* (Cork: Mercier Press, 2004)

Bundren, Mary Rodgers, 'The Influence of Catholicism, Islam and Judaism on the Assisted Reproductive Technologies (ART) Bioethical and Legal Debate: A Comparative Survey of ART in Italy, Egypt and Israel', *University of Detroit Mercy Law Review*, vol. 84, no. 5, 2007, pp. 715–46

Burgin, Victor, *The End of Art Theory: Criticism and Postmodernity* (Atlantic Highlands, NJ: Humanities Press International, 1986)

Butler, Judith, 'Is Kinship Always–Already Heterosexual?' *Differences: A Journal of Feminist Cultural Studies*, vol. 15, no. 1, 2002, pp. 14–43

Butler, Judith, *The Psychic Life of Power* (Stanford: Stanford University Press, 1997)

Butler, Judith, *Bodies that Matter* (New York: Routledge, 1993)

Butler, Judith, *Gender Trouble* (New York: Routledge, 1990)

Butler, Judith, and Joan Wallach Scott, *Feminists Theorize the Political* (New York: Routledge, 1992)

Byrne, Anne, 'Familist Ideology and Difficult Identities: "Never-Married" Women in Contemporary Irish Society', in Marilyn Cohen and Nancy J. Curtin (eds), *Reclaiming Gender: Transgressive Identities in Modern Ireland* (New York: St Martin's Press, 1999)

Byrne, Anne, Ricca Edmondson and Tony Varley, 'Introduction', in Conrad Arensberg and Solon T. Kimball, *Family and Community in Ireland*, 3rd edn (Ennis: Clasp Press, 2001)

Carolan, Mary, 'Existence of Embryos Outside Womb Precarious', *The Irish Times*, 16 November 2006 (http://www.irishtimes.com/newspaper/ireland/2006/1116/1163060665594.html [accessed 1 November 2012])

Carr, Bruce R., Richard E. Blackwell and Ricardo Azziz, *Essential Reproductive Medicine* (New York: McGraw–Hill, 2005), pp. 29–53

Cassidy, Luke, 'Court says frozen embryos "not unborn"', *The Irish Times*, 15 November 2006 (http://www.irishtimes.com/newspaper/breaking/2006/1115/breaking36.html [accessed 1 November 2012])

Catechism of the Catholic Church, http://www.vatican.va/archive/ccc_css archive/catechism/p122a3p2.htm#490 [accessed 1 November 2012]

Center for Genetics and Society Canadian Parliament Approves the 'Assisted Human Reproduction Act,' A Model of Responsible Policy. 2004 http://www.geneticsandsociety.org/article.php?id_335 (Accessed March 19, 2008)

Central Statistics Office, *Report on Vital Statistics* (http://www.cso.ie.news andevents/pressreleases/2006pressreleases/reportonvitalstatistics2004/ [accessed 20 December 2012])

Centre for Reproductive Rights. 'Fact Sheet, A, B, C, v. Ireland'. http://reproductiverights.org/sites/crr.civicactions.net/files/documents/crr_ABC_Fa ctsheet.pdf April 2012 Accessed July 26, 2013

Citizens Information, 'Family Rights and the Irish Constitution' (http://www.citizensinformation.ie/categories/government-in-ireland/irish-constitution-1/rights-of-the-family [accessed 1 November 2012])

Clear, Catriona, *Social Change and Everyday Life in Ireland 1850–1922* (Manchester: Manchester University Press, 2007)

Cohen, Marilyn, and Nancy J. Curtin, *Reclaiming Gender: Transgressive Identities in Modern Ireland* (New York: St Martin's Press, 1999)

Collier, Jane Fishburne, and Sylvia Junko Yanagisako (eds), *Gender and Kinship: Essays Towards a Unified Analysis* (Stanford: Stanford University Press, 1987)

Commission on Assisted Human Reproduction, *Report of the Commission on Assisted Human Reproduction* (Dublin: Stationery Office, 2005)

Commission to Inquire into Child Abuse, Commission Report, 2009, http://www.childabusecommission.com/rpt/pdfs/CICA-Execu-tive%20Summary.pdf [accessed 1 November 2012]

Congregation for the Doctrine of the Faith, *Donum Vitae (Instruction on Respect for Human Life in its Origin and on the Dignity of Procreation)* (Vatican City: Libreria Editrice Vaticana, 1987)

Connolly, Linda, *The Irish Women's Movement: From Revolution to Devolution* (Basingstoke: Palgrave, 2002)

Conrad, Katherine, *Locked in the Family Cell* (Madison, WI: The University of Wisconsin Press, 2004)

Conrad, Katherine, 'Fetal Ireland: National Bodies and Political Agency', *Éire/Ireland: Interdisciplinary Journal of Irish Studies*, vol. XXXVI, 2001

Conroy, Pauline, 'Maternity Confined: The Struggle for Fertility Control', in Patricia Kennedy (ed.), *Motherhood in Ireland* (Cork: Mercier Press, 2004)

Conway, Eileen, 'Motherhood Interrupted: Adoption in Ireland', in Patricia Kennedy (ed.), *Motherhood in Ireland* (Cork: Mercier Press, 2004)

Coulter, Carol, 'Court again calls for law on assisted reproduction', *The Irish Times*, 16 December 2009 (http://www.irishtimes.com/newspaper/opinion/2009/1216/1224260759286.html [accessed 1 November 2012]

Coulter, Carol, 'Ruling made public "in interests of child"', *The Irish Times*, 27 February 2006 (http://www.irishtimes.com/newspaper/ireland/2006/0227/1140626820833.html [accessed 1 November 2012]

Coulter, Carol, 'Entering a moral maze', *The Irish Times*, 8 July 2006

Coulter, Carol, 'Council's new guideline on IVF has huge implications for the family', *The Irish Times*, 26 March 2004 (http://www.irishtimes.com/newspaper/opinion/2004/0326/1079399149387.html [accessed 1 November 2012]

Coulter, Carol, 'Donation of embryos gets ethical go–ahead', *The Irish Times*, 24 March 2004 (http://www.irishtimes.com/newspaper/ireland/2004/0324/1079399145528.html [accessed 1 November 2012]

Coulter, Carol, '"Hello Divorce, Goodbye Daddy": Women, Gender and the Divorce Debate', in Anthony Bradley and Maryann Gialanella Valiulis (eds), *Gender and Sexuality in Modern Ireland* (Amherst, MA: University of Massachusetts Press, 1997), pp. 275–98

Crotty, William J., and David E. Schmitt, *Ireland and the Politics of Change* (London: Longman, 1998)

Csordas, Thomas J. *Body/Meaning/Healing* (Basingstoke: Palgrave Macmillan, 2002)

Csordas, Thomas J. *Embodiment and Experience: The Existential Ground of Culture and Self*, vol. 2 (Cambridge: Cambridge University Press, 1994)

Curtin, Nancy J. '"A Nation of Abortive Men": Gendered Citizenship and Early Irish Republicanism', in Cohen and Curtin (eds), *Reclaiming Gender*

Daly, Mary E. 'Marriage, Fertility and Women's Lives in Twentieth-Century Ireland (c. 1900–c. 1970)', *Women's History Review*, vol. 15, no. 4, 2006, pp. 571–85

Daly, Mary E. '"Oh Kathleen Ní Houlihan, Your Way's a Thorny Way!" The Condition of Women in Twentieth-Century Ireland', in Bradley and Gialanella Valiulis (eds), *Gender and Sexuality in Modern Ireland*

Daston, Lorraine, 'The Moral Economy of Science', *Osiris*, no. 10, 1995, pp. 3–26

Daston, Lorraine, and Fernando Vidal, *The Moral Authority of Nature* (Chicago: University of Chicago Press, 2004)

de Lacey, S. 'Parent Identity and "Virtual" Children: Why Patients Discard Rather than Donate Unused Embryos', *Human Reproduction*, vol. 20, no. 6, 2005, pp. 1661–9

Delaney, Flo, 'Infertility: The Silent Period', in Patricia Kennedy (ed.), *Motherhood in Ireland* (Cork: Mercier Press, 2004)

Dillon, Michele, *Debating Divorce: Moral Conflict in Ireland* (Lexington, KY: University Press of Kentucky, 1993)

Dreyfus, Hubert L., Paul Rabinow and Michel Foucault, *Michel Foucault: Beyond Structuralism and Hermeneutics*, 2nd edn (Chicago: University of Chicago Press, 1983)

Earle, Sarah, and Gayle Letherby, 'Conceiving Time? Women Who Do or Do Not Conceive', *Sociology of Health and Illness*, vol. 29, no. 2, 2007, pp. 233–50

Earle, Sarah, and Gayle Letherby, *Gender, Identity and Reproduction: Social Perspectives* (London: Palgrave, 2003)

Edwards, Jeanette 'Incorporating Incest: Gamete, Body and Relation in Assisted Conception', *Journal of the Royal Anthropological Institute*, vol. 10, no. 4, 2004, pp. 755–74

Edwards, Jeanette *Born and Bred: Idioms of Kinship and New Reproductive Technologies in England* (Oxford: Oxford University Press, 2000)

Edwards, Jeanette, 'Explicit Connections: Ethnographic Enquiry in North-West England', in Jeanette Edwards, Sarah Franklin, Eric Hirsch, Frances Price and Marilyn Strathern (eds), *Technologies of Procreation: Kinship in the Age of Assisted Conception* (London: Routledge, 1999[1993])

ElectionsIreland.org (http://electionsireland.org/results/referendum/summary. cfm [accessed 1 November 2012]

EurActive.com, The Irish EU Treaty Referendum, 20 May 2008 (http://www. euractiv.com/en/future-eu/irish-eu-treaty-referendum/article-172508 [accessed 1 November 2012])

Eur-Lex, Official Journal of the European Union, 'Treaty of Lisbon Amending the Treaty on European Union and the Treaty Establishing the European Community, Signed at Lisbon, 13 December 2007 (http://eur-lex. europa.eu/JOHtml.do?uri=OJ:C:2007:306:SOM:EN:HTML [accessed 1 November 2012])

European Commission Eurobarometer Flash EB No 245: Post-referendum survey in Ireland (http://ec.europa.eu/public_opinion/flash/fl_245_full_en.pdf [accessed 1 November 2012])

European Society for Human Reproduction and Embryology (ESHRE) (http://www.eshre.com/page.aspx/15 [accessed 1 November 2012])

Ewing, Katherine Pratt, 'Revealing and Concealing: Interpersonal Dynamics and the Negotiation of Identity in the Interview', *Ethos*, vol. 34, no. 1, 2006, pp. 88–192

Fahey, T., Bernadette C. Hayes and Richard Sinnott, *Conflict and Consensus: A*

Study of Values and Attitudes in the Republic of Ireland and Northern Ireland (Dublin: Institute of Public Administration (IPA), 2005)

Fahey, Tony, and Catherine Anne Field, *Families in Ireland: An Analysis of Patterns and Trends* (Dublin: Stationery Office, 2008)

Finlay, Andrew, *Nationalism and Multiculturalism: Irish Identity, Citizenship and the Peace Process*, vol. 4 (Münster: LIT Verlag, 2004)

Finnegan, F., *Do Penance or Perish* (Oxford: Oxford University Press, 2004)

Foster, Roy, 'Re-inventing the Past', in Andrew Higgins Wyndham (ed.), *Re-imagining Ireland* (Charlottesville, VA: University of Virginia Press, 2006)

Foster, Roy, *Modern Ireland, 1600–1972* (London: Allen Lane, 1988)

Foucault, Michel, 'Afterword: The Subject and Power', in Hubert L. Dreyfus and Paul Rabinow (eds), *Michel Foucault: Beyond Structuralism and Hermeneutics* (Chicago: University of Chicago Press, 1983)

Foucault, Michel, *The History of Sexuality* (New York: Pantheon Books, 1978)

Foucault, Michel, *Discipline and Punish: The Birth of the Prison* (New York: Pantheon Books, 1977)

Foucault, Michel, and Colin Gordon, *Power/Knowledge: Selected Interviews and Other Writings, 1972–1977* (New York: Pantheon Books, 1980)

Franklin, Sarah, 'Origin Stories Revisited: IVF as an Anthropological Project', *Culture, Medicine and Psychiatry*, vol. 30, no. 4, 2006, pp. 547–55

Franklin, Sarah, 'Biologization Revisited: Kinship Theory in the Context of the New Biologies', in Sarah Franklin and Susan McKinnon (eds), *Relative Values: Reconfiguring Kinship Studies* (Durham, NC: Duke University Press, 2001), pp. 302–28

Franklin, Sarah, 'Making Representations: The Parliamentary Debate on the Human Fertilization and Embryology Act', in Edwards *et al.* (eds), *Technologies of Procreation*

Franklin, Sarah, *Embodied Progress: A Cultural Account of Assisted Conception* (London: Routledge, 1997)

Franklin, Sarah, and Margaret M. Lock, *Remaking Life and Death: Towards an Anthropology of the Biosciences* (Santa Fe: School of American Research Press, 2003)

Franklin, Sarah, and Susan McKinnon, *Relative Values: Reconfiguring Kinship Studies* (Durham, NC: Duke University Press, 2001)

Friedman, Russell, and John W. James, 'The Myth of the Stages of Dying, Death and Grief', *Skeptic*, vol. 14, no. 2, 2008, pp. 37–41

Frith, Lucy, Ann Jacoby and Mark Gabbany, 'Ethical Boundary-Work in the Infertility Clinic', *Sociology of Health and Illness*, vol. 33, no. 4, 2011, pp. 570–85

Fuller, Louise, *Irish Catholicism Since 1950: The Undoing of a Culture* (Dublin: Gill & Macmillan, 2004)

Gal, Susan, 'Between Speech and Silence: The Problematics of Research on Language and Gender', in Michaela Di Leonardo (ed.), *Gender at the Crossroads of Knowledge: Feminist Anthropology in the Postmodern Era* (Berkeley: University of California Press, 1991)

Gal, Susan, and Gail Kligman, *The Politics of Gender After Socialism: A Comparative-Historical Essay* (Princeton, NJ: Princeton University Press, 2000)

Galligan, Yvonne, 'The Changing Roles of Women', in Crotty and Schmitt (eds), *Ireland and the Politics of Change*

Gartland, Fiona. 'Genetic mother wins surrogacy case', *The Irish Times*, 5 March 2013

Gibbon, Peter, and Chris Curtin, 'The Stem Family in Ireland Reconsidered', *Comparative Studies in Society and History*, vol. 25, 1983, pp. 393–5

Gibbon, Peter, and Chris Curtin, 'The Stem Family in Ireland', *Comparative Studies in Society and History*, vol.20, 1978, pp. 429–53

Gibbons, P.J., and Collette Keane, 'Playing second fiddle to Mammy', *Irish Examiner*, 20 March 2004

Gilligan, Carol, *Mapping the Moral Domain: A Contribution of Women's Thinking to Psychological Theory and Education* (Cambridge, MA: Harvard University Press, 1988)

Gilligan, Carol, *In a Different Voice: Psychological Theory and Women's Development* (Cambridge, MA: Harvard University Press, 1982)

Ginsburg, Faye D. *Contested Lives: The Abortion Debate in an American Community* (Berkeley: University of California Press, 1998)

Ginsburg, Faye D., and Rayna Rapp, *Conceiving the New World Order: The Global Politics of Reproduction* (Berkeley: University of California Press, 1995)

Glenn, C. *Unspoken: A Rhetoric of Silence* (Carbondale, IL: Southern Illinois University Press, 2004)

Gmelch, Sharon, *Irish Life and Traditions* (Dublin: The O'Brien Press, 1986)

Good, Byron, *Medicine, Rationality and Experience: An Anthropological Perspective* (Cambridge: Cambridge University Press, 1994)

Goodenough, Ward, *Description and Comparison in Cultural Anthropology* (Chicago: Aldine Publishing Company, 1970)

Gray, Breda, 'Gendering the Irish Diaspora', *Women's Studies International Forum*, vol. 23, no. 2, 2000, pp. 167–85

Gray, Breda, *Women and the Irish Diaspora* (London: Routledge, 2004)

Greil, Arthur L. 'Infertile Bodies: Medicalization, Metaphor and Agency', in Marcia C. Inhorn and Frank van Balen (eds), *Infertility Around the Globe* (Berkeley: University of California Press, 2002)

Greil, Arthur L. 'Infertility and Psychological Distress: A Critical Review of the Literature', *Social Science and Medicine*, vol. 45, no. 11, 1997, pp. 1679–1704

Greil, Arthur L. 'A Secret Stigma: The Analogy Between Infertility and Chronic Illness and Disability', *Advances in Medical Sociology*, vol. 2, 1991, pp. 17–38

Guilbride, Alexis, 'Infanticide: The Crime of Motherhood', in Patricia Kennedy (ed.), *Motherhood in Ireland* (Cork: Mercier Press, 2004)

Haimes, Erica, 'Issues of Gender in Gamete Donation', *Social Science and Medicine*, vol. 36, no. 1, 1993, pp. 85–93

Haimes, Erica, 'Recreating the Family? Policy Considerations Relating to the "New" Reproductive Technologies', in Maureen McNeil, Ian Varcoe and

Steven Yearly (eds), *The New Reproductive Technologies* (London: Macmillan, 1990)

Haraway, Donna Jeanne, *Modest_Witness@Second_Millenium.FemaleMan©_Meets_OncoMouse™* (New York: Routledge, 1997)

Haraway, Donna Jeanne, *Simians, Cyborgs and Women: The Reinvention of Nature* (New York: Routledge, 1991)

Hardiman, Niamh and Christopher Whelan, 'Changing Values', in Crotty and Schmitt (eds), *Ireland and the Politics of Change*

Harrington, J.A. 'Citizenship and the Biopolitics of Post-Nationalist Ireland', *Journal of Law and Society*, vol. 32, 2005, pp. 429–49

Healy, Morgan, '"I Don't Want to Get into This, It's Too Controversial": How Irish Women Politicians Conceptualise the Abortion Debate', in Jennifer Schweppe (ed.), *The Unborn Child, Article 40.3.3 and Abortion in Ireland: Twenty-Five Years of Protection?* (Dublin: The Liffey Press, 2008)

Herzfeld, Michael, *Cultural Intimacy: Social Poetics in the Nation-State* (New York: Routledge, 2005)

Hesketh, Tom, *The Second Partitioning of Ireland? The Abortion Referendum of 1983* (Dun Laoghaire: Brandsma Books, 1990)

Human Fertilisation and Embryology Authority (HFEA) (http://www.hfea.gov.uk/en/368.html)

Hilliard, Betty 'Changing Irish Attitudes to Marriage and Family in Cross-National Comparison', in Betty Hilliard and Máire Nic Ghiolla Phádraig (eds), *Changing Ireland in International Comparison* (Dublin: The Liffey Press, 2007)

Hilliard, Betty, 'Motherhood, Sexuality and the Catholic Church', in Patricia Kennedy (ed.), *Motherhood in Ireland* (Cork: Mercier Press, 2004)

Hirsch, Eric, 'Negotiated Limits: Interviews in South-East England', in Edwards *et al.* (eds), *Technologies of Procreation*

'Morality and the Social Sciences', in G. Weisz (ed.), *Social Science Perspectives on Medical Ethics* (Boston: Kinwer Academic, 1990)

Hogan, Senan, 'Lack of IVF legislation keeps couples childless, health committee hears', *Irish Examiner*, 16 September 2005

Holland, Kitty, 'Frozen in a legal limbo', *The Irish Times*, 22 July 2006 (http://www.irishtimes.com/newspaper/newsfeatures/2006/0722/1152913530201.html [accessed 1 November 2012])

Holy Bible, Book of Genesis in Standard Text Version (Cambridge: Cambridge University Press, 2005) http://qe2aproxy.mun.ca/login?url=http://www.credoreference.com/vol/110 *Dáil Debates* (http://historical-debates.oireachtas.ie/index.html [accessed 1 November 2012])

House of the Oireachtas Protection of Life During Pregnancy Bill 2013.http://www.oireachtas.ie/viewdoc.asp?fn=/documents/bills28/acts/2013/a3513.pdf. Accessed 19 August 2013

Hug, Crystel, *The Politics of Sexual Morality in Ireland* (London: Macmillan, 1999)

Iglesias, Teresa, *The Dignity of the Individual: Issues of Bioethics and Law* (Dublin: Pleroma Press, 2001)

Inglis, Tom, *Truth, Power and Lies: Irish Society and the Case of the Kerry Babies* (Dublin: UCD Press, 2003)

Inglis, Tom, *Lessons in Irish Sexuality* (Dublin: UCD Press, 1998)

Inglis, Tom, *Moral Monopoly: The Rise and Fall of the Catholic Church in Modern Ireland* (Dublin: University College Dublin Press, 1998[1987]

Inhorn, Marcia, 'Making Muslim Babies: IVF and Gamete Donation in Sunni Versus Shi'a Islam', *Culture, Medicine and Psychiatry*, vol. 30, no. 4, 2006, pp. 427–50

Inhorn, Marcia, 'The "Local" Confronts the "Global": Infertile Bodies and the New Reproductive Technologies in Egypt', in Marcia Inhorn and Frank van Balen (eds), *Infertility Around the Globe* (Berkeley: University of California Press, 2002)

Inhorn, Marcia, *Quest for Conception: Gender, Fertility, and Egyptian Medical Traditions* (Philadelphia: University of Pennsylvania Press, 1994)

Inhorn, Marcia, and Frank van Balen, *Infertility Around the Globe* (Berkeley: University of California Press, 2002)

Interdisciplinary Committee for Ethics in Human Research, Memorial University (http://www.mun.ca/research/researchers/ethics_committee.php [accessed 1 November 2012])

Irish Catholic Bishops' Committee for Bioethics, *Towards a Creative Response to Infertility* (Dublin: Veritas, 2006 [2005]) (http://www.catholicbishops.ie/wp-content/uploads/images/docs/towardsacreativeresponse.pdf [accessed 1 November 2012])

Irish Catholic Bishops' Conference, 'Irish Catholic Bishops Committee for Bioethics Assisted Human Reproduction: Facts and Ethical Issues' (http://www.catholicbishops.ie/bioethics/389 [accessed 1 November 2012])

Irish Medical Council, *Guide to Ethical Conduct and Behaviour and Fitness to Practice*, 6th edn, 2004 (http://www.medicalcouncil.ie/News-and-Publications/Publications/Professional-Conduct-Ethics/Ethical%20Guide%202004.pdf [accessed 20 December 2012])

Irish Medical Council *Guide to Ethical Conduct and Behaviour and Fitness to Practice* 5th edn (http://www.medicalcouncil.ie/_fileupload/standards/Ethical_Guide_6th_Edition.pdf)

Jacobus, Mary, Evelyn Fox Keller and Sally Shuttleworth, *Body/Politics: Women and the Discourses of Science* (London: Routledge, 1990)

Joyce, Rosemary A., 'Feminist Theories of Embodiment and Anthropological Imagination: Making Bodies Matter', in Pamela L. Geller and Miranda K. Stockett (eds), *Feminist Anthropology: Past, Present and Future* (Philadelphia: University of Pennsylvania Press, 2006), pp. 43–55

Kahn, Susan Martha, 'Making Technology Familiar: Orthodox Jews and Infertility Support, Advice and Inspiration', *Culture, Medicine and Psychiatry*, vol. 30, no. 4, 2006, pp. 467–80

Kahn, Susan Martha, 'Rabbis and Reproduction: The Uses of New Reproductive Technologies Among Ultraorthodox Jews in Israel', in Inhorn and van Balen (eds) *Infertility Around the Globe*

Kane, Aideen, and Edel O'Brien, *Making Babies*, RTÉ documentary (Dublin: Mint Productions, 2004)

Kearns, Martha, 'Mammies' boys show appreciation for the women they love most in the world, *Irish Independent*, 5 March 2005 (http://www.independent.ie/national-news/mammies-boys-show-appreciation-for-the-women-they-love-most-in-the-world-267648.html [accessed 1 November 2012])

Kennedy, Finola, 'A Social Revolution Within an Economic Revolution: Changes in Family Life in Ireland', in Felix Larkin (ed.), *Librarians, Poets and Scholars: A Festschrift for Dónall Ó Luanaigh* (Dublin: Four Courts Press, 2007)

Kennedy, Patricia, *Motherhood in Ireland* (Cork: Mercier Press, 2004)

Kenny, Mary, *Goodbye to Catholic Ireland* (London: Sinclair-Stevenson, 1997)

Kleinman, Arthur, *What Really Matters* (Oxford: Oxford University Press, 2006)

Kleinman, Arthur, *Writing at the Margin: Discourse Between Anthropology and Medicine* (Berkeley: University of California Press, 1995)

Kleinman, Arthur, *The Illness Narratives: Suffering, Healing and the Human Condition* (New York: Basic Books, 1988)

Konrad, Monica, *Nameless Relations* (New York: Berghahn Books, 2005)

Kübler-Ross, Elisabeth, *On Death and Dying* (New York: Quality Paperbacks, 1973 [1970])

Kübler-Ross, Elisabeth, and David Kessler, *On Grief and Grieving: Finding the Meaning of Grief Through the Five Stages of Loss* (New York: Simon & Schuster, 2005)

Lamphere, Louise, 'The Domestic Sphere of Women and the Public World of Men: The Strengths and Limitations of an Anthropological Dichotomy', in Caroline B. Brettell and Carolyn F. Sargent (eds), *Gender in Cross-Cultural Perspective* (Upper Saddle River, NJ: Prentice Hall, 2001)

Latour, Bruno, *We Have Never Been Modern* (Cambridge, MA: Harvard University Press, 1993)

Layne, Linda L. 'Pregnancy Loss, Stigma, Irony and Masculinities: Reflections on and Future Directions for Research on Religion in the Global Practice of IVF', *Culture, Medicine and Psychiatry*, vol. 30, no. 4, 2006, pp. 537–45

Layne, Linda L. 'Making Memories: Trauma, Choice and Consumer Culture in the Case of Pregnancy Loss', in Janelle S. Taylor, Linda L. Layne and Danielle F. Wozniak (eds), *Consuming Motherhood* (London: Rutgers University Press, 2004)

Layne, Linda L. 'Baby Things as Fetishes? Memorial Goods, Simulacra and the "Realness" Problem of Pregnancy Loss', in Helena Ragoné and France Winddance Twine (eds), *Ideologies and Technologies of Motherhood: Race, Class, Sexuality and Nationalism* (London: Routledge, 2000)

Lentin, Ronit 'Constitutionally Excluded: Citizenship and (Some) Irish Women', in Nira Yuval-Davis and Pnina Werbner (eds), *Women, Citizenship and Difference* (London: Zed Books, 1999)

Leonard, Lori, 'Problematizing Fertility: "Scientific" Accounts and Chadian Women's Narratives', in Inhorn and Balen (eds), *Infertility Around the Globe*

Letherby, Gayle, 'Challenging Dominant Discourses: Identity and Change and the Experience of "Infertility" and "Involuntary Childlessness"', *Journal of Gender Studies*, vol. 11, no. 3, 2002, pp. 277–88

Letherby, Gayle, 'Childless and Bereft? Stereotypes and Realities in Relation to "Voluntary" and "Involuntary" Childlessness and Womanhood' *Sociological Inquiry*, vol. 72, no. 1, Winter 2002, pp. 7–20

Letherby, Gayle, 'Other than Mother and Mothers as Others: The Experience of Motherhood and Non-Motherhood in Relation to "Infertility" and "Involuntary Childlessness"', *Women's Studies International Forum*, vol. 22, no. 3, 1999, pp. 359–72

Letherby, Gayle, and Sarah Earle, *Gender, Identity and Reproduction* (New York: Palgrave Macmillan, 2003)

Letherby, Gayle, and Catherine Williams, 'Non-motherhood: Ambivalent Autobiographies', *Feminist Studies*, vol. 25, no. 3, 1999, pp. 719–28

Lock, Margaret, *Twice Dead: Organ Transplants and the Reinvention of Death* (Berkeley: University of California Press, 2002)

Lock, Margaret, 'The Tempering of Medical Anthropology: Troubling Categories', *Medical Anthropology Quarterly*, vol. 15, no. 4, 2001, pp. 478–92

Lock, Margaret, 'Contesting the Natural in Japan: Moral Dilemmas and Technologies of Dying', *Culture, Medicine and Psychiatry*, vol. 19, no. 1, 1995

Lock, Margaret M., and Patricia A. Kaufert (eds), *Pragmatic Women and Body Politics* (Cambridge: Cambridge University Press, 1998)

MacKinnon, Catharine A. *Toward a Feminist Theory of the State* (Cambridge, MA: Harvard University Press, 1989)

Madden, Deirdre, *Medicine, Ethics and the Law* (Dublin: Butterworth (Ireland) Ltd., 2002)

Madden, Deirdre, 'Article 40.3.3 and Assisted Reproduction in Ireland', in Jennifer Schweppe (ed.), *The Unborn Child, Article 40.3.3 and Abortion in Ireland: Twenty-Five Years of Protection?* (Dublin: The Liffey Press, 2008)

Maguire, Moira J. 'The Changing Face of Catholic Ireland: Conservatism and Liberalism in the Ann Lovett and Kerry Babies Scandals', *Feminist Studies*, vol. 27, no. 2, 2001, pp. 335–58

Mahmood, Saba, *Politics of Piety: The Islamic Revival and the Feminist Subject* (Princeton, NJ: Princeton University Press, 2005)

Managh, Ray, 'Judge speaks of "deep regret" in baby decision', *Irish Independent*, 16 September 2006 (http://www.independent.ie/national-news/judge-speaks-of-deep-regret-in-baby-decision-78630.html [accessed 1 November 2012])

Marcus, George, 'Ethnography In/Of the World System: The Emergence of the Multi-Sited Ethnography', *Annual Review of Anthropology*, vol. 24, 1995, pp. 95–117

Marcus, George, *Ethnography Through Thick and Thin* (Princeton, NJ: Princeton University Press, 1998)

Martin, Angela K., 'Death of a Nation: Transnationalism, Bodies and Abortion in

Late Twentieth-Century Ireland', in Tamar Mayar (ed.), *Gender Ironies of Nationalism: Sexing the Nation* (London: Routledge, 2000)

Martin, Emily, *Flexible Bodies: Tracking Immunity in American Culture from the Days of Polio to the Age of AIDS* (Boston: Beacon Press, 1994)

Martin, Emily, 'The Egg and the Sperm: How Science has Constructed a Romance Based on Stereotypical Male–Female Roles', *Signs: Journal of Women in Culture and Society*, vol. 16, no. 3, 1991, pp. 485–501

Martin, Emily, *The Woman in the Body: A Cultural Analysis of Reproduction* (Boston: Beacon Press, 1987)

Mac Cárthaigh, Seán, 'European Court decision could affect citizenship vote', *Irish Examiner*, 18 May 2004

McDonald, Brian, 'Party time as miracle 500 enjoy birthday', *Irish Independent*, 21 April 2008 (http://www.independent.ie/national-news/party-time-as-miracle-500-enjoy-birthday-1353856.html [accessed 1 November 2012])

McDonald, Dearbhail, 'Baby Ann returned to parents', *Irish Independent*, 8 June 2007 (http://www.independent.ie/national-news/baby-ann-returned-to-parents-693265.html [accessed 1 November 2012])

McDonnell, Orla, 'New Reproductive Technologies and Public Discourse: From Biopolitics to Bioethics', unpublished PhD dissertation, University College Cork, 2001

McDonnell, Orla, 'Shifting Debates on New Reproductive Technology: Implications for Public Discourse in Ireland', in Patrick O'Mahony (ed.), *Nature, Risk and Responsibility: Discourses of Biotechnology* (New York: Routledge, 1999)

McDonnell, Orla, and Jill Allison, 'From Biopolitics to Bioethics: Church, State, Medicine and Assisted Reproduction Technology in Ireland', *Sociology of Health and Illness*, vol. 28, no. 6, 2006, pp. 817–37

McElroy, Damien. 'Irish consultant rejects accusation she refused abortion in "Catholic country"', *Daily Telegraph*, 10 April 2013

McKinnon, Susan, 'The Economies in Kinship and the Paternity of Culture: Origin Stories in Kinship Theory', in Franklin and McKinnon (eds), *Relative Values*

McKinnon, Susan, and Sydel Silverman, *Complexities: Beyond Nature and Nurture* (Chicago: University of Chicago Press, 2005)

McNay, Lois, 'Agency, Anticipation, Indeterminacy in Feminist Theory', *Feminist Theory*, vol. 4, no. 2, 2003, pp. 139–48

McQuillan, Julia, 'Frustrated Fertility: Infertility and Psychological Distress Among Women', *Journal of Marriage and the Family*, vol. 65, no. 4, 2003, pp. 1007–18

Meaney, Gerardine, *Sex and Nation: Women in Irish Culture and Politics* (Dublin: Attic Press, 1991)

Meyers, Kevin, 'An Irishman's Diary', *The Irish Times*, 8 February 2005

Moane Geraldine, *Gender and Colonialism: A Psychosocial Analysis of Oppression and Liberation* (New York: Palgrave, 1999)

Moody, T.W., and F.X. Martin, *The Course of Irish History*, 4th edn (Lanham, MD: Roberts Rinehart Publishers, 2001)

Morgan, Lynn, 'Embryo Tales', in Sarah Franklin and Margaret M. Lock (eds), *Remaking Life and Death: Towards an Anthropology of the Biosciences* (Santa Fe: School of American Research Press, 2003)

Murphy, Francis D., Helen Buckley and Larain Joyce, *The Ferns Report*, presented by the Ferns Inquiry to the Minister for Health and Children (Dublin: Stationery Office, 2005)

Murphy, Michelle, 'Liberation Through Control of the Body Politics of US Radical Feminism', in Lorraine Daston and Fernando Vidal (eds), *The Moral Authority of Nature* (Chicago: University of Chicago Press, 2004)

Nachtigall, Robert D. 'Secrecy: An Unresolved Issue in the Practice of Donor Insemination', *American Journal of Obstetrics and Gynecology*, vol. 168, 1993, pp. 1846–53

Nachtigall, Robert D., Gay Becker and Mark Wozny, 'The Effects of Gender-Specific Diagnosis on Men's and Women's Response to Infertility', *Fertility and Sterility*, vol. 54, 1992, pp. 113–21

Nagl, Sylvia, 'Biomedicine and Moral Agency in a Complex World', in Margit Shildrick and Roxanne Mykitiuk (eds), *Ethics of the Body: Postconventional Challenges* (Cambridge, MA: The MIT Press, 2005)

Nash, Catherine, 'Embodied Irishness: Gender, Sexuality and Irish Identities', in Brian Graham (ed.), *In Search of Ireland: A Cultural Geography* (London: Routledge, 1997)

National Infertility Support and Information Group (NISIG) (www.nisig.ie [accessed 1 November 2012])

Neimeyer, Robert A. (ed.), *Meaning, Reconstruction and the Experience of Loss* (Washington, DC: American Psychological Association, 2001)

O'Boyle, Neil, 'Addressing Multiculturalism? Conservatism and Conformity; Access and Authenticity in Irish Advertising' in *Translocations: The Irish Migration, Race and Social Transformation Review*, 2006, vol. 1:1

O'Brennan, John, 'Ireland Says No (Again): The 12 June 2008 Referendum on the Lisbon Treaty', *Parliamentary Affairs*, vol. 62, no. 2, 2009, pp. 258–77

O'Brien, Carl, Rate of foreign adoptions in Ireland one of Europe's highest', *The Irish Times*, 19 June 2007

O'Brien, Carl, 'The identity issue: how donated eggs and sperm are redefining parenthood', *The Irish Times*, 21 November 2011

O'Connell, Angela, 'Jet Trails, Train Rails and Emails', conference paper presented at 'Feminisms: Within and Without' conference, National University of Ireland, Galway, July 2005

O'Donnell, Mary, *Reading the Sunflowers at Night* (Dublin: Salmon Publishing, 1990)

Office of the Taoiseach, *Constitution of Ireland* (http://www.taoiseach.gov.ie/attached_files/Pdf%20files/Constitution%20of%20IrelandNov2004.pdf [accessed 1 November 2012])

Ó Gráda, Cormac, *Éirvana* (Dublin: UCD Centre for Economic Research Working Papers Series WP08/12, 2008), pp. 1–19

O'Keefe, Cormac, 'FF to stop Ireland being a magnet to migrants', *Irish Examiner*, 4 June 2004

Oliver, Kelly, 'Antigone's Ghost: Undoing Hegel's *Phenomenology of Spirit*', *Hypatia*, vol. 11, no. 1, 1996, pp. 67–90

O'Loughlin, Ann, 'No state protection for frozen embryos', *Irish Independent*, 6 October 2006

O'Neill, Mr Justice Iarfhlaith, Speech by Referendum Commission Chairman, Press Briefing, 4 June 2008 (http://www.refcom.ie/en/Past-Referendums-/Lisbon-Treaty-2008/Report-on-the-referendum-on-the-Lisbon-Treaty-2008/Report-on-the-referendum-on-the-Lisbon-Treaty-2008.pdf [accessed on 12 December 2012])

O'Regan, Eilish, Shane Phelan and Michael Brennan, 'Fertility clinics and ministers targeted in "live bullet" campaign', *Irish Independent*, 11 March 2008 (http://www.independent.ie/health/latest-news/fertility-clinics-and-ministers-targeted-in-live-bullet-campaign-1313157.html [accessed 1 November 2012])

O'Reilly, Emily, *Masterminds of the Right* (Dublin: Attic Press, 1992)

Ortner, Sherry B. *Making Gender: The Politics and Erotics of Gender* (Boston, MA: Beacon Press, 1996)

Ortner, Sherry B. 'Is Female to Male as Nature is to Culture?' in Michelle Rosaldo and Louise Lamphere (eds), *Women, Culture and Society* (Stanford: Stanford University Press, 1974), pp. 67–88

Ortner, Sherry B. and Harriet Whitehead (eds), *Sexual Meanings: The Cultural Construction of Gender and Sexuality* (Cambridge: Cambridge University Press, 1981)

O'Sullivan, Catherine, Jennifer Schweppe and Eimear Spain, 'Article 40.3.3 and the Protection of Life During Pregnancy Bill 2013: The Impetus for and process of legislative change', *Irish Journal of Legal Studies* Vol.3(3) 2013, pps. 1-17

O'Sullivan, Claire, 'Cancer drug trial decision "bizarre"', *Irish Examiner*, 4 October 2005

O'Toole, Fintan, 'Skin colour query sours census', *The Irish Times*, 4 April 2006 (http://www.irishtimes.com/newspaper/opinion/2006/0404/1142365530664.html [accessed 1 November 2012])

Pashigan, Melissa J. 'Conceiving the Happy Family: Infertility and Marital Politics in Northern Vietnam', in Inhorn and van Balen (eds), *Infertility Around the Globe*

Paxson, Heather, 'Reproduction as Spiritual Kin Work: Orthodoxy, IVF and the Moral Economy of Motherhood in Greece', *Culture, Medicine and Psychiatry*, vol. 30, 2006, pp. 481–505

Paxson, Heather, *Making Modern Mothers: Ethics and Family Planning in Urban Greece* (Berkeley: University of California Press, 2004)

Paxson, Heather, 'With Or Against Nature? IVF, Gender and Reproductive Agency in Athens, Greece', *Social Science and Medicine*, vol. 56, no. 9, 2003, pp. 1853–66

Peace, Adrian J. *A World of Fine Difference: The Social Architecture of a Modern Irish Village* (Dublin: UCD Press, 2001)

Petchesky, Rosalind Pollack, 'The Body as Property: A Feminist Re-Vision', in Ginsburg and Rapp (eds), *Conceiving the New World Order*

Petchesky, Rosalind Pollack, 'Foetal Images: The Power of Visual Culture in the Politics of Reproduction', in Michelle Stanworth (ed.), *Reproductive Technologies: Gender, Motherhood and Medicine* (Cambridge: Polity Press, 1987)

Pfeffer, Naomi, *The Stork and the Syringe: A Political History of Reproductive Medicine* (Oxford: Blackwell Publishers, 1993)

Pfeffer, Naomi, and Anne Woollett, *The Experience of Infertility* (London: Virago Press, 1983)

Price, Frances, 'Beyond Expectation: Clinical Practices and Clinical Concerns', in Edwards *et al.* (eds), *Technologies of Procreation,* Edwards, Jeanette, Sarah Franklin, Eric Hirsch, Frances Price and Marilyn Strathern (eds), *Technologies of Procreation: Kinship in the Age of Assisted Conception* (London: Routledge, 1999 [1995])

Rabinow, Paul, 'Epochs, Presents, Events', in Margaret Lock, Allan Young and Alberto Cambrosio (eds), *Living and Working with the New Medical Technologies* (Cambridge: Cambridge University Press, 2000)

Rabinow, Paul, *The Foucault Reader: Foucault, Michel, 1926–1984*, 1st edn (New York: Pantheon Books, 1984)

Ragoné, Helena, and France Winddance Twine, *Ideologies and Technologies of Motherhood: Race, Class, Sexuality and Nationalism* (New York: Routledge, 2000)

Rapp, Rayna, 'Gender, Body and Biomedicine: How Some Feminist Concerns Dragged Reproduction to the Center of Social Theory', *Medical Anthropology Quarterly*, vol. 15, no. 4, 2001, pp. 466–77

Rapp, Rayna, *Testing Women, Testing the Fetus: The Social Impact of Amniocentesis in America* (London: Routledge, 1999)

Raymond, Janice G. *Women as Wombs: Reproductive Technologies and the Battle Over Women's Freedom* (San Francisco: HarperSanFrancisco, 1994)

Reissman, Catherine Kohler, 'Analysis of Personal Narratives', in James A. Holstein and Jaber F. Gubrium (eds), *Inside Interviewing: New Lenses, New Concerns* (London: Sage Publications, 2003), pp. 331–46

Reissman, Catherine Kohler, 'Positioning Gender Identity in Narratives of Infertility: South Indian Women's Lives in Context', in Inhorn and van Balen (eds), *Infertility Around the Globe*

Reissman, Catherine Kohler, 'Stigma and Everyday Resistance Practices: Childless Women in South India', *Gender and Society*, vol. 14, 2000, pp. 111–35

Reissman, Catherine Kohler, 'Strategic Uses of Narrative in the Presentation of Self and Illness', *Social Science and Medicine*, vol. 30, 1990, pp.1195–1200

Rich, Adrienne, *Of Woman Born: Motherhood as Experience and Institution*, 1st edn (New York: Norton, 1976)

Roberts, Elizabeth, 'Extra Embryos: The Ethics of Cryopreservation in Ecuador and Elsewhere', *American Ethnologist*, vol. 34, 2007, pp. 182–99

Roberts, Elizabeth, 'God's Laboratory: Religious Rationalities and Modernity in Ecuadorian In Vitro Fertilization', *Culture, Medicine and Psychiatry*, vol. 30, no. 4, 2006, pp. 507–36

Roche, Barry 'Stem cell vote by UCC governors paves way for campus research', *The Irish Times*, 29 October 2008

Rosaldo, Michelle Z. 'The Use and Abuse of Anthropology: Reflections on Feminism and Cross-Cultural Understanding', *Signs: Journal of Women in Culture and Society*, vol. 5, no. 3, 1980, pp. 389–417

Russell, Helen, Emer Smyth and Philip J. O'Connell, 'Gender Differences in Pay Among Recent Graduates: Private Sector Employees in Ireland', *Journal of Youth Studies*, vol. 13, no. 2, April, 2010, pp. 213–33

Ryan-Sheridan, Susan, *Women and the New Reproductive Technologies in Ireland* (Cork: Cork University Press, 1994)

Sandelowski, Margarete, *With Child in Mind: Studies of the Personal Encounter with Infertility* (Philadelphia: University of Pennsylvania Press, 1993)

Schenker, J.G. 'Women's Reproductive Health: Monotheistic Religious Perspectives', *International Journal of Gynecology and Obstetrics*, vol. 70, no. 1, 2000, pp. 77–86

Scheper-Hughes, Nancy, *Saints, Scholars and Schizophrenics: Mental Illness in Rural Ireland*, 20th anniversary edn (Berkeley: University of California Press, 2001)

Schneider, David Murray, *A Critique of the Study of Kinship* (Ann Arbor, MI: University of Michigan Press, 1984)

Schneider, David Murray, *American Kinship: A Cultural Account*, 2nd edn (Chicago: University of Chicago Press, 1980)

Scott, Joan, 'Experience', in Judith Butler and Joan Scott (eds), *Feminists Theorise the Political* (London: Routledge, 1992), pp. 22–40

Seward, Rudy Ray, Richard A. Stivers, Donal G. Igoe, Iftekhar Amin and Deborah Cosimo, 'Irish Families in the Twentieth Century: Exceptional Or Converging?' *Journal of Family History*, vol. 30, no. 4 (2005), pp. 410–30

Shanley, Mary Lyndon, *Making Babies, Making Families* (Boston: Beacon Press, 2001)

Shaw, Rhonda, 'Rethinking Reproductive Gifts as Body Projects', *Sociology*, vol. 42, no. 1, 2008, pp. 11–28

Shildrick, Margrit, 'Beyond the Body of Bioethics: Challenging the Conventions', in Margit Shildrick and Roxanne Mykitiuk (eds), *Ethics of the Body: Postconventional Challenges* (Cambridge, MA: The MIT Press, 2005)

Shildrick, Margrit, *Leaky Bodies and Boundaries: Feminism, Postmodernism and (Bio)Ethics* (London: Routledge, 1997)

Sills, Eric, and Sarah Murphy, 'Determining the Status of Non-Transferred Embryos in Ireland: A Conspectus of Case Law and Implications for Clinical IVF Practice' (2009, available from www.biomedcentral.com [accessed 1 November 2012])

Smyth, Ailbhe, 'A Sadistic Farce: Women and Abortion in the Republic of Ireland, 1992', in Ailbhe Smyth (ed.), *The Abortion Papers Ireland* (Dublin: Attic Press, 1992

Smyth, Jamie, 'Second poll on Lisbon to be held before end of October', *The Irish Times*, 11 December 2008 (http://www.irishtimes.com/newspaper/breaking/2008/1211/breaking2.html [accessed 1 November 2012])

Smyth, Lisa, 'From Rights to Compassion: The D Case and Contemporary Abortion Politics', in Jennifer Schweppe (ed.), *The Unborn Child, Article 40.3.3 and Abortion in Ireland: Twenty-Five Years of Protection?* (Dublin: The Liffey Press, 2008)

Smyth, Lisa, *Abortion and Nation: The Politics of Reproduction in Contemporary Ireland* (Farnham, Surrey: Ashgate, 2005)

Speed, Anne, 'The Struggle for Reproductive Rights: A Brief History in its Political Context', in Smyth (ed.), *The Abortion Papers Ireland*

Stevens, Jacqueline, 'Methods of Adoption: Eliminating Genetic Privilege', in Sally Haslanger and Charlotte Witt (eds), *Adoption Matters: Philosophical and Feminist Essays* (Ithaca, NY: Cornell University Press, 2005)

Stevens, Jacqueline, *Reproducing the State* (Princeton, NJ: Princeton University Press, 1999)

Strathern, Marilyn, *Kinship, Law and the Unexpected: Relatives are Always a Surprise* (New York: Cambridge University Press, 2005)

Strathern, Marilyn, 'A Question of Context' (Introduction to 1st edition), in Edwards *et al.* (eds), *Technologies of Procreation*

Strathern, Marilyn, *After Nature: English Kinship in the Late Twentieth Century* (Cambridge: Cambridge University Press, 1992)

Strathern, Marilyn, *Reproducing the Future: Essays on Anthropology, Kinship and the New Reproductive Technologies* (Manchester: Manchester University Press, 1992)

Taylor, Janelle S., Linda L. Layne and Danielle F. Wozniak, *Consuming Motherhood* (New Brunswick, NJ: Rutgers University Press, 2004)

Taylor, Lawrence J. 'There Are Two Things that People Don't Like to Hear About Themselves: The Anthropology of Ireland and the Irish View of Anthropology', *South Atlantic Quarterly*, vol. 96, 1996, pp. 213–26

Taylor, Lawrence J. *Occasions of Faith: An Anthropology of Irish Catholics* (Philadelphia: University of Pennsylvania Press, 1995)

Taylor, Lawrence J. 'Stories of Power, Powerful Stories', in Ellen Badone (ed.), *Religious Orthodoxy and Popular Faith in European Society* (Princeton, NJ: Princeton University Press, 1990)

Thompson, Claris M. 'God is in the Details: Comparative Perspectives on the Intertwining of Religion and Assisted Reproductive Technologies', *Culture, Medicine and Psychiatry*, vol. 30, no. 4, 2006, pp. 557–61

Thompson, Claris M. 'Fertile Ground: Feminists Theorize Infertility', in Inhorn and van Balen (eds), *Infertility Around the Globe*

Thompson, Claris M. 'Strategic Naturalizing: Kinship in an Infertility Clinic', in Franklin and McKinnon (eds), *Relative Values*, p. 175

Thompson, E.P. 'The Moral Economy of the English Crowd', *Past and Present*, vol. 50, no. 76, 1971, pp. 76–136

Throop, Elizabeth, *Net Curtains and Closed Doors: Intimacy, Family and Public Life in Dublin* (Westport, CT: Bergin & Garvey, 1999)

Traina, Christine, Eugenia Georges, Marcia Inhorn, Susan Kahn and Maura Ryan, 'Compatible Contradictions: Religions and the Naturalization of Assisted Reproduction', in B. Andrew Lustig, Baruch A. Brody and Gerald

P. McKenny (eds), *Altering Nature. Volume Two: Religion, Biotechnology and Public Policy* (Dordrecht, Netherlands: Springer, 2008)

Tsing, Anna Lowenhaupt, *In the Realm of the Diamond Queen: Marginality in an Out-of-the-Way Place* (Princeton, NJ: Princeton University Press, 1993)

Turner, Bryan S. *The Body and Society: Explorations in Social Theory* (Oxford: Blackwell, 1984)

Valiulis, Maryann Gialanella and Anthony Bradley, *Gender and Sexuality in Modern Ireland* (Amherst, MA: University of Massachusetts Press, 1997)

Valiulis, Maryann Gialanella and Mary O'Dowd, *Women and Irish History: Essays in Honour of Margaret MacCurtain* (Dublin: Wolfhound Press, 1997)

Van Balen, Frank, 'The Psychologisation of Infertility', in Inhorn and Van Balen (eds), *Infertility Around the Globe*

Van Balen, Frank, and T.C.M. Trimbos-Kemper, 'Factors Influencing the Well-being of Long-Term Infertile Couples', *Journal of Psychosomatic Obstetrics and Gynecology*, vol. 15, 1994, pp. 157–64

Van den Akker, Olga, 'A Review of Family Donor Constructs: Current Research and Future Directions', *Human Reproduction Update*, 19 September 2005, pp. 1–11

Vayena, Effy, Patrick Rowe, David Griffin, Paul Van Look and Tomris Turmen, 'Foreword', in Effy Vayena, Patrick Rowe and David Griffin (eds), *Current Practices and Controversies in Assisted Reproduction* (Geneva: World Health Organization, 2002)

Walsh, David, Mary L. Ma and Eric Scott Sills, 'The Evolution of Health Policy Guidelines for Assisted Reproduction in the Republic of Ireland, 2004–2009', *Health Research Policy and Systems*, vol. 9, no. 28, 2011

Walsh, Jimmy, 'Mater castigated over cancer drug test', *The Irish Times*, 6 October 2005

Walsh, Judy, and Fergus Ryan, *The Rights of De Facto Couples* (Dublin: Irish Human Rights Commission, 2006)

Warnock, Mary, *Making Babies: Is There a Right to Have Children?* (Oxford: Oxford University Press, 2002)

Warnock, Mary, *A Question of Life: The Warnock Report on Human Fertilisation and Embryology* (Oxford: Blackwell, 1985)

Waterfield, Bruno, 'Irish abortion law key factor in death of Savita Halappanavar, official report finds', http://www.telegraph.co.uk/news/worldnews/europe/ireland/10119109/Irish-abortion-law 13 June 2013. Accessed 25 July 2013

Weston, Kath, 'Kinship, Controversy and the Sharing of Substance: The Race/Class Politics of Blood Transfusion', in Franklin and McKinnon (eds), *Relative Values*

Weston, Kath, *Families We Choose: Lesbians, Gays, Kinship*, 2nd edn (New York: Columbia University Press, 1997)

Whyte, John Henry, *Church and State in Modern Ireland, 1923–1979*, 2nd edn (Dublin: Gill & Macmillan, 1980)

Wills, Clair, 'Women, Domesticity and the Family: Recent Feminist Work in Irish

Cultural Studies', *Cultural Studies*, vol. 15, no. 1, 2001, pp. 33–57

Wright, Victoria C., Laura A. Schrieve, Meredith A. Reynolds and Gary Jeng, 'Assisted Reproduction Technology Surveillance: United States 2000', *Morbidity and Mortality Weekly*, vol. 52, no. SS-9, August 2003, pp. 1–16

Yanagisako, Sylvia Junko, and Carol Lowery Delaney, *Naturalizing Power: Essays in Feminist Cultural Analysis* (New York: Routledge, 1995)

Yeates, Nicola, 'Gender, Familism and Housing: Matrimonial Property Rights in Ireland', *Women's Studies International Forum*, vol. 22, no. 6, 1999, pp. 607–18

Yuval-Davis, Nira *Gender & Nation*. London: Sage Publications, 1997.

Zigon, Jarrett, *Morality: An Anthropological Perspective* (Oxford: Berg, 2008)

Zwicker, Heather, 'Between Mater and Matter: Radical Novels by Republican Women', in Cohen and Curtin (eds), *Reclaiming Gender*

Newspaper Sources (by date)

Irish Examiner

'Maternity scam: citizenship referendum justified', *Irish Examiner*, 27 May 2004

Irish Independent

'Concern over unnecessary caesarians', *Irish Independent*, 13 June 2001

'Wary doctors favour caesarean deliveries', *Irish Independent*, 29 August 2001 (http://www.independent.ie/national-news/wary-doctors-favour-caesarean-deliveries-337074.html [accessed 1 November 2012])

The Irish Times

'Medical ethics of old', *The Irish Times*, 6 October 2005, p. 17.

'Taoiseach says government will act on Ferns Report', *The Irish Times*, 25 October 2005, p. 17 (http://www.irishtimes.com/newspaper/newsfeatures/2006/0708/1146660098 845.html [accessed 1 November 2012])

'Court rules man did not give consent over embryos', *The Irish Times*, 18 July 2006 (http://www.irishtimes.com/newspaper/breaking/2006/0718/breaking51.ht ml [accessed 1 November 2012])

'State to pay costs in embryos case', *The Irish Times*, 22 November 2006 (http://www.irishtimes.com/newspaper/breaking/2006/1122/breaking51.ht ml [accessed 1 November 2012])

'Lisbon Treaty rejected by Irish electorate', *The Irish Times*, 13 June 2008 (http://www.irishtimes.com/newspaper/breaking/2008/0613/breaking1.html [accessed 1 November 2012])

'The Adoption Act', *The Irish Times*, 5 November 2010 (http://www.irishtimes.com/newspaper/opinion/2010/1105/1224282726307.h tml [accessed 1 November 2012])

Notes and References

INTRODUCTION

1 Effy Vayena, Patrick Rowe, David Griffin, Paul Van Look and Tomris Turmen, 'Foreword', in Effy Vayena, Patrick Rowe and David Griffin (eds), *Current Practices and Controversies in Assisted Reproduction* (Geneva: World Health Organization, 2002). The widely accepted definition of infertility used by medical and health policy institutions is the one given by the World Health Organization, which describes it as 'the failure to conceive after one year of unprotected sexual intercourse'.

2 The concept of *The Presence of Absence* came to Elsa when she inverted the phrase 'the absence of presence' taken from the work of artist and theorist Victor Burgin published in 1986 in a collected volume, *The End of Art Theory: Criticism and Post-Modernity*. Elsa thought Burgin's ideas provided valuable insight into the technique of merging painting and photography, a technique she later incorporated into her own work.

3 Sylvia Janko Yanagisako and Carol Lowery Delaney, *Naturalizing Power: Essays in Feminist Cultural Analysis* (New York: Routledge, 1995), p. 5.

4 Ibid., p. 9.

5 Paul Rabinow, *The Foucault Reader: Foucault, Michel, 1926–1984*, 1st edn (New York: Pantheon Books, 1984).

6 Michel Foucault, 'Afterword: The Subject and Power', in Hubert L. Dreyfus and Paul Rabinow (eds), *Michel Foucault: Beyond Structuralism and Hermeneutics* (Chicago: University of Chicago Press, 1983), p. 208.

7 João Guilherme Biehl, Byron Good and Arthur Kleinman, *Subjectivity: Ethnographic Investigations* (Berkeley: University of California Press, 2007), p. 14.

8 Seyla Benhabib, *Feminist Contentions: A Philosophical Exchange* (New York: Routledge, 1995).

9 Judith Butler, 'Contingent Foundations in', in Seyla Benhabib, *Feminist Contentions: A Philosophical Exchange* (New York: Routledge, 1995), p. 41.

10 Louis Althusser, *Essays on Ideology* (London: Verso, 1970).

11 Heléna Ragoné and Frances Winddance Twine, *Ideologies and Technologies of Motherhood: Race, Class, Sexuality and Nationalism* (New York: Routledge, 2000), p. 1. Ragoné and Twine argue that ideologies of motherhood are part of a wider hegemony that 'posits the unquestioned existence of racial matching, exclusively heterosexual family formations and unassisted or

"natural" reproduction, unequal economic privilege and the idea of "perfect" babies'.

12 I draw here on the concept of 'naturalising power' described by Sylvia Yanagisako and Carol Delaney in which they suggest that 'differentials of power come already embedded in culture ... [where] power appears natural, inevitable, even god-given'. See Yanagisako and Delaney, *Naturalizing Power*, p. 1.

13 Sarah Earle and Gayle Letherby, *Gender, Identity and Reproduction: Social Perspectives* (London: Palgrave, 2003), p. 3; see also 'Conceiving Time? Women Who Do or Do Not Conceive', *Sociology of Health and Illness*, vol. 29, no. 2, 2007, pp. 233–50, by the same authors.

14 Judith Butler, *Bodies that Matter* (New York: Routledge, 1993), p. 28; see also *Gender Trouble* (New York: Routledge, 1990), by the same author.

15 Thomas Csordas, *Body/Meaning/Healing* (Basingstoke: Palgrave Macmillan, 2002), p. 2; see also *Embodiment and Experience: The Existential Ground of Culture and Self*, vol. 2 (Cambridge: Cambridge University Press, 1994), by the same author; Byron Good, *Medicine, Rationality and Experience: An Anthropological Perspective* (New York: Cambridge University Press, 1994); Bryan Turner, *The Body and Society: Explorations in Social Theory* (Oxford: Blackwell, 1984).

16 Michelle Rosaldo (1980) argues that while reproduction is obviously a biologically distinctive fact of difference, social science research has tended to construct categories and dichotomies of analysis such as public and private as a means of explaining differences in access to power and prestige along biological lines. She notes that '[m]inimally, it would appear that certain biological facts – women's role in reproduction and, perhaps male strength – have operated in a non-necessary but universal way to shape and reproduce male dominance' (1980:396). She argues that instead of looking at what women do, we should focus on the meanings of those roles and the way biological difference has become 'an excuse rather than a cause for any sexism we observe' (ibid:400).

17 Ana Maria Alonso, 'The Use and Abuse of Feminist Theory: Fear, Dust and Commensality', in Alejandro Lugo and Bill Maurer (eds), *Gender Matters: Rereading Michelle Rosaldo* (Ann Arbor, MI: University of Michigan Press, 2000), pp. 221–31; Rosemary Joyce, 'Feminist Theories of Embodiment and Anthropological Imagination: Making Bodies Matter', in Pamela L. Geller and Miranda K. Stockett (eds), *Feminist Anthropology: Past, Present and Future* (Philadelphia: University of Pennsylvania Press, 2006), pp. 43–55; Sherry B. Ortner, *Making Gender: The Politics and Erotics of Gender* (Boston: Beacon Press, 1996); Rayna Rapp, 'Gender, Body and Biomedicine: How Some Feminist Concerns Dragged Reproduction to the Center of Social Theory', *Medical Anthropology Quarterly*, vol. 15, no. 4, 2001, pp. 466–77.

18 Thomas Csordas, *Embodiment and Experience: The Existential Ground of Culture and Self*, vol. 2 (Cambridge: Cambridge University Press, 1994), p. 2.

19 Joan Scott, 'Experience', in Judith Butler and Joan Scott (eds), *Feminists Theorize the Political* (London: Routledge, 1992), p. 25.

20 Tom Inglis, *Moral Monopoly: The Rise and Fall of the Catholic Church in Modern Ireland* (Dublin: UCD Press, 1998 [1987]).

21 Arthur Kleinman, *What Really Matters* (Oxford: Oxford University Press, 2006).

22 Jarrett Zigon, *Morality: An Anthropological Perspective* (Oxford: Berg, 2008).

23 Mary Douglas, *Purity and Danger* (London: Routledge, 2002); Good, *Medicine, Rationality and Experience*; Kleinman, *What Really Matters*; Zigon, *Morality: An Anthropological Perspective*.

24 Christine Traina, Eugenia Georges, Marcia Inhorn, Susan Kahn and Maura Ryan, 'Compatible Contradictions: Religions and the Naturalization of Assisted Reproduction', in B. Andrew Lustig, Baruch A. Brody and Gerald P. McKenny (eds), *Altering Nature. Volume Two: Religion, Biotechnology and Public Policy* (Dordrecht, Netherlands: Springer, 2008), p. 19.

25 Margaret M. Lock and Patricia A. Kaufert (eds), *Pragmatic Women and Body Politics* (Cambridge: Cambridge University Press, 1998).

26 Lorraine Daston, 'The Moral Economy of Science', *Osiris*, no. 10, 1995, pp. 3–26. Daston describes how her use of moral economy differs from that of many political economists such as E.P. Thompson. She defines a moral economy as 'a web of affect-saturated values that stand in a well-defined relationship to one another [...], a balanced system of emotional forces, with equilibrium points and constraints' (1995:4). She notes that quantification, empiricism and objectivity are part of a brisk trade in ideals that at once infuse science with emotional appeal and defer to 'facticity'. See also E.P. Thompson, 'The Moral Economy of the English Crowd', *Past and Present*, vol. 50, no. 76, 1971, pp. 76–136; Margaret Lock, 'The Tempering of Medical Anthropology: Troubling Categories', *Medical Anthropology Quarterly*, vol. 15, no. 4, 2001, pp. 478–92.

27 Margaret Lock uses an example from her own work on organ donation in Japan and North America to animate Daston's point. Lock notes that physicians universally draw upon the same set of, purportedly, objective criteria in making a diagnosis of brain death. She argues, however, that in a 'moral economy of objectivity', the value of objectivity as a tool for ethical decisions is culturally shaped by the meaning of brain death itself. Thus objectivity, as an attribute or value of science, has different implications in different places (ibid:486).

28 Mary Bouquet, 'Making Kinship, with an Old Reproductive Technology', in Sarah Franklin and Susan McKinnon (eds), *Relative Values: Reconfiguring Kinship Studies* (Durham, NC: Duke University Press, 2001); Sarah Franklin, *Embodied Progress: A Cultural Account of Assisted Conception* (London: Routledge, 1997); Sarah Franklin, 'Biologization Revisited: Kinship Theory in the Context of the New Biologies', in Franklin and McKinnon (eds), *Relative Values*; Susan McKinnon, 'The Economies in Kinship and the Paternity of Culture: Origin Stories in Kinship Theory', in

Franklin and McKinnon (eds), *Relative Values*; Kath Weston, 'Kinship, Controversy and the Sharing of Substance: The Race/Class Politics of Blood Transfusion', in Franklin and McKinnon (eds), *Relative Values*; see also, by the same author, *Families We Choose: Lesbians, Gays, Kinship*, 2nd edn (New York: Columbia University Press, 1997).

29 Rapp, Gender, Body and Biomedicine', p. 469; see also *Testing Women, Testing the Fetus: The Social Impact of Amniocentesis in America* (London: Routledge, 1999).

30 See Victoria C. Wright, Laura A. Schrieve, Meredith A. Reynolds and Gary Jeng, 'Assisted Reproduction Technology Surveillance: United States 2000', *Morbidity and Mortality Weekly*, vol. 52, no. SS-9, August 2003, pp. 1–16. For a discussion on American infertility and ART practices see the CDC Morbidity and Mortality Weekly Report (Wright *et al.* 2003:6). See also the report from the WHO meeting on 'Medical, Ethical and Social Aspects of Assisted Reproduction' which states, 'in general one in ten couples experiences primary or secondary infertility but infertility rates vary amongst countries from less than 5% to more than 30%'. Vayena, Rowe, Griffin, Look and Turmen, 'Foreword', in Vayean, Rowe and Griffin (eds), *Current Practices and Controversies in Assisted Reproduction*, p. xv.

31 Italy and Germany, for example, both have laws that prohibit embryo freezing. In countries where freezing is allowed, such as Canada, the US and the UK, among others, the number of embryos replaced during a single treatment cycle is regulated by legislation or by medical ethics regulations. For a list of countries with legislation governing ART see Commission on Assisted Human Reproduction (CAHR), *Report of the Commission on Assisted Human Reproduction* (Dublin: Stationery Office, 2005).

32 Commission on Assisted Human Reproduction Report of the Commission on Assisted Human Reproduction (Dublin: Stationery Office, 2005); and Susan Ryan-Sheridan, *Women and the New Reproductive Technologies in Ireland* (Cork: Cork University Press, 1994).

33 Depending on the report, numbers of IVF births worldwide are estimated to have reached between one and three million.

34 The Assisted Human Reproduction Act, passed in 2004, established the Assisted Human Reproduction Agency Canada (AHRAC) as a regulatory and licensing body. However, in 2012, the federal government closed the AHRAC and transferred its regulatory functions to other government departments within Health Canada, including the Health Products and Food Branch (HPFB). This move has been described as a response to a Supreme Court of Canada ruling regarding the limits of Health Canada's jurisdiction in matters related to assisted human reproduction as a health-care issue, acknowledging the provincial governments' authority to make decisions around health care coverage and administration in their respective jurisdictions. http://www.ahrc-pac.gc.ca/v2/index-eng.php.

35 Mary Warnock, *Making Babies: Is There a Right to Have Children?* (Oxford: Oxford University Press, 2002); and *A Question of Life: The Warnock Report*

on *Human Fertilisation and Embryology* (Oxford: Blackwell, 1985).

36 CAHR, *Report of the Commission on Assisted Human Reproduction*; Orla McDonnell, 'Shifting Debates on New Reproductive Technology: Implications for Public Discourse in Ireland', in Patrick O'Mahony (ed.), *Nature, Risk and Responsibility: Discourses of Biotechnology* (New York: Routledge, 1999).

37 McDonnell, 'Shifting Debates on New Reproductive Technology', p. 71; see also Susan Ryan-Sheridan, *Women and the New Reproductive Technologies in Ireland* (Cork: Cork University Press, 1994), p. 4. After three attempts in ten years, Canada passed the Assisted Human Reproduction Act in 2004. The government established the Assisted Human Reproduction Agency Canada (AHRAC) as a regulatory and licensing body. It was disbanded after just a couple of years when a provincial court challenge found that the oversight infringed on provincial jurisdiction for healthcare administration. No oversight body has been established in its place.

38 CAHR, *Report of the Commission on Assisted Human Reproduction*, p. v.

39 I use the term post-Catholic to accommodate the fact that while dominant social influences in Ireland have changed, the relevance of Catholicism as a formative influence in many political institutions as well as the lives of many Irish people endures. The idea of a post-Catholic Ireland emerged in a number of conversations with friends in academia in Ireland. I thank Orla McDonnell in particular for her insights on this idea.

40 George Marcus, 'Ethnography In/Of the World System: The Emergence of the Multi-Sited Ethnography', *Annual Review of Anthropology*, vol. 24, 1995, pp. 95–117; and *Ethnography Through Thick and Thin* (Princeton, NJ: Princeton University Press, 1998).

41 Among the forty women who participated in my study, three were not infertile themselves but had volunteered to be egg donors at Irish clinics. Of the remaining thirty-seven women, thirty had undergone some kind of medical treatment for their infertility even if they had not all gone for *in vitro* fertilisation.

42 The Travellers are Ireland's indigenous population of gypsies. Also known as 'tinkers', they are one of many itinerant groups throughout Europe who are similar to the Romany but according to Sharon Gmelch (1986) remain among the least assimilated. The Travellers are a socially and economically marginalised group who are often misunderstood as a result of their nomadic lifestyle. While they attempt to maintain their way of life in order to distinguish themselves as a unique ethnic group they are under pressure to settle since their way of life often puts them in conflict with social norms in mainstream Irish society. For further research see Marie Claire Van Hout (2010): 'The Irish Traveller Community: Social Capital and Drug Use' *Journal of Ethnicity in Substance Abuse*, vol. 9, no. 3, pp. 186–205; Nan, Sharon Gmelch, *The Life of an Irish Travelling Woman* (New York: W.W. Norton & Co, 1986)

43 I met with women in the Traveller community on several occasions. I had two meetings with women who were involved in providing social services

and community outreach. I attended two community events organised for women in the Traveller community and talked to many women about my work. There was no response to my invitation for participation and no one acknowledged that infertility was a problem for anyone they knew. One woman quietly mentioned that her niece had recently had several miscarriages and she would pass my information along in case she wanted to talk to me. Similarly, my conversations at the local charity network run by the St Vincent de Paul Society did not garner any support or interest.

44 Jill Allison, 'Conceiving Silence: Infertility as Discursive Contradiction in Ireland', *Medical Anthropology Quarterly*, vol. 25, no. 1, 2011.

45 Franklin, *Embodied Progress*; Faye D. Ginsburg, *Contested Lives: The Abortion Debate in an American Community* (Berkeley: University of California Press, 1998); Marcia Inhorn, *Quest for Conception: Gender, Fertility and Egyptian Medical Traditions* (Philadelphia: University of Pennsylvania Press, 1994); Emily Martin, *Flexible Bodies: Tracking Immunity in American Culture from the Days of Polio to the Age of AIDS* (Boston: Beacon Press, 1994); and *The Woman in the Body: A Cultural Analysis of Reproduction* (Boston: Beacon Press, 1987); Rapp, 'Gender, Body and Biomedicine, p. 469; and *Testing Women, Testing the Fetus*; Catherine Kohler Reissman, 'Analysis of Personal Narratives', in James A. Holstein and Jaber F. Gubrium (eds), *Inside Interviewing: New Lenses, New Concerns* (London: Sage Publications, 2003); and 'Positioning Gender Identity in Narratives of Infertility: South Indian Women's Lives in Context', in Marcia C. Inhorn and Frank van Balen (eds), *Infertility Around the Globe* (Berkeley: University of California Press, 2002); and 'Stigma and Everyday Resistance Practices: Childless Women in South India', *Gender and Society*, vol. 14, 2000; and 'Strategic Uses of Narrative in the Presentation of Self and Illness', *Social Science and Medicine*, vol. 30, 1990, pp.1195–1200.

46 Katherine Pratt Ewing, 'Revealing and Concealing: Interpersonal Dynamics and the Negotiation of Identity in the Interview', *Ethos*, vol. 34, no. 1, 2006, p. 90.

47 Gay Becker *The Elusive Embryo: How Women and Men Approach New Reproductive Technologies* (Berkeley: University of California Press, 2000); Inhorn, *Quest for Conception*; Gayle Letherby, 'Other than Mother and Mothers as Others: The Experience of Motherhood and Non-Motherhood in Relation to "infertility" and "involuntary childlessness"', *Women's Studies International Forum*, vol. 22, no. 3, 1999, pp. 359–72; Frank Van Balen, 'The Psychologisation of Infertility', in Inhorn and Van Balen (eds), *Infertility Around the Globe*.

48 Ruth Behar, *The Vulnerable Observer: Anthropology that Breaks Your Heart* (Boston: Beacon Press, 1996), p. 174.

49 Roy Foster, 'Re-inventing the Past', in Andrew Higgins Wyndham (ed.), *Re-imagining Ireland* (Charlottesville, VA: University of Virginia Press, 2006), p. 186. Foster suggests this occurs because people can only think about the past through their own experiences and can only 'map the future on analogies of the past'.

1. FAMINE'S TRACES

1 Katherine Conrad, *Locked in the Family Cell* (Madison, WI: University of Wisconsin Press, 2004).

2 Ibid., p. 10.

3 T.W. Moody and F.X. Martin, *The Course of Irish History*, 4th edn (Lanham, MD: Roberts Rinehart Publishers, 2001), p. 240. A shift from subdivision of family land holdings to impartible land inheritance reduced the number of potential heirs and kept farms intact as viable economic units. The formation of the Land League in 1879 spearheaded changes that virtually abolished rural tenancy, paving the way for a new emphasis and a wider access to land ownership.

4 Ruth-Ann Harris, in Marilyn Cohen and Nancy J. Curtin (eds), *Reclaiming Gender: Transgressive Identities in Modern Ireland* (New York: St Martin's Press, 1999), p. 207.

5 Anne Byrne, 'Familist Ideology and Difficult Identities: "Never-Married" Women in Contemporary Irish Society', in Marilyn Cohen and Nancy J. Curtin (eds), *Reclaiming Gender: Transgressive Identities in Modern Ireland* (New York: St Martin's Press, 1999); Crystel Hug, *The Politics of Sexual Morality in Ireland* (London: Macmillan, 1999); Tom Inglis, *Lessons in Irish Sexuality* (Dublin: UCD Press, 1998); Nancy Scheper-Hughes, *Saints, Scholars and Schizophrenics: Mental Illness in Rural Ireland*, 20th anniversary edn (Berkeley: University of California Press, 2001).

6 Finola Kennedy, 'A Social Revolution Within an Economic Revolution: Changes in Family Life in Ireland', in Felix Larkin (ed.), *Librarians, Poets and Scholars: A Festschrift for Dónall Ó Luanaigh* (Dublin: Four Courts Press, 2007).

7 Tom Inglis, *Moral Monopoly: The Rise and Fall of the Catholic Church in Modern Ireland* (Dublin: UCD Press, 1998 [1987].

8 Louise Fuller, *Irish Catholicism Since 1950: The Undoing of a Culture* (Dublin: Gill & Macmillan, 2004), p. 35; Mary Kenny, *Goodbye to Catholic Ireland* (London: Sinclair-Stevenson, 1997), p. 229.

9 William J. Crotty and David E. Schmitt (eds), *Ireland and the Politics of Change* (London: Longman, 1998); Michele Dillon, *Debating Divorce: Moral Conflict in Ireland* (Lexington, KY: University Press of Kentucky, 1993); Inglis, *Moral Monopoly*; Lawrence Taylor, *Occasions of Faith: An Anthropology of Irish Catholics* (Philadelphia: University of Pennsylvania Press, 1995); and 'Stories of Power, Powerful Stories', in Ellen Badone (ed.), *Religious Orthodoxy and Popular Faith in European Society* (Princeton, NJ: Princeton University Press, 1990).

10 Mary E. Daly, '"Oh Kathleen Ní Houlihan, Your Way's a Thorny Way!" The Condition of Women in Twentieth-Century Ireland', in Anthony Bradley and Maryann Gialanella Valiulis (eds), *Gender and Sexuality in Modern Ireland* (Amherst, MA: University of Massachusetts Press, 1997), p. 117. Daly cautions that it is simplistic to link high rates of marital fertility only to the influence of Catholicism in the banning of contraception since other European countries such as France, Spain and Italy, all of which restricted

access to contraception, had falling fertility rates in the same time frame. See also Pauline Conroy, 'Maternity Confined: The Struggle for Fertility Control', in Patricia Kennedy (ed.), *Motherhood in Ireland* (Cork: Mercier Press, 2004).

11 Claire Wills, 'Women, Domesticity and the Family: Recent Feminist Work in Irish Cultural Studies', *Cultural Studies*, vol. 15, no. 1, 2001, p. 45.

12 Ibid., p. 45; see also Kennedy, 'A Social Revolution within an Economic Revolution'.

13 Margot Gayle Backus, *The Gothic Family Romance: Heterosexuality, Child Sacrifice and the Anglo-Irish Colonial Order* (Durham, NC: Duke University Press, 1999); Nancy J. Curtin, '"A Nation of Abortive Men": Gendered Citizenship and Early Irish Republicanism', in Marilyn Cohen and Nancy J. Curtin (eds), *Reclaiming Gender: Transgressive Identities in Modern Ireland* (New York: St Martin's Press, 1999); Angela K. Martin, 'Death of a Nation: Transnationalism, Bodies and Abortion in Late Twentieth-Century Ireland', in Tamar Mayar (ed.), *Gender Ironies of Nationalism: Sexing the Nation* (London: Routledge, 2000); Heather Zwicker, 'Between Mater and Matter: Radical Novels by Republican Women', in Cohen and Curtin (eds), *Reclaiming Gender*.

14 Katherine Conrad, *Locked in the Family Cell* (Madison: The University of Wisconsin Press, 2004); Nancy J. Curtin, '"A Nation of Abortive Men": Gendered Citizenship and Early Irish Republicanism', in Marilyn Cohen and Nancy J. Curtin, (eds), *Reclaiming Gender: Transgressive Identities in Modern Ireland* (New York: St. Martin's Press, 1999); Breda Gray, Gendering the Irish Diaspora. *Women's Studies International Forum,* vol. 23, no. 2, 2000, pp. 167–85; Lisa Smyth, *Abortion and Nation: The Politics of Reproduction in Contemporary Ireland* (Hants, England: Ashgate Publishing Ltd., 2005); Maryann Gialanella Valiulis and Mary O'Dowd, *Women & Irish History: Essays in Honour of Margaret MacCurtain* (Dublin: Wolfhound Press: Irish American Book Co., 1997).

15 Nancy J. Curtin, '"A Nation of Abortive Men", pp. 38–40.

16 Tom Inglis, *Moral Monopoly*, p. 188. See also Clair Wills, "Women, domesticity and the family: Recent feminist work in Irish Cultural Studies." *Cultural Studies*, vol. 15, no. 1, 2001, pp. 33–57.

17 Angela Bourke, Irish Stories of Weather, Time and Gender: St. Brigid. In *Reclaiming Gender: Transgressive Identities in Modern Ireland*. Marilyn Cohen and Nancy J. Curtin, (eds) pp. 13–32 (New York: St. Martin's Press, 1999), p. 17.

18 Humphreys, in Patricia Kennedy (ed.), *Motherhood in Ireland* (Cork, Ireland: Mercier Press, 2004)

19 Catriona Clear, *Social Change and Everyday Life in Ireland 1850–1922* (Manchester: Manchester University Press, 2007).

20 Even prior to 1937, the homogenous character of Irishness was being cemented around the Gaelic identity. The roots of struggle and the construction of an authentic Irish identity in a postcolonial nation incorporated

the notion of a homogenous Gaelic and Catholic population exacerbating the seemingly intractable political divisions between Northern Ireland and the Republic. See Andrew Finlay, *Nationalism and Multiculturalism: Irish Identity, Citizenship and the Peace Process*, vol. 4 (Münster: LIT Verlag, 2004) and Ronit Lentin, 'Constitutionally Excluded: Citizenship and (Some) Irish Women', in Nira Yuval-Davis and Pnina Werbner (eds), *Women, Citizenship and Difference* (London: Zed Books, 1999). Gaelic language revival was, for example, being encouraged as a means of perpetuating the nationalist ideal of common heritage.

21 Ailbhe Smyth, 'A Sadistic Farce: Women and Abortion in the Republic of Ireland, 1992', in Ailbhe Smyth (ed.), *The Abortion Papers Ireland* (Dublin: Attic Press, 1992), p. 87.

22 Bunreacht na hÉireann. De Valera espoused a vision of Ireland as a nation concerned not with economic growth and material wealth but with a moral and simple rural life described as 'a land whose countryside would be bright with cosy homesteads, whose fields and villages would be joyous with the sounds of industry, with the romping of sturdy children, the contests of athletic youth and the laughter of comely maidens, whose firesides would be forums for the wisdom of serene old age. It would, in a word, be the home of a people living the life that God desires that man should live.' Crotty and Schmitt (eds), *Ireland and the Politics of Change*, p. 3.

23 Bunreacht na hÉireann quoted in Crotty and Schmitt (eds), *Ireland and the Politics of Change*, p. 14.

24 Conrad, *Locked in the Family Cell*.

25 Kennedy, 'A Social Revolution Within an Economic Revolution', p. 157.

26 Yvonne Galligan, 'The Changing Roles of Women', in Crotty and Schmitt (eds), *Ireland and the Politics of Change*, p. 109; see also Geraldine Moane, *Gender and Colonialism: A Psychosocial Analysis of Oppression and Liberation* (New York: Palgrave, 1999).

27 Helen Russell, Emer Smyth and Philip J. O'Connell, 'Gender Differences in Pay Among Recent Graduates: Private Sector Employees in Ireland', *Journal of Youth Studies*, vol. 13, no. 2, 2010, p. 230.

28 Gerardine Meaney, *Sex and Nation: Women in Irish Culture and Politics* (Dublin: Attic Press, 1991), p. 6.

29 Kennedy, 'A Social Revolution Within an Economic Revolution', p. 166.

30 Adrian Peace, *A World of Fine Difference: The Social Architecture of a Modern Irish Village* (Dublin: UCD Press, 2001).

31 The website documents of the All-Party Oireachtas Committee on the Constitution describe its programme as continuing the work of previous committees established in 1996 and 1997, 'aimed at renewing the Constitution in all its parts, for implementation over a number of years. The task is unprecedented: no other state with the referendum as its sole mechanism for constitutional change has set itself so ambitious an objective.'

32 All-Party Oireachtas Committee on the Constitution, *Tenth Progress Report: The Family* (Dublin: Stationery Office, 2006), p. 122.

33 I made a submission to the committee in January 2005, supporting a wider, more inclusive definition of family that extended beyond a hetero-normative, marriage-based institution. I was urged to undertake this by some friends in the lesbian community in Cork who felt they were not included in the definition of family as it stood. The final recommendation in the 2006 report reads in full:

> In the case of the family, the committee takes the view that an amendment to extend the definition of the family would cause deep and long-lasting division in our society and would not necessarily be passed by a majority. Instead of inviting such anguish and uncertainty, the committee proposes to seek through a number of other constitutional changes and legislative proposals to deal in an optimal way with the problems presented to it in the submissions (p. 122).

34 Judy Walsh and Fergus Ryan, *The Rights of De Facto Couples* (Dublin: Irish Human Rights Commission, 2006), p. 6.

35 See also Byrne, 'Familist Ideology and Difficult Identities'; Conrad, *Locked in the Family Cell* for discussion about the difficulties associated with gaining recognition for alternative forms of family and partnerships.

36 Anne Byrne, Ricca Edmondson and Tony Varley, 'Introduction', in Conrad Arensberg and Solon T. Kimball, *Family and Community in Ireland*, 3rd edn (Ennis: Clasp Press, 2001); Conrad, *Locked in the Family Cell*; Lisa Smyth, *Abortion and Nation: The Politics of Reproduction in Contemporary Ireland* (Farnham, Surrey: Ashgate, 2005).

37 In fact the average age of 'unwed mothers' in 1990 was 23.6 years whereas in 2006 it had risen to 27.1 years. Cormac Ó Gráda, *Éirvana* (Dublin: UCD Centre for Economic Research, Working Papers Series WP08/12, 2008), p. 10.

38 Tom Hesketh, *The Second Partitioning of Ireland? The Abortion Referendum of 1983* (Dun Laoghaire: Brandsma Books, 1990), p. 2.

39 Emily O'Reilly, *Masterminds of the Right* (Dublin: Attic Press, 1992); Smyth, *Abortion and Nation*.

40 *Dáil Debates*, vol. 339, 9 February 1983, paragraph 1386.

41 Smyth, 'A Sadistic Farce', p. 17; see also Katherine Conrad, 'Fetal Ireland: National Bodies and Political Agency', *Éire/Ireland: Interdisciplinary Journal of Irish Studies*, vol. XXXVI, 2001, p. 169. Conrad argues that 'Protocol 17 was designed to protect "Irish morality" from the purview of European law . . . ensur[ing] that a particular version of Ireland continued to be reproduced even as it linked itself more fully with Europe'. Like the previous measures which banned contraceptives and divorce, this measure was framed as protecting Ireland's valuable moral and social assets from *outside* influence even as Ireland itself was very much *inside* the EU.

42 The 'X' Case was complicated because, in fact, the girl's parents had taken her out of the country to access a termination of her pregnancy. The court order demanding they return was issued after they inquired about the need for DNA evidence against the accused rapist. The police informed the authorities of the court, who then issued the injunction and order to

return based on Article 40.3.3. The case was widely debated publicly, sparked widespread protest and served to highlight the difficulty such social policies can present for individual lives and situations (see Conrad, 'Fetal Ireland'; Smyth, 'A Sadistic Farce'; Smyth, *Abortion and Nation*); Lawrence Taylor, 'There Are Two Things that People Don't Like to Hear About Themselves: The Anthropology of Ireland and the Irish View of Anthropology', *South Atlantic Quarterly*, vol. 96, 1996, pp. 213–26.

43 Morgan Healy, '"I Don't Want to Get into This, It's Too Controversial": How Irish Women Politicians Conceptualise the Abortion Debate', in Jennifer Schweppe (ed.), *The Unborn Child, Article 40.3.3 and Abortion in Ireland: Twenty-Five Years of Protection?* (Dublin: The Liffey Press, 2008), p. 67.

44 Dr Mary Henry introduced the private member's bill in relation to the Olviedo Convention (the European Convention on Human Rights and Biotechnology), brought forward by the Council of Europe in 1997. The purpose of the convention was to promote respect for human rights and dignity in light of advances in biomedical technology. She later expressed concern in debates and various articles that Ireland remained, in 2002, one of the few nations who had not signed the convention. While the UK had also not signed the convention, Senator Henry noted that they had legislation in place that provided protection and bioethical guidance around the practices of ART; http://www.oireachtas.ie/documents/bills28/bills/1999/0799/b799.pdf [accessed 30 October 2012]; http:/homepage.tinet.ie/~mary-henry/debates/adjourn/4dec02.htm [accessed 30 October 2012].

45 The commission consisted of a committee of twenty-five members with diverse backgrounds as legal and ethics scholars, medical practitioners, scientists and theologians but no priests or representatives of the Catholic Church hierarchy or any other church. In addition there were nine participants in working groups who were possessed of similar diversity in their expertise. Together they worked for four years conducting surveys, researching the practices involved in ART and exploring the policies of other states in Europe and beyond.

46 Commission on Assisted Human Reproduction (CAHR), *Report of the Commission on Assisted Human Reproduction* (Dublin: Stationery Office, 2005), p. 78.

47 Conrad, *Locked in the Family Cell*; Angela K. Martin, 'Death of a Nation: Transnationalism, Bodies and Abortion in Late Twentieth-Century Ireland', in Tamar Mayar (ed.), *Gender Ironies of Nationalism: Sexing the Nation* (London: Routledge, 2000).

48 Smyth, *Abortion and Nation*, p. 2.

49 Orla McDonnell, 'New Reproductive Technologies and Public Discourse: From Biopolitics to Bioethics', unpublished PhD dissertation, University College Cork, 2001. I follow McDonnell in her emphasis on Foucault's concept of biopolitics here as it describes the exercise of power in activities aimed at regulating the production of populations through the reproductive activities of individuals.

50 Chrystel Hug, *The Politics of Sexual Morality in Ireland* (London: Macmillan, 1999); Catherine Nash, 'Embodied Irishness: Gender, Sexuality and Irish Identities', in Brian Graham (ed.), *In Search of Ireland: A Cultural Geography* (London: Routledge, 1997).

2. MOTHERHOOD CONTESTED

1 Christine Battersby, *The Phenomenal Woman: Feminist Metaphysics and the Patterns of Identity* (New York: Routledge, 1998), p. 16.

2 Sadly, in 2008 the village had to cancel its parade as one of the pubs closed in the wake of declining population. See http://news.bbc.co.uk/2/hi/uk_news/northern_ireland/7302135.stm

3 Changes were being made to laws while I was doing my fieldwork and many pubs began to prohibit entrance by children after 8 or 8.30 pm, but even prior to these changes it was most common for children to be in pubs only during afternoon and very early evening hours.

4 P.J. Gibbons and Collette Keane, 'Playing Second Fiddle to Mammy', *Irish Examiner*, 20 March 2004; see also Martha Kearns, 'Mammies' boys show appreciation for the women they love most in the world', *Irish Independent*, 5 March 2005.

5 Pierre Bourdieu, *Outline of a Theory of Practice* (Cambridge: Cambridge University Press, 1977). In his work on social capital Bourdieu draws connections between enduring social class distinctions and access to knowledge and social practices which are products themselves of class distinctions. Similarly, the middle-class norms of gift-giving and response to commercial pressure in the media would constitute participatory forms of social capital in a family-oriented society. See also Janelle S. Taylor, Linda L. Layne and Danielle F. Wozniak (eds), *Consuming Motherhood* (New Brunswick, NJ: Rutgers University Press, 2004).

6 Neil O'Boyle (2004) describes the use of 'culture' by Irish commercial advertising as part of the 'symbolic endorsement of the dominant cultural code'.

7 Nancy Scheper-Hughes, *Saints, Scholars and Schizophrenics: Mental Illness in Rural Ireland*, 20th anniversary edn (Berkeley: University of California Press, 2001), pp. 231–2. See Scheper-Hughes for a discussion of the tension between secrecy and social interest in the sex and reproduction of newly married couples in rural Ireland in the 1970s. See also Jill Allison, 'Conceiving Silence: Infertility as Discursive Contradiction in Ireland', *Medical Anthropology Quarterly*, vol. 25, no. 1, 2011, pp. 1–21.

8 I recall being in a taxi one evening and the male driver engaged me in conversation, asking where I was from and why I was in Ireland. When I had explained something about my research he asked me if I had heard the expression and its meaning. He also suggested I use it for a thesis title – a common event in my work as many people offered such title suggestions. He did not tell me whether his knowledge of the expression was born of personal experience but his instant willingness to offer something to my research made me suspect that perhaps he had an infertility story of his own.

9 Flo Delaney, 'Infertility: The Silent Period', in Patricia Kennedy (ed.), *Motherhood in Ireland* (Cork: Mercier Press, 2004), p. 73.

10 Katherine Conrad, *Locked in the Family Cell*; Nancy J. Curtin, 'A Nation of Abortive Men'; Lisa Smyth, *Abortion and Nation*.

11 Louis Althusser, *Essays on Ideology* (London: Verso, 1970) pp. 46–48.

12 Judith Butler, *Bodies that Matter and Gender Trouble*.

13 Jane's story reminded me of Angela Bourke's story of a woman who was burned in the fireplace of her cottage by her husband and father and a number of other male relatives. Bridget Cleary's husband defended his actions which led to his wife's death by arguing that an illness was a sign that she had been taken by fairies and replaced with a 'changeling'. The burning was described in court and in the community as an effort to force the changeling to confess and facilitate the return of the real Bridget. Bourke points out that Bridget and Michael Cleary did not have children and that Bridget was under a cloud of suspicion and thought to be odd for not having become a mother after marriage. See Angela Bourke, *The Burning of Bridget Cleary: A True Story* (London: Pimlico, 1999).

14 Elizabeth Throop, *Net Curtains and Closed Doors: Intimacy, Family and Public Life in Dublin* (Westport, CT: Bergin & Garvey, 1999). Throop draws on Scheper-Hughes in part for her analysis of the measure of achieved adulthood reflected in having children.

15 Heather Paxson, *Making Modern Mothers: Ethics and Family Planning in Urban Greece* (Berkeley: University of California Press, 2004), p. 220.

16 Melissa Pashigian, 'Conceiving the Happy Family: Infertility and Marital Politics in Northern Vietnam', in Marcia C. Inhorn and Frank van Balen (eds), *Infertility Around the Globe* (Berkeley: University of California Press, 2002).

17 Marcia Inhorn, 'The "Local" Confronts the "Global": Infertile Bodies and the New Reproductive Technologies in Egypt', in Inhorn and van Balen (eds), *Infertility Around the Globe*; and *Quest for Conception: Gender, Fertility and Egyptian Medical Traditions* (Philadelphia: University of Pennsylvania Press, 1994).

18 Catherine Kohler Reissman, 'Positioning Gender Identity in Narratives of Infertility: South Indian Women's Lives in Context', in Inhorn and van Balen (eds), *Infertility Around the Globe*; and ' Stigma and Everyday Resistance Practices: Childless Women in South India', *Gender and Society*, vol. 14, 2000, pp. 111–35.

19 Gay Becker, *The Elusive Embryo: How Women and Men Approach New Reproductive Technologies* (Berkeley: University of California Press, 2000); and *Disrupted Lives: How People Create Meaning in a Chaotic World* (Berkeley: University of California Press, 1997).

20 This definition of family was made evident to me early on in my research as I began taking classes to learn the Irish language at University College Cork. The first week the instructor described the meaning of the word *clan* or family in Irish as 'a man, his wife and their children'.

21 Heather Paxson, 'Reproduction as Spiritual Kin Work: Orthodoxy, IVF and the Moral Economy of Motherhood in Greece', *Culture, Medicine and Psychiatry*, vol. 30, 2006; see also Michael Herzfeld, *Cultural Intimacy: Social Poetics in the Nation-State* (New York: Routledge, 2005).

22 Aideen Kane and Edel O'Brien, *Making Babies* (Dublin: Mint Productions, 2004).

23 Herzfeld, *Cultural Intimacy*, p. 16.

24 Faye Ginsberg, *Contested Lives: The Abortion Debate in an American Community* (Berkeley: University of California Press, 1998), p. 141.

25 Nicola Yeates, 'Gender, Familism and Housing: Matrimonial Property Rights in Ireland', *Women's Studies International Forum*, vol. 22, no. 6, 1999, p. 608. The choice of the word 'familism' can be contentious in anthropology but it is often used by scholars of Irish history and family politics and I include it as part of the descriptive context for my work. It does not relate to the work of Edward Banfield (1958) whose controversial analysis of rural Mediterranean societies described an unwillingness to act on behalf of the well-being of community. His central tenet was that 'amoral familism' operates when people 'maximise the material, short-run advantage of the nuclear family; assume that all others will do likewise'. See Edward C. Banfield, *The Moral Basis for a Backward Society* (Glencoe, IL: Free Press, 1958), p. 85. Instead, the use of familism in the social science literature on Ireland refers to social, institutional and political structures that serve to perpetuate the definition of an idealised hetero-normative marital family. For more descriptions of familism in Ireland see Ann Byrne, 'Familist Ideology and Difficult Identities: "Never-Married" Women in Contemporary Irish Society', in Cohen and Curtin (eds), *Reclaiming Gender*.

26 Tony Fahey and Catherine Anne Field, *Families in Ireland: An Analysis of Patterns and Trends* (Dublin: Stationery Office, 2008), p. 7.

27 Ibid. Divorce has only been legally available in Ireland since 1995, following a national referendum.

28 In addition, according to a report commissioned by the Irish Human Rights Commission in 2006, marriage rates increased from 4.3 per 1,000 of the population in 1995 to 5.1 in 2004. This can be compared to the rate in 1951 which was only slightly higher at 5.4. Judy Walsh and Fergus Ryan, *The Rights of De Facto Couples* (Dublin: Irish Human Rights Commission, 2006), p. 2.

29 Cohabiting couples represented 11.6 percent of all family units in 2006 compared with 8.4 percent in 2002 and, according to the Central Statistics Office, represents the fastest growing type of family unit. The majority, almost two thirds, were couples without children but the fact that 33 percent did have children points again to the shift away from the predominance of marriage as a precursor to parenthood. Central Statistics Office press release, 31 May 2007 http://www.cso.ie/en/newsandevents/pressreleases/2007pressreleases/2006censusofpopulation-volume3-householdcompositionfamilyunit sandfertility/ [accessed on 29 November 2012]; see also Fahey and Field, *Families in Ireland*.

30 Betty Hilliard, 'Changing Irish Attitudes to Marriage and Family in Cross-National Comparison', in Betty Hilliard and Máire Nic Ghiolla Phádraig (eds), *Changing Ireland in International Comparison* (Dublin: The Liffey Press, 2007).

31 Central Statistics Office press release, 31 May 2007 http://www.cso.ie/en/newsandevents/pressreleases/2007pressreleases/2006censusofpopulation-volume3-householdcompositionfamilyunitsandfertility/ [accessed on 29 November 2012].

32 Cormac Ó Grada, *Éirvana* (Dublin: UCD Centre for Economic Research Working Papers Series WP08/12, 2008)

33 As I note in the Introduction, the analytical value of this construction has been challenged by feminists as essentialist and an imposition of a value structure that fails to account for the overlap and blurring of public and private or public and domestic space. See Louise Lamphere, 'The Domestic Sphere of Women and the Public World of Men: The Strengths and Limitations of an Anthropological Dichotomy', in Caroline B. Brettell and Carolyn F. Sargent (eds), *Gender in Cross-Cultural Perspective* (Upper Saddle River, NJ: Prentice Hall, 2001). It is also linked, historically, to the social, economic and political structures that depend upon and enhance its use. However, it remains an organisational concept for many people in Ireland when talking about family, gender and the past.

34 Pauline Conroy, 'Maternity Confined: The Struggle for Fertility Control', in Kennedy (ed.), *Motherhood in Ireland*, p. 138.

35 Ibid., p. 128.

36 Adrienne Rich, *Of Woman Born: Motherhood as Experience and Institution*, 1st edn (New York: Norton, 1976).

37 Michelle Murphy, 'Liberation Through Control of the Body Politics of US Radical Feminism', in Lorraine Daston and Fernando Vidal (eds), *The Moral Authority of Nature* (Chicago: University of Chicago Press, 2004); see also Michelle Z. Rosaldo, 'The Use and Abuse of Anthropology: Reflections on Feminism and Cross-Cultural Understanding', *Signs: Journal of Women in Culture and Society*, vol. 5, no. 3, 1980, pp. 389–417.

38 See 'An Irishman's Diary', *The Irish Times*, 8 February 2005.

39 Moira J. Maguire, 'The Changing Face of Catholic Ireland: Conservatism and Liberalism in the Ann Lovett and Kerry Babies Scandals', *Feminist Studies*, vol. 27, no. 2, 2001, pp. 335–58.

40 Ginsburg, *Contested Lives*, p. 143 (emphasis in original).

41 As I discussed in the introduction to this chapter, the Irish Census for 2006 notes that cohabiting couples represented the fastest-growing type of family unit; 11.6% of all households fitted this model, up from 8.4% only 4 years earlier http://www.cso.ie/en/newsandevents/pressreleases/2007pressreleases/2006censusofpopulation-volume3-householdcompositionfamilyunitsandfertility/ [accessed on 29 November 2012].

42 Patricia Burke Brogan, 'The Magdalen Experience', in Kennedy (ed.), *Motherhood in Ireland*; Alexis Guilbride, 'Infanticide: The Crime of Motherhood', in Kennedy (ed.), *Motherhood in Ireland*; F. Finnegan, *Do*

Penance or Perish (Oxford: Oxford University Press, 2004).

43 Seyla Banhabid: *Feminist Contentions: A Philosophical Exchange* (New York: Routledge, 1995); Lois McNay: 'Agency, Anticipation, Indeterminacy in Feminist Theory', *Feminist Theory*, vol. 4, no. 2, 2003, pp. 139–48.

44 Ginsburg, *Contested Lives*, p. 144.

45 For a discussion on the concept of the financially and socially worthy parent, see Gayle Letherby, 'Other than Mother and Mothers as Others: The Experience of Motherhood and Non-Motherhood in Relation to "infertility" and "involuntary childlessness"', *Women's Studies International Forum*, vol. 22, no. 3, 1999.

46 Naomi Pfeffer, *The Stork and the Syringe: A Political History of Reproductive Medicine* (Oxford: Blackwell Publishers, 1993); Janice G. Raymond, *Women as Wombs: Reproductive Technologies and the Battle Over Women's Freedom* (San Francisco: Harper, 1994); Margarete Sandelowski, *With Child in Mind: Studies of the Personal Encounter with Infertility* (Philadelphia: University of Pennsylvania Press, 1993).

47 Sarah Earle and Gayle Letherby, 'Conceiving Time? Women Who Do or Do Not Conceive', *Sociology of Health and Illness*, vol. 29, no. 2, 2007, pp. 233–50; and *Gender, Identity and Reproduction: Social Perspectives* (London: Palgrave, 2003); Rosalind Pollack Petchesky, 'The Body as Property: A Feminist Re-Vision', in Faye D. Ginsburg and Rayna Rapp (eds), *Conceiving the New World Order* (Berkeley: University of California Press, 1995); and 'Foetal Images: The Power of Visual Culture in the Politics of Reproduction', in Michelle Stanworth (ed.), *Reproductive Technologies: Gender, Motherhood and Medicine* (Cambridge: Polity Press, 1987).

48 Paxson, *Making Modern Mothers*, pp. 65–6.

49 Letherby and Williams (1999) also describe the social construction of childless women as selfish and the difficulty feminists have in representing adequately the emotional and social challenges posed by 'involuntary' childlessness in comparison to the celebration of a choice to be child-free.

50 Paxson, *Making Modern Mothers*, p. 35.

51 Eileen Conway, 'Motherhood Interrupted: Adoption in Ireland', in Kennedy (ed.), *Motherhood in Ireland*, p. 190.

52 Sarah Franklin, *Embodied Progress: A Cultural Account of Assisted Conception* (London: Routledge, 1997), p. 131.

53 See Kennedy (ed.), *Motherhood in Ireland*.

54 Bourdieu, *Outline of a Theory of Practice*.

55 Ana Maria Alonso, 'The Use and Abuse of Feminist Theory: Fear, Dust and Commensality', in Alejandro Lugo and Bill Maurer (eds), *Gender Matters: Rereading Michelle Rosaldo* (Ann Arbor, MI: University of Michigan Press, 2000), pp. 223–4. See also Ginsburg and Rapp, *Conceiving the New World Order*.

56 Gaye Becker, *Elusive Embryo 2000* notes a similar frustration in her multi-sited and extensive collection of interviews in the US. She was also unable to access people who were in lower income brackets despite attempts to recruit a wide range of participants in her various studies. Among my

attempts were discussions with community service groups such as St Vincent de Paul and the people working with Travellers in Cork City. A group of women in the Traveller community, whom I befriended, laughed out loud when I told them what I was researching. They all noted that as far as they were concerned conception was only problematic if one could not control it. Since I did not meet anyone who told a different story it is difficult to judge the extent to which childlessness affected couples among the Traveller community. Certainly their practice of marrying very young would maximise women's reproductive potential but infertility would, presumably, still be an issue for at least some men and women in the community. See Sharon Gmelch, *Irish Life and Traditions* (Dublin: The O'Brien Press, 1986) for more on the Travellers.

3. CONCEIVING NONCONFORMITY

1 See Judith Butler, *Bodies that Matter* (New York: Routledge, 1993); *Gender Trouble* (New York: Routledge, 1990); 'Is Kinship Always-Already Heterosexual?' *Differences: A Journal of Feminist Cultural Studies*, vol. 15, no. 1, 2002, pp. 14–43. While the term 'hetero-normative' is often used by Judith Butler it is not exclusive to her work. I use it here to reinforce the relationship between heterosexual relationships and reproduction as an assumed norm to which all other sexual and reproductive relationships are compared or contrasted.

2 Saba Mahmood, *Politics of Piety: The Islamic Revival and the Feminist Subject* (Princeton, NJ: Princeton University Press, 2005), p. 153.

3 Michelle Murphy, 'Liberation Through Control of the Body Politics of US Radical Feminism', in Lorraine Daston and Fernando Vidal (eds), *The Moral Authority of Nature* (Chicago: University of Chicago Press, 2004).

4 I chose Sarah as a pseudonym here not entirely randomly as it alludes to the biblical story of Sarah and Abraham who waited many years to become parents with the assistance of God.

5 FSH or follicle stimulating hormones is measured to determine whether the hormonal balance in a woman's body is likely to support natural or assisted conception. High levels of FSH secreted from the pituitary gland suggest menopause or ovarian failure and can reduce the likelihood of success in IVF. Bruce R. Carr *et al. Essential Reproductive Medicine.* (Toronto: McGraw Hill, 2005)

6 The short notice was a feature of the circumstances as Sarah adopted her child in an African country to which she had relocated. This was standard procedure apparently once the assessments had been done and the placement ordered.

7 Several of my participants recalled hearing from the nuns in school about the 'missions' in Africa and the need to help the little black children there. Collections and prayers for the missions were apparently common even if the actual information about them was vague.

8 Ann Murphy, 'I didn't want to let the opportunity to have a baby pass me by while I was waiting for Mr Right', *Irish Independent*, 21 May 2008.

9 For the story of Sarah and Abraham see the Book of Genesis, Chapters 15, 17, 18 and 21 in the King James version of the Holy Bible.

10 Anna Lowenhaupt Tsing, *In the Realm of the Diamond Queen: Marginality in an Out-of-the-Way Place* (Princeton, NJ: Princeton University Press, 1993), pp. 114–17. Tsing describes how gender plays a role in the complex social and economic meaning of childbirth among the Meritus Dayaks in Indonesia. She notes that men have different aims in achieving status and economic independence linked to marriage and fathering children whereas women's 'readiness' to be mothers is often more subjectively determined.

11 In 2009 a clinic in Kilkenny began to provide fertility treatment services for single women. Since then a couple of other clinics have followed suit, removing the condition that couples be married.

12 This form of ART involves stimulating the ovaries to produce more than one egg in a cycle, but rather than removing the eggs, as occurs in IVF, the cycle is monitored by frequent ultrasound examinations to determine the exact timing of ovulation. When this occurs, sperm (either donor or partner's) is inserted into the uterus by a small tube to facilitate the best opportunity for fertilisation. The process is less technical, less invasive and less costly.

13 Commission on Assisted Human Reproduction (CAHR), *Report of the Commission on Assisted Human Reproduction* (Dublin: Stationery Office, 2005), p. 137.

14 Angela O'Connell, 'Jet Trails, Train Rails and Emails', conference paper presented at 'Feminisms: Within and Without' conference, National University of Ireland, Galway, July 2005.

15 Katherine Conrad, *Locked in the Family Cell* (Madison, WI: University of Wisconsin Press, 2004), pp. 21–2.

16 Tom Inglis, *Moral Monopoly: The Rise and Fall of the Catholic Church in Modern Ireland* (Dublin: UCD Press, 1998 [1987]), p. 97; see also Conrad, *Locked in the Family Cell*; Crystel Hug, *The Politics of Sexual Morality in Ireland* (London: Macmillan, 1999).

17 CAHR, *Report of the Commission on Assisted Human Reproduction*. The CAHR report cites the case of MhicMhathúna v. Ireland [1995] in which Article 41.3.1 was tested with respect to the provision of 'child-centred financial support to one-parent families'. The Supreme Court judgement stated that such provision did not amount to a failure in the constitutional duty to protect marriage, since such payments could not be seen as 'an inducement not to marry'.

4. CONCEIVING OF GRIEVING

1 Gayle Letherby, 'Challenging Dominant Discourses: Identity and Change and the Experience of "Infertility" and "Involuntary Childlessness"', *Journal of Gender Studies*, vol. 11, no. 3, 2002, pp. 277–88; and 'Childless and Bereft? Stereotypes and Realities in Relation to "Voluntary" and "Involuntary" Childlessness and Womanhood', *Sociological Inquiry*, vol. 72, no. 1, Winter 2002, pp. 7–20.

2 Linda Layne, 'Making Memories: Trauma, Choice and Consumer Culture in the Case of Pregnancy Loss', in Janelle S. Taylor, Linda L. Layne and Danielle F. Wozniak (eds), *Consuming Motherhood* (London: Rutgers University Press, 2004), p. 129; see also, by the same author, 'Pregnancy Loss, Stigma, Irony and Masculinities: Reflections on and Future Directions for Research on Religion in the Global Practice of IVF', *Culture, Medicine and Psychiatry*, vol. 30, no. 4, 2006, pp. 537–45; and 'Baby Things as Fetishes? Memorial Goods, Simulacra and the "Realness" Problem of Pregnancy Loss', in Helena Ragoné and France Winddance Twine (eds), *Ideologies and Technologies of Motherhood: Race, Class, Sexuality and Nationalism* (London: Routledge, 2000).

3 Louis Althusser, *Essays on Ideology* (London: Verso, 1970).

4 Judith Butler, *Gender Trouble* (New York: Routledge, 1990).

5 Letherby 'Challenging Dominant Discourses', p. 277.

6 Elisabeth Kübler-Ross, *On Death and Dying* (New York: Quality Paperbacks, 1973 [1970]); and Elisabeth Kübler-Ross and David Kessler, *On Grief and Grieving: Finding the Meaning of Grief Through the Five Stages of Loss* (New York: Simon & Schuster, 2005). The notion that grief follows stages or an established pattern is associated with the work of Elizabeth Kübler-Ross in the 1970s. As a psychiatrist with an interest in helping terminally ill patients have a better experience with end of life issues, Kübler-Ross published her widely cited volume *On Death and Dying*. She argues for a series of stages that dying people might experience before ultimately (if ever) accepting their situation, and she later extended this perspective in *On Grief and Grieving*. Her rather rigid construction of stages has been challenged as both unsupported and perhaps even unhelpful in more recent literature. See Russell Friedman and John W. James, 'The Myth of the Stages of Dying, Death and Grief', *Skeptic*, vol. 14, no. 2, 2008, pp. 37–41; Robert A. Neimeyer (ed.), *Meaning, Reconstruction and the Experience of Loss* (Washington, DC: American Psychological Association, 2001). While other people talked about grief in different ways, Elsa was the only participant to mention *stages* of grieving, but her association with the support network suggests it was an organisational motif for people in that forum.

7 Marcia Inhorn, *Quest for Conception: Gender, Fertility and Egyptian Medical Traditions* (Philadelphia: University of Pennsylvania Press, 1994).

8 Heather Paxson, *Making Modern Mothers: Ethics and Family Planning in Urban Greece* (Berkeley: University of California Press, 2004). Paxson found that there was an emphasis on motherhood as completing a woman's identity in her work in Greece.

9 Gayle Letherby, 'Other than Mother and Mothers as Others: The Experience of Motherhood and Non-Motherhood in Relation to "Infertility" and "Involuntary Childlessness"', *Women's Studies International Forum*, vol. 22, no. 3, 1999, pp. 359–72.

10 Arthur Greil, 'A Secret Stigma: The Analogy Between Infertility and Chronic Illness and Disability', *Advances in Medical Sociology*, vol. 2, 1991,

pp. 17–38; Gay Becker, *The Elusive Embryo: How Women and Men Approach New Reproductive Technologies* (Berkeley: University of California Press, 2000); Naomi Pfeffer and Anne Woollett, *The Experience of Infertility* (London: Virago Press, 1983).

11 Julia McQuillan, 'Frustrated Fertility: Infertility and Psychological Distress Among Women', *Journal of Marriage and the Family*, vol. 65, no. 4, 2003, pp. 1007–18.

12 Linda Nicholson, 'Introduction' in Seyla Benhabib, *Feminist Contentions: A Philosophical Exchange* (New York: Routledge, 1995).

13 Gay Becker, *Disrupted Lives: How People Create Meaning in a Chaotic World* (Berkeley: University of California Press, 1997).

14 An ectopic pregnancy occurs when the fertilised egg does not travel from the fallopian tubes into the womb, but rather implants and begins to grow inside the tube itself. Since the fallopian tube is not much larger in diameter than a human hair and is well supplied with blood vessels, this can very rapidly become a potentially life-threatening event for a woman as the embryo continues to grow and threatens to rupture the tube. Surgical treatment to remove the embryo often leaves a woman with scarring in the tube and frequently the only recourse is removal of the fallopian tube altogether, leading to a reduction in potential fertility.

15 Ann Byrne, 'Familist Ideology and Difficult Identities: "Never-Married" Women in Contemporary Irish Society', in Marilyn Cohen and Nancy J. Curtin (eds), *Reclaiming Gender: Transgressive Identities in Modern Ireland* (New York: St Martin's Press, 1999), p. 72; see also Katherine Conrad, 'Fetal Ireland: National Bodies and Political Agency', *Éire/Ireland, Interdisciplinary Journal of Irish Studies*, vol. XXXVI, 2001. The rhetorical construction of mother Ireland and the morality implied by what Lisa Smyth identifies as the idiomatic 'pro-life nation' have been used to consolidate and sustain ideological distinctions between Ireland and its former coloniser as well as other nations of the EU. See Nancy J. Curtin, '"A Nation of Abortive Men": Gendered Citizenship and Early Irish Republicanism', in Cohen and Curtin (eds), *Reclaiming Gender*; Lisa Smyth, *Abortion and Nation: The Politics of Reproduction in Contemporary Ireland* (Farnham, Surrey: Ashgate, 2005).

16 Becker, *Disrupted Lives*, p. 142. Emphasis original.

17 In some cases infertility is absolute and final, as in the case of early menopause, hysterectomy, hormonal imbalances, trauma to reproductive organs, surgical sterilisation and azoospermatosis (absence of sperm).

18 Sarah Franklin, *Embodied Progress*, p. 155 and Gay Becker, *Disrupted Lives*, p. 122.

19 Thomas Csordas, *Body, Meaning, Healing*.

20 Sarah Franklin, *Embodied Progress*.

21 Embryo transfer (ET) is the process of inserting, via a fine plastic tube, one or more embryos into the uterus of a woman who has taken hormonal treatments in order to maximise the chance of the embryos 'implanting' or adhering and beginning to grow.

22 In the process of IVF, fertilised eggs are left to incubate in the lab for between two and five days before being returned to the womb or frozen. During this time they are often 'graded' for quality and assessed for cell division progress or signs of 'fragmentation'. See Bruce R. Carr, Richard E. Blackwell and Ricardo Azziz, *Essential Reproductive Medicine* (New York: McGraw-Hill, 2005), pp. 568–9.

23 Mary Jacobus, Evelyn Fox Keller and Sally Shuttleworth, *Body/Politics: Women and the Discourses of Science* (London: Routledge, 1990), p. 1.

24 Sarah Franklin, *Embodied Progress: A Cultural Account of Assisted Conception* (London: Routledge, 1997) p. 145.

25 National Infertility Support and Information Group (http://www.nisig.ie).

26 Jill Allison, 'Conceiving Silence: Infertility as Discursive Contradiction in Ireland', *Medical Anthropology Quarterly*, vol. 25, no. 1, 2011, pp. 1–21.

27 Franklin, *Embodied Progress*, p. 123.

5. Eggs, Sperm and Conceptions of a Moral Nature

1 Sylvia Junko Yanagisako and Carol Lowery Delaney, *Naturalizing Power: Essays in Feminist Cultural Analysis* (New York: Routledge, 1995).

2 Kelly Oliver, 'Antigone's Ghost: Undoing Hegel's *Phenomenology of Spirit'*, *Hypatia*, vol. 11, no. 1, 1996, pp. 67–90; see also Sherry B. Ortner and Harriet Whitehead (eds), *Sexual Meanings: The Cultural Construction of Gender and Sexuality* (Cambridge: Cambridge University Press, 1981); Jacqueline Stevens, *Reproducing the State* (Princeton, NJ: Princeton University Press, 1999).

3 Kelly Oliver, 'Antigone's Ghost', p. 70.

4 Sarah Franklin, 'Biologization Revisited: Kinship Theory in the Context of the New Biologies', in Sarah Franklin and Susan McKinnon (eds), *Relative Values: Reconfiguring Kinship Studies* (Durham, NC: Duke University Press, 2001); and 'Making Representations: The Parliamentary Debate on the Human Fertilization and Embryology Act', in Jeanette Edwards, Sarah Franklin, Eric Hirsch, Frances Price and Marilyn Strathern (eds), *Technologies of Procreation: Kinship in the Age of Assisted Conception* (London: Routledge, 1999 [1993]); Bruno Latour, *We Have Never Been Modern* (Cambridge, MA: Harvard University Press, 1993); Margaret Lock, *Twice Dead: Organ Transplants and the Reinvention of Death* (London: University of California Press, 2002); and 'Contesting the Natural in Japan: Moral Dilemmas and Technologies of Dying', *Culture, Medicine and Psychiatry*, vol. 19, no. 1, 1995.

5 The Immaculate Conception of Mary is associated with her perpetual virginity described by Pope Pius IX in 1854 as 'preserved from the stain of original sin'. *Catechism of the Catholic Church*, http://www.vatican.va/archive/ccc_css/archive/catechism/p122a3p2.htm#490

6 For a discussion on the impact of religious views on bioethics debates in a cross-cultural context, see Mary Rodgers Bundren, 'The Influence of Catholicism, Islam and Judaism on the Assisted Reproductive Technologies (ART) Bioethical and Legal Debate: A Comparative Survey of ART in Italy,

Egypt and Israel', *University of Detroit Mercy Law Review*, vol. 84, no. 5, 2007, pp. 715–46.

7 Lorraine Daston and Fernando Vidal, *The Moral Authority of Nature* (Chicago: University of Chicago Press, 2004), p. 1.

8 Jarrett Zigon, *Morality: An Anthropological Perspective* (Oxford: Berg, 2008).

9 Aditya Bhardadwaj, 'Sacred Conceptions: Clinical Theodicies, Uncertain Science and Technologies of Procreation in India', *Culture, Medicine and Psychiatry*, vol. 30, no. 4, 2006, pp. 451–65; and 'Sacred Modernity: Religion, Infertility and Technoscientific Conception Around the Globe', *Culture, Medicine and Psychiatry*, vol. 30, no. 4, 2006, pp. 423–45.

10 Marcia Inhorn, 'Making Muslim Babies: IVF and Gamete Donation in Sunni Versus Shi'a Islam', *Culture, Medicine and Psychiatry*, vol. 30, no. 4, 2006, pp. 427–50; and 'The "Local" Confronts the "Global": Infertile Bodies and the New Reproductive Technologies in Egypt', in Marcia Inhorn and Frank van Balen (eds), *Infertility Around the Globe* (Berkeley: University of California Press, 2002).

11 Susan Martha Kahn, 'Making Technology Familiar: Orthodox Jews and Infertility Support, Advice and Inspiration', *Culture, Medicine and Psychiatry*, vol. 30, no. 4, 2006, pp. 467–80; and 'Rabbis and Reproduction: The Uses of New Reproductive Technologies Among Ultraorthodox Jews in Israel', in Inhorn and van Balen (eds) *Infertility Around the Globe*.

12 Linda L. Layne, 'Pregnancy Loss, Stigma, Irony and Masculinities: Reflections on and Future Directions for Research on Religion in the Global Practice of IVF', *Culture, Medicine and Psychiatry*, vol. 30, no. 4, 2006, pp. 537–45; Claris M. Thompson, 'God is in the Details: Comparative Perspectives on the Intertwining of Religion and Assisted Reproductive Technologies', *Culture, Medicine and Psychiatry*, vol. 30, no. 4, 2006, pp. 557–61.

13 Heather Paxson, 'Reproduction as Spiritual Kin Work: Orthodoxy, IVF and the Moral Economy of Motherhood in Greece', *Culture, Medicine and Psychiatry*, vol. 30, no. 4, 2006, pp. 481–505.

14 This kind of simultaneous accommodation and resistance to the formal views of the Roman Catholic Church resonates with other examples of anti-clericalism in Europe. See Ellen Badone, *Religious Orthodoxy and Popular Faith in European Society* (Princeton, NJ: Princeton University Press, 1990); and Caroline B. Brettell, 'Breton Folklore of Anticlericalism', in Ellen Badone (ed.), *Religious Orthodoxy and Popular Faith in European Society* (Princeton, NJ: Princeton University Press, 1990).

15 Orla McDonnell, 'New Reproductive Technologies and Public Discourse: From Biopolitics to Bioethics', unpublished PhD dissertation, University College Cork, 2001; Orla McDonnell and Jill Allison, 'From Biopolitics to Bioethics: Church, State, Medicine and Assisted Reproduction Technology in Ireland', *Sociology of Health and Illness*, vol. 28, no. 6, 2006, pp. 817–37.

16 Irish Catholic Bishops' Conference, 'Irish Catholic Bishops Committee for Bioethics Assisted Human Reproduction: Facts and Ethical Issues', *http://www.catholicbishops.ie/bioethics/389* [accessed 1 November 2012].

17 McDonnell, 'New Reproductive Technologies and Public Discourse'. McDonnell describes the public backlash in the media, reflected in a large number of calls to popular radio talk shows, letters to the editors of national newspapers and calls to support groups in protest against the archbishop's remarks.

18 The Irish Catholic Bishops' Committee for Bioethics was formed in 1996 as a sub-committee of the Irish Catholic Bishops' Joint Healthcare Commission. In 2007 it became the Irish Catholic Bishops' Consultative Group.

19 Irish Catholic Bishops' Committee for Bioethics, *Towards a Creative Response to Infertility* (Dublin: Veritas, 2006 [2005]), p. 5 (http://www.catholic bishops.ie/wp-content/uploads/images/docs/towardsacreative response.pdf [accessed 1 November 2012]).

20 The papal encyclical (letter) *Humanae Vitae* was issued by Pope Paul VI on 25 July 1968, to re-affrim the Catholic Church's position on the meaning of conjugal love, parental responsibility and its disapproval of artificial means of contraception. It emphasises instead the 'fundamental nature of the marriage act, while uniting husband and wife in the closest intimacy, also renders them capable of generating new life – and this as a result of laws written into the actual nature of man and of woman' (http://www. vatican.va/holy_father/paul_vi/encyclicals/documents/hf_p–vi_enc_ 25071968_humanae–vitae_en.html) [accessed on 29 November 2012].

21 Heather Paxson, *Making Modern Mothers: Ethics and Family Planning in Urban Greece* (Berkeley: University of California Press, 2004) p. 227.

22 Irish Catholic Bishops' Committee for Bioethics, *Towards a Creative Response to Infertility*.

23 Deidre Madden, 'Article 40.3.3 and Assisted Reproduction in Ireland', in Jennifer Schweppe (ed.), *The Unborn Child, Article 40.3.3 and Abortion in Ireland: Twenty-Five Years of Protection?* (Dublin: The Liffey Press, 2008).

24 This stance is reminiscent of the response by the hierarchy to the Mother and Child Scheme six decades earlier wherein providing care to women and children was feared for its potential to encourage behaviour regarded as immoral by the church, such as the use of contraception (Hug 1999:84; see also Browne 1986; Whyte 1980).

25 Latour, *We Have Never Been Modern*, p. 3.

26 The other couple, Paul and Lara, had joined an Evangelical Christian church but did not cite their infertility problems or treatment issues as having exclusively precipitated this shift.

27 This description is a synthesis of information from Bruce R. Carr, Richard E. Blackwell and Ricardo Azziz, *Essential Reproductive Medicine* (New York: McGraw-Hill, 2005) as well as detailed participant descriptions of treat-ment, information given to me by fertility medicine practitioners in clinics.

28 Donna Haraway, *Simians, Cyborgs and Women: The Reinvention of Nature* (New York: Routledge, 1991), p. 154.

29 Sarah Franklin, *Embodied Progress: A Cultural Account of Assisted Conception* (London: Routledge, 1997).

30 A less invasive procedure known as intrauterine insemination (IUI) involves taking collected sperm, washing out the less desirable ones and concentrating the remainder and inserting this optimum sperm directly into the uterus with a plastic catheter. It is much less costly, does not always necessitate the use of hormonal support for the woman and can sometimes overcome male factor infertility problems, forestalling the need for IVF.

31 Lucy Fith, Ann Jacoby and Mark Gabbany, 'Ethical Boundary-Work in the Infertility Clinic', *Sociology of Health and Illness*, vol. 33, no. 4, 2011, p. 571.

32 Ibid., p. 576; see also Barry Hoffmaster, 'Morality and the Social Sciences', in G. Weisz (ed.), *Social Science Perspectives on Medical Ethics* (Boston: Kinwer Academic, 1990).

33 Angela Martin, 'Death of a Nation: Transnationalism, Bodies and Abortion in Late Twentieth-Century Ireland', in Tamar Mayar (ed.), *Gender Ironies of Nationalism: Sexing the Nation* (London: Routledge, 2000).

34 Paxson, *Making Modern Mothers*, p. 15.

35 Jeanette Edwards, 'Explicit Connections: Ethnographic Enquiry in North-West England', in Edwards *et al.* (eds), *Technologies of Procreation*; Robert D. Nachtigall, 'Secrecy: An Unresolved Issue in the Practice of Donor Insemination', *American Journal of Obstetrics and Gynecology*, vol. 168, 1993, pp. 1846–53; Robert D. Nachtigall, Gay Becker and Mark Wozny, 'The Effects of Gender-Specific Diagnosis on Men's and Women's Response to Infertility', *Fertility and Sterility*, vol. 54, 1992, pp. 113–21.

36 Erica Haimes, 'Issues of Gender in Gamete Donation', *Social Science and Medicine*, vol. 36, no.1, 1993, p. 85.

37 Frances Price, 'Beyond Expectation: Clinical Practices and Clinical Concerns', in Edwards *et al.* (eds), *Technologies of Procreation*, p. 56.

38 Emily Martin, 'The Egg and the Sperm: How Science has Constructed a Romance Based on Stereotypical Male–Female Roles', *Signs: Journal of Women in Culture and Society*, vol. 16, no. 3, 1991, pp. 485–501.

39 Gayle Letherby and Sarah Earle, *Gender, Identity and Reproduction* (New York: Palgrave Macmillan, 2003), p. 53.

40 Franklin, *Embodied Progress*.

41 GIFT is useful in cases of one blocked fallopian tube or where fertilisation rates have been high but embryos have failed to implant during regular IVF. It is also useful where there has been difficulty transferring embryos to the womb following IVF. See Carr *et al.*, *Essential Reproductive Medicine*, p. 535.

42 Sperm can also be recovered from the vagina after intercourse and subsequently inserted into the fallopian tube by laparoscopy. J.G. Schenker, 'Women's Reproductive Health: Monotheistic Religious Perspectives', *International Journal of Gynecology and Obstetrics*, vol. 70, no. 1, 2000, pp. 77–86.

43 NaPro originated in the US and has been available in Ireland since 1998. Its practitioners claim its efficacy in treating a variety of gynaecological and reproductive problems including infertility, recurrent miscarriage and a number of menstrual problems (http://www.fertilitycare.ie [accessed 1 November 2012]).

44 At the time of writing, the number of practitioners of NaPro has apparently increased to six. NaPro Fertility Care, http://www.fertilitycare.ie/ FertilityCareIreland.htm; [accessed 29 November 2012] see also Brian McDonald, 'Party time as miracle 500 enjoy birthday', *Irish Independent*, 21 April 2008.

45 I was also rather shocked to have been confronted by a very large, bloodied figure of Jesus on a cross, mounted on the wall in the staircase that led to the medical library at the UCC Hospital in Cork. Nobody ascending or descending that staircase could fail to notice the imposing figure looming over them.

46 The presence of veterinary medicine practitioners at this conference is symbolic of the complexity of the issues around science, nature and morality with respect to assisted reproduction. Much of the 'science' and many of the cutting-edge developments come from the realm of agricultural practice where controlling and enhancing fertility and reproduction are important aspects of agricultural production.

47 Tom Inglis, *Truth, Power and Lies: Irish Society and the Case of the Kerry Babies* (Dublin, UCD Press, 2003), pp. 144–6.

48 Inhorn and van Balen (eds), *Infertility Around the Globe*.

49 Trans-epididymal sperm aspiration in which sperm are taken surgically from the testicles in cases where very few sperm are produced.

6. CONCEPTIONS OF CONTENTION

1 David Schneider, *American Kinship: A Cultural Account*, 2nd edn (Chicago: University of Chicago Press, 1980), p. 23.

2 Sylvia Nagl, 'Biomedicine and Moral Agency in a Complex World', in Margit Shildrick and Roxanne Mykitiuk (eds), *Ethics of the Body: Postconventional Challenges* (Cambridge, MA: The MIT Press, 2005), p. 167.

3 Monica Konrad, *Nameless Relations* (New York: Berghahn Books, 2005), p. 241.

4 Susan McKinnon and Sydel Silverman, *Complexities: Beyond Nature and Nurture* (Chicago: University of Chicago Press, 2005); see also Jacqueline Stevens, 'Methods of Adoption: Eliminating Genetic Privilege', in Sally Haslanger and Charlotte Witt (eds), *Adoption Matters: Philosophical and Feminist Essays* (Ithaca, NY: Cornell University Press, 2005).

5 Sarah Franklin, 'Making Representations: The Parliamentary Debate on the Human Fertilization and Embryology Act', in Jeanette Edwards, Sarah Franklin, Eric Hirsch, Frances Price and Marilyn Strathern (eds), *Technologies of Procreation: Kinship in the Age of Assisted Conception* (London: Routledge, 1999 [1993]).

6 Rhonda Shaw, 'Rethinking Reproductive Gifts as Body Projects', *Sociology*, vol. 42, no. 1, 2008, p. 12; see also Nagl, 'Biomedicine and Moral Agency in a Complex World'; Margrit Shildrick, 'Beyond the Body of Bioethics: Challenging the Conventions', in Margit Shildrick and Roxanne Mykitiuk (eds), *Ethics of the Body: Postconventional Challenges* (Cambridge, MA: The MIT Press, 2005).

7 Carol Gilligan, *Mapping the Moral Domain: A Contribution of Women's Thinking to Psychological Theory and Education* (Cambridge, MA: Harvard University Press, 1988); and *In a Different Voice: Psychological Theory and Women's Development* (Cambridge, MA: Harvard University Press, 1982); see also Margrit Shildrick, *Leaky Bodies and Boundaries: Feminism, Postmodernism and (Bio)Ethics* (London: Routledge, 1997).

8 Kath Weston, 'Kinship, Controversy and the Sharing of Substance: The Race/Class Politics of Blood Transfusion', in Sarah Franklin and Susan McKinnon (eds), *Relative Values: Reconfiguring Kinship Studies* (Durham, NC: Duke University Press, 2001).

9 Altruistic donors are those who do not have a relative or friend for whom they are donating, but rather donate eggs for use by anyone on the waiting list at the discretion of the clinic. In Ireland, they are reimbursed for any 'expenses' such as travel costs, drugs and medical costs incurred.

10 Carl O'Brien, 'The identity issue: how donated eggs and sperm are redefining parenthood', *The Irish Times*, 21 November 2011.

11 The Irish Catholic Bishops' Conference paper titled *Towards a Creative Response to Infertility* was first issued as a statement in response to the CAHR report in 2005 and re-published as a document in 2006.

12 Irish Catholic Bishops' Conference, *Towards a Creative Response to Infertility* (Dublin: Veritas, 2006 [2005]), p. 23 (emphasis added)(http://www.catholic bishops.ie/wp-content/uploads/images/docs/towardsacreative response.pdf [accessed 1 November 2012]).

13 Marilyn Strathern, 'A Question of Context' (Introduction to 1st edition), in Edwards *et al.* (eds), *Technologies of Procreation*, p. 175.

14 Konrad, *Nameless Relations*, p. 241.

15 Ibid., p. 104; see also Ward Goodenough, *Description and Comparison in Cultural Anthropology* (Chicago: Aldine Publishing Company, 1970).

16 This ruling was controversial in light of presiding Judge MacMenamin's statement that 'by virtue of their marriage, the natural parents had become a family unit within the meaning of the Constitution, creating a constitutional presumption that the appropriate place for the upbringing and education of a child was within the family unit'. See Ray Managh, 'Judge speaks of "deep regret" in baby decision', *Irish Independent*, 16 September 2006; see also Dearbhail McDonald, 'Baby Ann returned to parents', *Irish Independent*, 8 June 2007.

17 The Adoption Act of 2010 provides a legal mechanism for considering the best interests of a child rather than the interests of the marital family as paramount and does not guarantee the dissolution of an adoption order in the case that birth parents marry.

18 See also Jacqueline Stevens, *Reproducing the State* (Princeton, NJ: Princeton University Press, 1999) for a discussion on the mechanisms through which naturalised meanings of birth are legally codified in the process of determining what constitutes families and membership in political society.

19 Commission on Assisted Human Reproduction (CAHR), *Report of the*

Commission on Assisted Human Reproduction (Dublin: Stationery Office, 2005), pp. 46–7.

20 Many countries have regulations that ensure some information on donors will be available to a child produced with donor gametes. The UK, Sweden, Canada, Austria, the Netherlands and New Zealand have laws providing some measure of access to information or identity for offspring of donor gametes. See Mary Lyndon Shanley, *Making Babies, Making Families* (Boston: Beacon Press, 2001); Shaw, 'Rethinking Reproductive Gifts as Body Projects', pp. 11–28; Olga van den Akker, 'A Review of Family Donor Constructs: Current Research and Future Directions', *Human Reproduction Update*, 19 September 2005, pp. 1–11.

21 HFEA regulations changed on 1 April 2005 to state that some 'identifying information' about gamete donors would be available, if requested, to any children born as a result of their donation. Donors are protected from any financial responsibility to offspring (http://www.hfea.gov.uk/en/368.html).

22 Commission on Assisted Human Reproduction (http://www.dohc.ie/publications/pdf/cahr.pdf).

23 Eric Hirsch, 'Negotiated Limits: Interviews in South-East England', and Frances Price, 'Beyond Expectation: Clinical Practices and Clinical Concerns', both in Edwards *et al.*, *Technologies of Procreation*.

24 Marilyn Strathen, *After Nature: English Kinship in the Late Twentieth Century* (Cambridge: Cambridge University Press, 1992), p. 151; see also Stevens, 'Methods of Adoption' for discussions on the implications of privileging genetic and biological motherhood in law.

25 Claris Thompson, 'Strategic Naturalizing: Kinship in an Infertility Clinic', in Franklin and McKinnon (eds), *Relative Values*, p. 175.

26 Heather Paxson, 'With Or Against Nature? IVF, Gender and Reproductive Agency in Athens, Greece', *Social Science and Medicine*, vol. 56, no. 9, 2003, p. 1862.

27 Shaw, 'Rethinking Reproductive Gifts as Body Projects', p. 20.

28 Konrad, *Nameless Relations*, p. 7.

29 Konrad's *Nameless Relations* published in 2005 was written at the time of the HFEA consultations in the UK that ultimately led to changes in legislation that now guarantee children of donor conceptions access to information about their donor parent when they reach the age of 18.

30 Kay refers to a common practice in clinics that offer donor egg treatment. People who are on a waiting list for donor eggs can bring a sibling or friend to the clinic as a donor but have the option of letting her donate to the woman who is at the top of the waiting list. As a recruiter, their name then goes to the top of the list and they receive eggs from the next available donor. Some people prefer this option as it allows for some distance between donor and recipient and removes the issue of a donor feeling a conflicted sense of parenthood to a child they might also have a social relationship with. For example, someone who recruits their own sister or a close

friend as a donor might find it easier to create this social separation between the child and the donor.

31 Strathern, 'A Question of Context'. See also Konrad, *Nameless Relations*.
32 Frances Price, 'Beyond Expectation: Clinical Practices and Clinical Concerns', in Jeanette Edwards, Sarah Franklin, Eric Hirsch, Frances Price and Marilyn Strathern (eds.) *Technologies of Procreation: Kinship in the Age of Assisted Conception* (London: Routledge 1999 [1993]). See also Rhonda Shaw, 'Rethinking Reproductive Gifts as Body Projects', *Sociology*, vol. 42, no. 1, 2008, pp. 11–25.
33 Konrad, *Nameless Relations*, p. 241.
34 Hirsch, 'Negotiated Limits', p. 106; see also Jeanette Edwards, 'Explicit Connections: Ethnographic Enquiry in North-West England'in Edwards *et al.* (eds), *Technologies of Procreation*.
35 Emily Martin, 'The Egg and the Sperm: How Science has Constructed a Romance Based on Stereotypical Male–Female Roles', *Signs: Journal of Women in Culture and Society*, vol. 16, no. 3, 1991, pp. 485–501; Nagl, 'Biomedicine and Moral Agency in a Complex World'.
36 Marcia Inhorn, 'Making Muslim Babies: IVF and Gamete Donation in Sunni Versus Shi'a Islam', *Culture, Medicine and Psychiatry*, vol. 30, no. 4, 2006, pp. 427–50; Susan Martha Kahn, 'Making Technology Familiar: Orthodox Jews and Infertility Support, Advice and Inspiration', *Culture, Medicine and Psychiatry*, vol. 30, no. 4, 2006, pp. 467–80; Konrad, *Nameless Relations*.
37 Gay Becker, *The Elusive Embryo: How Women and Men Approach New Reproductive Technologies* (Berkeley: University of California Press, 2000), p. 134.
38 Frank van Balen and T.C.M. Trimbos-Kemper, 'Factors Influencing the Well-being of Long-Term Infertile Couples', *Journal of Psychosomatic Obstetrics and Gynecology*, vol. 15, 1994, pp. 157–64.
39 This emphasis on the overriding investment of pregnancy and birth for women who use donor eggs was identified in Becker's (2000) study of couples in the US. Paxson also describes the importance of the 'blood, a biologizable idiom of relatedness' in Greece as something that is attributed to the gestational period and therefore more strongly influenced by the mother (2003:1862).
40 Becker, *The Elusive Embryo*; see also Marcia Inhorn and Frank van Balen (eds), *Infertility Around the Globe* (Berkeley: University of California Press, 2002) for a discussion on the use of ICSI in Egypt where sperm donation is not culturally accepted, and Kahn, 'Making Technology Familiar' for a description of the issues of donor sperm among Orthodox Jews in Israel where the emphasis is on maternal transmission of ethnic heritage. Jewish men are prohibited from being donors but women can use donor sperm from non-Jewish donors.
41 For a more detailed discussion on the importance of the 'witness' in the making of scientific truth, see Donna Haraway's *Modest_Witness@ Second_Millenium.FemaleMan©_Meets_OncoMouse™* (New York: Routledge, 1997).

42 Martin, 'The Egg and the Sperm'.

43 Judith Butler, *Bodies that Matter* (New York: Routledge, 1993).

44 The radio programme aired on the morning of 10 November 2004 and for several days following there were calls and emails regarding the programme, many of them negative and condemning of lesbian relationships and/or assisted reproduction.

45 With this service, conducted on the internet, the donor is paid 'expenses' amounting to around €100 or €200 but the service costs the recipient about €5,000 or more. The company originated in the UK. Women can contract for a 'donor' and have a vial of fresh semen delivered to their home within two hours of its collection. This necessarily implies the donor will be someone from within a fairly small radius and possibly someone a woman might know. In contrast, all donor sperm used at fertility clinics in Ireland is obtained from abroad. The service is primarily used by lesbian couples who need sperm in order to procreate within their relationship. However, the health implications are obvious in that, while the donors are initially screened for any health risks, no ongoing monitoring of donors can be assured.

46 Mr Fergal Goodman was principal officer in the Department of Health and Children and spoke before the Committee of Health and Children. See Oireachtas Debates, Committee for Health and Children Assisted Human Reproduction: Presentation, 12 December 2006. (http://debates.oireachtas-.ie/HEJ/2006/12/12/00003.asp [accessed on 6 December 2012]).

7. EMBRYOS AND THE ETHICS OF AMBIVALENCE

1 Sean Hogan, 'Lack of IVF legislation keeps couples childless, health committee hears', *Irish Examiner*, 16 September 2005. In fact while the information in this article suggests that a thousand babies a year are born in Ireland as a result of IVF, the European Society for Human Reproduction and Embryology (ESHRE) published statistics for 2005 indicating that just 301 births occurred as a result of IVF treatment in Ireland (http://www.eshre. com/page.aspx/15 [accessed 1 November 2012]). The apparent discrepancy might be attributed to the difference between fertility treatments and IVF, where 8,000 couples may seek some form of treatment and 1,000 babies might indeed result but not all of them are as a result of IVF.

2 Italy passed legislation prohibiting embryo freezing in 2004 along with the clinical obligations to create a maximum of three embryos in IVF treatment and to return all embryos to the womb of the mother. Germany has restrictive laws that prohibit egg donation and embryo donation and limits the number of blastocysts created in treatment (Bartolucci 2008).

3 Lynn Morgan, 'Embryo Tales', in Sarah Franklin and Margaret M. Lock (eds), *Remaking Life and Death: Towards an Anthropology of the Biosciences* (Santa Fe: School of American Research Press, 2003), p. 289.

4 Rebecca Sullivan, 'An Embryonic Nation: Life Against Health in Canadian Biotechnological Discourse', *Communication Theory*, vol. 15, no. 1, 2005.

5 Lisa Smyth, *Abortion and Nation: The Politics of Reproduction in Contemporary Ireland* (Farnham, Surrey: Ashgate, 2005).

6 Eric Scott Sills and Sarah Ellen Murphy, 'Determining the Status of Non-Transferred Embryos in Ireland: A Conspectus of Case Law and Implications for Clinical IVF Practice' (2009, available from www.biomed-central.com [accessed 1 November 2012]).

7 Jarrett Zigon, *Morality: An Anthropological Perspective* (Oxford: Berg, 2008), p. 19.

8 Sills and Murphy, 'Determining the Status of Non-Transferred Embryos in Ireland'.

9 Margrit Schildrick, 'Beyond the Body of Bioethics: Challenging the Conventions', in Margit Shildrick and Roxanne Mykitiuk (eds), *Ethics of the Body: Postconventional Challenges* (Cambridge, MA: The MIT Press, 2005), p. 3.

10 Sarah Franklin, 'Biologization Revisited: Kinship Theory in the Context of the New Biologies', in Sarah Franklin and Susan McKinnon (eds), *Relative Values: Reconfiguring Kinship Studies* (Durham, NC: Duke University Press, 2001), p. 303.

11 Irish Catholic Bishops' Conference, *Towards a Creative Response to Infertility* (Dublin: Veritas, 2006 [2005]) (http://www.catholicbishops.ie/wp-content/uploads/images/docs/towardsacreativeresponse.pdf [accessed 1 November 2012])

12 See Jacqueline Stevens for a critical discussion of the assumption that the DNA from a single gamete, alone, makes a significant contribution to the personhood of an individual. 'Methods of Adoption: Eliminating Genetic Privilege', in Sally Haslanger and Charlotte Witt (eds), *Adoption Matters: Philosophical and Feminist Essays* (Ithaca, NY: Cornell University Press, 2005).

13 Marilyn Strathern, 'A Question of Context' (Introduction to 1st edition), in Jeanette Edwards, Sarah Franklin, Eric Hirsch, Frances Price and Marilyn Strathern (eds), *Technologies of Procreation: Kinship in the Age of Assisted Conception* (London: Routledge, 1999 [1993]).

14 Marilyn Strathern, *Kinship, Law and the Unexpected: Relatives are Always a Surprise* (New York: Cambridge University Press, 2005).

15 For a detailed description of the Catholic Church's meaning of 'dignity' as it relates to the Irish Constitution, see Teresa Iglesias, *The Dignity of the Individual: Issues of Bioethics and Law* (Dublin: Pleroma Press, 2001).

16 S.T. Asma, 'Abortion and the Embarrassing Saint [Thomas Aquinas]', *The Humanist*, vol. 54 (May/June 1994), pp. 30–3.

17 Michel Foucault and Colin Gordon, *Powerknowledge: Selected Interviews and Other Writings, 1972–1977* (New York: Pantheon Books, 1980).

18 Orla McDonnell 'New Reproductive Technologies and Public Discourse: From Biopolitics to Bioethics', PhD dissertation, University College Cork, 2001.

19 Orla McDonnell and Jill Allison, 'From Biopolitics to Bioethics: Church, State, Medicine and Assisted Reproduction Technology in Ireland', *Sociology of Health and Illness*, vol. 28, no. 6, 2006, pp. 817–37.

20 Irish Catholic Bishops' Conference, *Towards a Creative Response to Infertility*.

21 Commission on Assisted Human Reproduction (CAHR), *Report of the*

Commission on Assisted Human Reproduction (Dublin: Stationery Office, 2005), p. 12.

22 Elizabeth Roberts, 'Extra Embryos: The Ethics of Cryopreservation in Ecuador and Elsewhere', *American Ethnologist*, vol. 34, 2007, p. 194; see also Deidre Madden, *Medicine, Ethics and the Law* (Dublin: Butterworth Ireland Ltd., 2002).

23 Jimmy Walsh, 'Mater castigated over cancer drug test', *The Irish Times*, 6 October 2000; and Claire O'Sullivan, 'Cancer drug trial decision "bizarre"', *Irish Examiner*, 4 October 2005; 'Medical ethic of old', *The Irish Times*, 6 October 2005.

24 The day of the release of the report, the story was trumped by news of the sale of the Manchester United football club to an American businessman, relegating the story to the second page of most major newspapers.

25 Orla McDonnell, 'New Reproductive Technologies and Public Discourse: From Biopolitics to Bioethics', PhD dissertation, University College Cork, 2001. McDonnell had, in fact, in her work on the issue of public debate and assisted reproduction predicted that the abortion debate would shape the outcome of the CAHR and the challenges to producing legislation.

26 CAHR, *Report of the Commission on Assisted Human Reproduction*, p. 73–6. The letters came from Professor Gerry Whyte of the Law School at Trinity College Dublin and Christine O'Rourke from the Office of the Attorney General. Professor Whyte argued in favour of the 'human nature of the embryo' and for protection from the moment of fertilisation as opposed to implantation. Ms O'Rourke's objections were with respect to surrogacy and the need to protect the rights of 'birth mothers' and the recognition of a child's legal parentage from the moment of birth. She argued that proposals to award custody to commissioning parents according to 'intent of reproduction' would erode the power of a birth mother to change her mind and effectively separate her from her biological offspring while the dispute was in litigation.

27 Sarah Franklin, 'Making Representations: The Parliamentary Debate on the Human Fertilization and Embryology Act', in Edwards *et al.* (eds), *Technologies of Procreation*, p. 141.

28 Monica Konrad, *Nameless Relations* (New York: Berghahn Books, 2005). Konrad describes similar discursive patterns in debates leading up to changes to HEFA in 2004–5.

29 Congregation for the Doctrine of the Faith, *Donum Vitae (Instruction on Respect for Human Life in its Origin and on the Dignity of Procreation)* (Vatican City: Libreria Editrice Vaticana, 1987).

30 Luke Cassidy, 'Court says frozen embryos "not unborn"', *The Irish Times*, 15 November 2006; and Carol Coulter, 'Court again calls for law on assisted reproduction', *The Irish Times*, 16 December 2009.

31 See McDonnell, 'New Reproductive Technologies and Public Discourse'.

32 Strathern, 'A Question of Context', p. 180.

33 See Oireachtas Debates, Committee for Health and Children Debate on the Report of the Commission on Assisted Human Reproduction, 21 July 2005.

http://debates.oireachtas.ie/HEJ/2005/07/21/00003.asp [accessed on 12 December 2012].

34 An interesting contradiction in some respects since Deputy Twomey is himself a physician.

35 See *Dáil Éireann Debates*, vol. 717, no. 2, http://debates.oireachtas.ie/dail/2010/10/05/00028.asp [accessed 1 November 2012].

36 The couple had one child without ART but used IVF after suffering from secondary infertility.

37 See 'Entering a moral maze' and 'Ruling on embryos due later in the month', *The Irish Times*, 8 July 2006.

38 See 'Court rules man did not give consent over embryos', *The Irish Times*, 18 July 2006. See also extensive coverage of this case in numerous articles in the *The Irish Times*, 15 November 2006, 16 November 2006; *Irish Examiner*, 14 March 2006; and *Irish Independent*, 6 October 2006.

39 'State to pay costs in embryos case', *The Irish Times*, 22 November 2006. Helen Browne of NISIG argued that legislation was necessary for clarity and to provide a wider range of options for couples with extra embryos rather than simply transfer to the mother or indefinite cryo-preservation. Dr Berry Kiely, on the other hand, argued that all embryos must 'be given a chance of life' and suggested that Ireland enact legislation following the model in Germany which bans freezing.

40 The term 'implant' is an important one to clarify here as this does not refer to the act of placing the embryo in the womb but rather the physiological event of its adhering or attaching to the lining of the womb. I make this distinction because for many of the people I spoke with in the course of this research, the difference is enormous. During IVF, an embryo is 'transferred' to the womb but whether it implants or not is the deciding factor between success and failure. If IVF practitioners could actually 'implant' an embryo there would be more positive pregnancy tests following the procedure.

41 See 'Court says frozen embryos "not unborn"', *The Irish Times*, 15 November 2006; Ann O'Loughlin, 'No state protection for frozen embryos', *Irish Independent*, 6 October 2006.

42 Mary Carolan, 'Existence of embryos outside womb "precarious"', *The Irish Times*, 16 November 2006.

43 Carol Coulter, 'Court again calls for law on assisted reproduction', *The Irish Times*, 16 December 2009.

44 These events had, of course, not occurred until a year after my departure from Ireland. I use the story here to show the immanence of the moral dilemma and fragility of the ethical framework under which decisions were made during the time I was conducting my research.

45 Current Medical Council Guidelines can be found at http://www.medical-council.ie/News-and-Publications/Publications/Professional-Conduct-Eth ics/Ethical%20Guide%202004.pdf. These are the latest updated versions from 2009.

46 McDonnell, 'New Reproductive Technologies and Public Discourse'. McDonnell provides a complete transcription of the debate on the RTÉ current affairs show *Prime Time*. This procedure was itself not without risk as embryos could 'implant' in the cervix in rare cases, causing pain, infection and possible damage to the body of the woman.

47 CAHR, *Report of the Commission on Assisted Human Reproduction*, Appendix V.

48 Ibid., p. 23. I was told that letters are sent out annually requesting direction from couples with embryos frozen in clinics and embryologists said that people do sometimes request that they be destroyed.

49 Kitty Holland, 'Frozen in legal limbo', *The Irish Times*, 22 July 2006.

50 See storage costs at the HARI Unit at http://www.hari.ie/index. php?section=hari&page=costs; at the Clane Hospital Clinic at http://www.clanefertility.ie/prices/pre-treatment-tests.134.html; at the Kilkenny Clinic at http://www.thekilkennyclinic.com/pricelist.htm; and at the Sims International Fertility Clinic at http://www.sims.ie/_fileupload/Image/Sims_Schedule_of_Fees_09.pdf [all accessed 1 November 2012]. Some clinics include the first twelve months of freezing as part of the initial cost of the freezing process, which of course offers an incentive for people to pursue their frozen cycles within a year.

51 Sarah Franklin, *Embodied Progress*. Also see Gail Letherby 'Childless and Bereft? Stereotypes and Realities in Relation to "Voluntary" and "Involuntary" Childlessness and Womanhood', *Sociological Inquiry*, vol. 72, no. 1, Winter 2002 pp. 7–20.

52 Carol Coulter, 'Donation of embryos gets ethical go-ahead', *The Irish Times*, 25 March 2004.

53 Carol Coulter, 'Council's new guideline on IVF has huge implications for the family', *The Irish Times*, 26 March 2004.

54 Such constructions are not unique to bioethical or regulatory discourse in Ireland as a movement called 'Snowflake' operates to rescue frozen embryos in the US, positioning them as adoptable entities. See Elizabeth F.S. Roberts, 'Extra Embryos: The Ethics of Cryopreservation in Ecuador and Elsewhere', *American Ethnologist*, vol. 34, 2007, p. 195, n1); see also Sarah-Vaughan Brakman, 'Paradigms, Practices and Politics: Ethics and the Language of Human Embryo Donation/Rescue/Adoption', in M.J. Cherry and A.S. Iltis (eds), *Pluralistic Casuistry* (Dordrecht, Netherlands: Springer, 2007), pp. 191–210.

55 David Walsh, Mary L. Ma and Eric Scott Sills, 'The Evolution of Health Policy Guidelines for Assisted Reproduction in the Republic of Ireland, 2004–2009', *Health Research Policy and Systems*, vol. 9, no. 28, 2011.

56 Franklin, 'Biologization Revisited', p. 303.

57 Bruno Latour, *We Have Never Been Modern* (Cambridge, MA: Harvard University Press, 1993); Paul Rabinow, 'Epochs, Presents, Events', in Margaret Lock, Allan Young and Alberto Cambrosio (eds), *Living and Working with the New Medical Technologies* (Cambridge: Cambridge University Press, 2000); Marilyn Strathern, *After Nature: English Kinship in*

the Late Twentieth Century (Cambridge: Cambridge University Press, 1992).

58 Donna Haraway, *Simians, Cyborgs and Women: The Reinvention of Nature* (New York: Routledge, 1991).

59 Franklin, 'Biologization Revisited'.

60 Heather Paxson, *'Making Modern Mothers: Ethics and Family Planning in Urban Greece* (Berkeley: University of California Press, 2004); 'With Or Against Nature? IVF, Gender and Reproductive Agency in Athens, Greece', *Social Science and Medicine*, vol. 56, no. 9, 2003, pp. 1853–66.

61 Elizabeth Roberts, 'Extra Embryos: The Ethics of Cryopreservation in Ecuador and Elsewhere', *American Ethologist*, vol. 34, 2007, p. 181.

62 Mothercare is a popular British chain store specialising in maternity wear, baby clothes and baby items such as toys, furniture, books and assorted paraphernalia. It is a popular store in Ireland as well and caters to all the material 'needs' of expectant parents.

63 Morgan, 'Embryo Tales', pp. 274–6. Morgan describes how embryos came to be constituted as 'patients' or subjects of medical and scientific ministrations detached from the maternal body.

64 Heather Paxson, 'With or Against Nature: IVF, Gender and Reproductive Agency in Athens, Greece', *Social Science and Medicine*, vol. 56, no. 9, 2003, p. 1857.

65 Elizabeth Roberts, 'God's Laboratory: Religious Rationalities and Modernity in Ecuadorian In Vitro Fertilization', *Culture, Medicine and Psychiatry*, vol. 30, no. 4, 2006, pp. 507–36; see also Franklin and McKinnon, *Relative Values*; and Marilyn Strathern, *Reproducing the Future: Essays on Anthropology, Kinship and the New Reproductive Technologies* (Manchester: Manchester University Press, 1992) for broader discussions on the challenges ART poses to current frameworks of kinship.

66 Morgan, 'Embryo Tales'.

67 S. de Lacey, 'Parent Identity and "Virtual" Children: Why Patients Discard Rather than Donate Unused Embryos', *Human Reproduction*, vol. 20, no. 6, 2005, pp. 1661–9.

68 Morgan, 'Embryo Tales'.

69 Edwards *et al.* (eds), *Technologies of Procreation*.

70 Morgan, 'Embryo Tales'.

71 Margaret Lock and Pat Kaufert, *Pragmatic Women and Body Politics* (Cambridge: Cambridge University Press, 1998).

72 Sarah Franklin, *Embodied Progress*, p. 103.

73 Heather Paxson, *Making Modern Mothers*, p. 224.

74 Sarah Franklin, 'Origin Stories Revisited: IVF as an Anthropological Project', *Culture, Medicine and Psychiatry*, vol. 30, no. 4 p. 73. This can be linked to Daston's (1995) concept of the 'moral economy of science' where such values as hope might be conveyed as intrinsic to the practices involved in producing and acquiring embryos.

75 Jeanette Edwards, 'Incorporating Incest: Gamete, Body and Relation in Assisted Conception', *Journal of the Royal Anthropological Institute*, vol. 10, no.

4, 2004, pp. 755–74; *Born and Bred: Idioms of Kinship and New Reproductive Technologies in England* (Oxford: Oxford University Press, 2000); 'Explicit Connections: Ethnographic Enquiry in North-West England, in Edwards *et al.* (eds), *Technologies of Procreation*. Edwards' work is somewhat unique in that she conducted research on the use of ART, particularly donor gametes, among a wider group of people who constituted the general public. The material she collected reflects a wider set of perceptions than those confined to a group of people who have used or contemplated using ART themselves.

76 At the same time, the Adult Stem Cell Foundation, formed in 2012, calls for greater attention and research funding to be dedicated to the medical innovation that is possible with this research material, which is much less contentious and more easily available. 'Expert warns over stem cell future', *The Irish Times*, 18 April 2012.

77 Sarah Franklin, 'Origin Stories Revisited: IVF as an Anthropological Project', *Culture, Medicine and Psychiatry*, vol. 30, no.4, 2006, pp. 547–55.

8. CONCLUSION

1 Lorraine Daston and Fernando Vidal, *The Moral Authority of Nature* (Chicago: University of Chicago Press, 2004).

2 Carol Coulter, '"Hello Divorce, Goodbye Daddy": Women, Gender and the Divorce Debate', in Anthony Bradley and Maryann Gialanella Valiulis (eds), *Gender and Sexuality in Modern Ireland* (Amherst, MA: University of Massachusetts Press, 1997), p. 295.

3 Lisa Smyth, 'From Rights to Compassion: The D Case and Contemporary Abortion Politics', in Jennifer Schweppe (ed.), *The Unborn Child, Article 40.3.3 and Abortion in Ireland: Twenty-Five Years of Protection?* (Dublin: The Liffey Press, 2008), p. 61.

4 Sarah Pentz Bottini, 'Europe's Rebellious Daughter: Will Ireland Be Forced to Conform Its Abortion Law to That of Its Neighbors?', *Journal of Church and State*, vol. 49, no. 2, 2007, p. 241.

5 Lisa Smyth, *Abortion and Nation: The Politics of Reproduction in Contemporary Ireland* (Farnham, Surrey: Ashgate, 2005), p. 143.

6 J.A. Harrington, 'Citizenship and the Biopolitics of Post-Nationalist Ireland', *Journal of Law and Society*, vol. 32, 2005, p. 449.

7 Mr Justice Iarfhlaith O'Neill, Speech by Referendum Commission Chairman, Press briefing, 4 June 2008.

8 See 'Lisbon Treaty rejected by Irish electorate', *The Irish Times*, 13 June 2008. A second referendum vote is scheduled to be held in 2009. A second proposed vote will be held in 2009 and the EU has attached an annex to the agreement designed to reassure 'Ireland's requirements regarding maintenance of its traditional policy of neutrality are met; that the terms of the Lisbon Treaty will not affect the continued application of the provisions of the Constitution in relation to the right to life, education and the family; that in the area of taxation the Treaty of Lisbon makes no change of any kind.' (Jamie Smyth, 'Second poll on Lisbon to be held before end of October', *The Irish Times*, 11 November 2008.)

9   John O'Brennan, 'Ireland Says No (Again): The 12 June 2008 Referendum on the Lisbon Treaty', *Parliamentary Affairs*, vol. 62, no. 2, 2009, p. 258.

10 See European Commission Eurobarometer Flash EB no. 245: Post-referendum survey in Ireland (http://ec.europa.eu/public_opinion/flash/fl_245_full_en.pdf). In addition, a number of people suggested that the 'No' side was 'more convincing'.

11 Sarah Franklin, *Embodied Progress: A Cultural Account of Assisted Conception* (London: Routledge, 1997); Heather Paxson, *Making Modern Mothers: Ethics and Family Planning in Urban Greece* (Berkeley: University of California Press, 2004).

12 Gay Becker, *Disrupted Lives: How People Create Meaning in a Chaotic World* (Berkeley: University of California Press, 1997).

13 Michael Herzfeld, *Cultural Intimacy: Social Poetics in the Nation-State* (London: Routledge, 2005). For further analysis on the relationship between the meanings attributed to 'tradition' and the ethos of the Catholic Church see Claire Wills, 'Women, Domesticity and the Family: Recent Feminist Work in Irish Cultural Studies', *Cultural Studies*, vol. 15, no. 1, 2001, pp. 33–57; and Carol Coulter, '"Hello Divorce, Goodbye Daddy": Women, Gender and the Divorce Debate', in Anthony Bradley and Maryann Gialanella Valiulis (eds), *Gender and Sexuality in Modern Ireland* (Amherst, MA: University of Massachusetts Press, 1997).

14 Ó Gráda, Cormac, *Éirvana* (Dublin: UCD Centre for Economic Research Working Papers Series WP08/12, 2008), p. 10.

15 Susan Gal, 'Between Speech and Silence: The Problematics of Research on Language and Gender', in Michaela Di Leonardo (ed.), *Gender at the Crossroads of Knowledge: Feminist Anthropology in the Postmodern Era* (Berkeley: University of California Press, 1991), p. 175.

16 M.L. Achino-Loeb, *Silence: The Currency of Power* (New York: Berghahn Books, 2006); C. Glenn, *Unspoken: A Rhetoric of Silence* (Carbondale, IL: Southern Illinois University Press, 2004).

17 Orla McDonnell, 'New Reproductive Technologies and Public Discourse: From Biopolitics to Bioethics', unpublished PhD dissertation, University College Cork, 2001; and 'Shifting Debates on New Reproductive Technology: Implications for Public Discourse in Ireland', in Patrick O'Mahony (ed.), *Nature, Risk and Responsibility: Discourses of Biotechnology* (New York: Routledge, 1999); Susan Ryan-Sheridan, *Women and the New Reproductive Technologies in Ireland* (Cork: Cork University Press, 1994).

18 McDonnell, 'New Reproductive Technologies and Public Discourse'.

19 Deirdre Madden, *Medicine, Ethics and the Law* (Dublin: Butterworth (Ireland) Ltd., 2002); and 'Article 40.3.3 and Assisted Reproduction in Ireland', in Jennifer Schweppe (ed.), *The Unborn Child, Aritcle 40.3.3 and Abortion in Ireland: Twenty-Five Years of Protection?* (Dublin: The Liffey Press, 2008).

20 Barry Roche, 'Stem cell vote by UCC governors paves way for campus research', *The Irish Times*, 29 October 2008.

21 Negotiations to protect Ireland's constitutionally enshrined 'right to life of the unborn' against challenges from EU law arose again with the writing of the Lisbon Treaty in 2008, when a protocol was attached to the treaty in this regard. On 12 June 2008, 53.4% of voters in a referendum in Ireland voted to reject a constitutional amendment to ratify the treaty. While abortion politics was overshadowed by wider concerns for Ireland's ability to maintain military neutrality and issues of trade, the ongoing inclusion of the issue indicates the importance of Article 40.3.3 to the case for Ireland's unique political character within the EU (http://eur-lex.europa.eu/LexUriServ/LexUriServ.do?uri=OJ:C:2007:306:0165:0165:EN:PDF [accessed 1 November 2012]; see also http://www.euractiv.com/en/future-eu/irish-eu-treaty-referendum/article-172508 [accessed 1 November 2012].

22 Elizabeth F.S. Roberts, 'Extra Embryos: The Ethics of Cryopreservation in Ecuador and Elsewhere', *American Ethnologist*, vol. 34, 2007, pp. 182–99; and 'Abandonment and Accumulation: Embryonic Futures in the United States and Ecuador', *Medical Anthropology Quarterly*, vol. 25, no. 2, 2011, pp. 232–253. The stem cell debate in the US took a similar turn under George W. Bush. The emergence of such organisations as Operation Snowflake, which finds 'adoptive parents' for abandoned embryos, is indicative of the contrasting political positions and emotional difficulties provoked by embryos as entities with multiple possibilities.

23 Eilish O'Regan, 'Fertility clinics and ministers targeted in "live bullet" campaign', *Irish Independent*, 11 March 2008.

AFTERWORD

1 Centre for Reproductive Rights. 'Fact Sheet, A, B, C, v. Ireland'. http://reproductiverights.org/sites/crr.civicactions.net/files/documents/crr_ABC_Factsheet.pdf April 2012

2 Catherine O'Sullivan, Jennifer Schweppe and Eimear Spain. 'Article 40.3.3 and the Protection of Life During Pregnancy Bill 2013: The Impetus for and process of legislative change', *Irish Journal of Legal Studies* Vol. 3 (3) 2013, pps 1–17.

3 Bruno Waterfield, 'Irish abortion law key factor in death of Savita Halappanavar, official report finds', http://www.telegraph.co.uk/news/worldnews/europe/ireland/10119109/Irish-abortion-law 13 June 2013. Accessed 25 July 2013.

4 Damien McElroy, 'Irish consultant rejects accusation she refused abortion in "Catholic country"', *Daily Telegraph* 10 April 2013.

5 House of the Oireachtas Protection of Life During Pregnancy Bill 2013. http://www.oireachtas.ie/viewdoc.asp?fn=/documents/bills28/acts/2013/a3513.pdf.

6 O'Sullivan Article 40.3.3 p. 10.

7 Fiona Gartland, 'Genetic mother wins surrogacy case, *The Irish Times*, March 5, 2013.

8 Ibid.

9 Commission on Assisted Reproduction. Report of the Commission of Assisted Reproduction 2005.

Index